At Europe's Edge

The Mediterranean Sea is now the deadliest region in the world for migrants. Although the death toll has been rising for many years, the EU response remains fragmented and short-sighted. Politicians frame these migration flows as an unprecedented crisis and emphasize migration control at the EU's external boundaries. In this context, *At Europe's Edge* investigates (1) why the EU prioritizes the fortification of its external borders; (2) why migrants nevertheless continue to cross the Mediterranean and to die at sea; and (3) how EU member states on the southern periphery respond to their new role as migration gatekeepers. The book addresses these questions by examining the relationship between the EU and Malta, a small state with an outsized role in migration politics as EU policies place it at the crosshairs of migration flows and controls. The chapters combine ethnographic methods with macro-level analyses to weave together policymaker, practitioner, and migrant experiences, and demonstrate how the Mediterranean is an important space for the contested construction of 'Europe'. *At Europe's Edge* provides rich insight into the unexpected level of influence Malta exerts on EU migration governance, as well as the critical role migrants and their clandestine journeys play in animating EU and Maltese migration policies, driving international relations, and producing Malta's political power. By centring on the margins, the book pushes the boundaries of our knowledge of the global politics of migration, asylum, and border security.

Cetta Mainwaring is an author and activist. She is currently a Lecturer in Sociology at the University of Glasgow. She holds a DPhil in International Relations from the University of Oxford and an MA in Sociology from City University, London. Dr Mainwaring's research lies at the intersection of migration, borders, and resistance. She is interested in how people move, seek asylum, and resist bordering practices. Her research projects have examined how European Union member states seek to control migration in the Mediterranean region and how these policies shape migrant experiences. This includes co-leading a collaborative, cross-regional project, 'Clandestine Migration Journeys', which analyzed the everyday experiences of migrants travelling without authorization and the ways they challenge and overcome restrictive policies and barriers they face along the route. She currently holds a UKRI Future Leaders Fellowship examining immigration detention, the way this failed policy travels internationally, and resistance to it in the UK, US, and Australia.

'*At Europe's Edge: Migration and Crisis in the Mediterranean* [is] an impressively comprehensive and polished piece of work, addressing discourses, policy and security in relation to migration in the Mediterranean, based on a methodologically robust study. The book eloquently weaves together the historical evolution of border policy and migration in the Mediterranean, while also bringing the current realities into focus … The author does not only centre migrant voices, but skilfully brings her interlocutors to life, by capturing in a few words their character, background or the impression that encounter left on her.'

2020 Annual Best Book Award of the 'International Politics of Migration, Refugees and Diaspora' Working Group of the British International Studies Association Committee

'The way that Mainwaring cements her discussion in ongoing empirical evidence is one of the greatest joys in this book … I found myself hooked by her attention to detail and have been following emerging events throughout this year as a result of the interest she has managed to pique. For Mainwaring this is not just research; *At Europe's Edge* reflects the determination of a type of academic activism (an intervention) that has been present in all the work of hers I have read to date.'

Richard Vogt, Independent Scholar

'It's all there, surgically taken apart by Ċetta Mainwaring in her excellent *At Europe's Edge*. Anyone who is serious about migration should buy and read this book.'

Mark Anthony Falzon, Professor and Head of Sociology, University of Malta

'*At Europe's Edge* is a compelling account … [and] a valuable resource; it is relevant not only for scholars of governance and migration research but also for the interested public, migrants' advocates, and politicians alike … Mainwaring's book is timely and much-needed, as dehumanizing events like the tuna-pen incident still happen, as a glance at recent news reports from April 2020 reveals.'

Dr Laura Otto, Goethe University, Frankfurt am Main

At Europe's Edge

Migration and Crisis in the Mediterranean

ĊETTA MAINWARING

OXFORD
UNIVERSITY PRESS

Great Clarendon Street, Oxford, OX2 6DP,
United Kingdom

Oxford University Press is a department of the University of Oxford.
It furthers the University's objective of excellence in research, scholarship,
and education by publishing worldwide. Oxford is a registered trade mark of
Oxford University Press in the UK and in certain other countries

First published 2019
First published in paperback 2023

Published in the United States of America by Oxford University Press
198 Madison Avenue, New York, NY 10016, United States of America

British Library Cataloguing in Publication Data
Data available

Library of Congress Cataloging in Publication Data
Data available

ISBN 978–0–19–884251–4 (Hbk.)
ISBN 978–0–19–888182–7 (Pbk.)

This book is dedicated to the people whose courage in crossing the seas, deserts, and borders of the world is so often answered with violence and oppression.

Acknowledgen

This work is the result of conversations, encounters, observations, and exchanges over many years, in different places, with many people. Foremost, I am indebted to those who gave their time and contributed to interviews and other conversations in Malta and in Brussels: fellow 'migrants', policymakers, bureaucrats, fishermen, border guards, activists, soldiers, politicians, and workers on the front lines in advocacy organizations, open centres, detention centres, and at sea. Without them, empty pages would follow.

I have been privileged to have inspiring and committed mentors during and after my graduate education. At City University, where I completed an MA in International Politics and Human Rights, Liza Schuster first kindled my interest in migration in the Mediterranean. She continues to be an academic role model. As a DPhil student at the University of Oxford, Franck Düvell, Kalypso Nicolaïdis, and Dimitar Bechev were critical in my training as a social scientist, pushing me to be rigorous and creative. My DPhil examiners—Nick Van Hear and Nick Vaughan-Williams—encouraged me to make the leap from thesis to book and continue to be mentors and friends, despite that journey having been much longer and more circuitous than they could have imagined. The friends I made during my years in Oxford remain some of my closest. My Oxford family—Janina Dill, Robin Markwica, and Nina Silove—are still emotional and intellectual cornerstones for me despite the distance between us. Melanie Griffiths' intellectual sharpness, humour, warmth, and company on dance floors and carers' retreats has enlivened the book and the journey.

At the University of Malta, Derek Lutterbeck was always generous, and is responsible for many research opportunities I had early on in my academic training. Maria Pisani remains an inspiring friend, scholar, and activist. She provided invaluable contacts, insights, and camaraderie during fieldwork.

The Wise Women I came to know in San Diego—Maria Cook, Jill Esbenshade, and Kristen Hill Maher—reignited my desire and rekindled my confidence to begin to transform my DPhil into a book manuscript. It would still be many years, but without their intellectual insights and camaraderie, I would have never started.

It was in Ontario, between the University of Waterloo and the Balsillie School of International Affairs, that I found my footing as an academic and shed disciplinary constraints. In part, this was because of the open-mindedness of and warm welcome from many colleagues in the UW Department of Sociology and Legal Studies, especially Suzan Ilcan, Dan O'Connor, and Rashmee Singh. In Waterloo and Toronto, students and colleagues provided a rich and nurturing community where friendships and intellectual collaborations blossomed with Alison Mountz, Jennifer Hyndman, Kim Rygiel, Honor Brabazon, and Margaret Walton-Roberts.

In my most recent academic home, the University of Glasgow, I have again had the good fortune to find a community of like-minded scholars. The Migration and Mobilities Research Group and the Writing Group have provided fertile ground for exploring ideas, critiquing work, and getting some writing done. In particular, I'd like to thank Rebecca Kay who has been not only the type of mentor one dreams of having but also a friend. She, Robert Gibb, and other 'MigMobers' provided incisive feedback on draft chapters. I'm also grateful to the Leverhulme Trust for their generous funding while I have been at Glasgow, which allowed me to complete the book.

Throughout my academic journey, I have had the privilege of writing with many inspirational co-authors, including Noelle Brigden, Maria Cook, Stephanie J. Silverman, Margaret Walton-Roberts, and Daniela DeBono. I am indebted to these women for making me a better writer and thinker and for contributing invaluably to the intellectual processes that led to this book.

At Oxford University Press, I would like to thank my editor, Dominic Byatt, for his encouragement and guidance throughout the review and publishing process. Assistant Commissioning Editor Céline Louasli and Editorial Assistant Matthew Williams also provided indispensable support. I was fortunate to have dedicated and astute anonymous reviewers; their critiques made this a better book. The New Internationalist, Olivier Clochard, Nicholas Lambert, and Migreurop generously allowed me to reprint the map on European Border Deaths.

My deepest thanks and affection go to all my family for their unfaltering support and love. In particular, my mother, Yana Mintoff, has read innumerable drafts of chapters, acted as an interpreter and research assistant in Malta, and has generally been my champion without reservation, as only a mother can. I cannot thank her enough. Throughout, my brother, Danny Mainwaring, offered light-hearted relief and much-needed perspective. He has also been an inspiring academic collaborator and co-author, read more iterations of the book than he probably cares to count, and always advised on being more exact with language. In Scotland, my father, Geoff Mainwaring, and step-mother, Karen Buist, have provided valuable discussions, encouragement, and endless hours of childcare that allowed for this book to be completed.

It is this family that raised me to be attuned to and fight against social inequalities and injustices, an education that shapes who I am and what I write about. They continue to inspire me in their own work and activism, and in their ability to balance anger at the world's inequalities and love for the people in it.

Last and not least, Carsten has always encouraged me to aim higher. His unwavering love and support have made this author a happy one. Our children, Sofia and the wee babe who will join us any day now, fill my life with more joy (and sleepless nights!) than I thought possible, reminding me how precious our lives are and how carelessly some people's continue to be treated.

Ċetta Mainwaring

Edinburgh, UK
November 2018

Contents

List of Illustrations

This is an intervention. A message from that space in the margin that is a site of creativity and power, that inclusive space where we recover our-selves, where we move in solidarity to erase the category of colonized/ colonizer. Marginality as a site of resistance. Enter that space. Let us meet there. Enter that space. We greet you as liberators.

bell hooks, 1990[1]

[1] Reprinted from 'Choosing the Margin as Space of Radical Openness' by bell hooks in *Framework: The Journal of Cinema and Media,* Vol. 36. Copyright © 1989 Wayne State University Press, with the permission of Wayne State University Press.

1

Notes from the Mediterranean

Shipwrecks, Politics, and Death

In May 2007, twenty-seven men from sub-Saharan Africa set sail from the Libyan port city of Zuwarah on a small, fibreglass boat. Overcrowded and unseaworthy, the boat remained adrift in the Mediterranean for six days. Two fishing boats had already ignored their calls of distress when the men deserted the sinking vessel and clambered onto the eighteen-inch, plastic walkway of a tuna pen being towed by the *Budafel*, a Maltese trawler. The captain informed the Maltese authorities, but refused to allow the men aboard his boat 'in case they turned violent and killed everyone'. He cited the security concerns of the four-man crew, as well as the risk of being burdened with responsibility for the migrants for an extended period (Kenyon 2009: 272).[1] The captain likewise refused to tow the migrants back to Malta, maintaining that he would lose millions of euros in tuna profit (Popham 2007a; Italian Refugee Council 2007).

Informed of the migrants' distress, the Maltese authorities also refused to dispatch a rescue boat and claimed responsibility lay with either Libya, in whose search and rescue area the migrants and trawler were found, or with Italy, because the boat was closer to the Italian island of Lampedusa than to Malta (European Union 2007). Political wrangling ensued, with the twenty-seven men left clinging to the tuna pen in rough seas for three days, according to their own accounts. Eventually, an Italian navy vessel arrived on the scene and transferred the migrants to Lampedusa.

The media ran the story under headlines denouncing 'Europe's shame', accompanied by aerial photographs of the men on the tuna pen.[2] In these accounts, state actors were rendered the protagonists, while the migrants remained victims, unspeaking and largely unseen. Indeed, even in the photographs chosen for print, the men are just small dots barely decipherable as

---

[1] The media also quoted the owner of the boat, who said 'As a Maltese, I'm prepared to assist people, but there's a limit to everything. What if these twenty-four strong men rebelled and tried to assume control of the boat?' (Hooper 2007).

[2] For example, *The Independent* ran a piece about the tuna pen incident on 28 May 2007. The front-page story included a picture of the men on the tuna pen and was entitled 'Europe's Shame: The Killing Seas of the Mediterranean' (Popham 2007a; cf. Amnesty International 2015a).

human. It would be a few years before journalist Paul Kenyon (2009) published *I am Justice*, a book that details the experiences and memories of one of the men aboard the boat. In his account, the migrants who crossed the Mediterranean transform from the silent, passive victims reflected on our television screens and in our newspapers to active participants in the drama.

Throughout their journeys out of Africa, the twenty-seven men negotiated their survival and mobility with friends, relatives, smugglers, border guards, fellow migrants, and other actors. In the middle of the Mediterranean, as their boat was sinking, and they faced armed crew members on the *Budafel* who insisted they carry on to Italy, they resisted, pleaded, reasoned, and eventually convinced the crew to allow them onto the narrow walkway surrounding the tuna pen. Even when they were abandoned on this walkway for days in desperate conditions—waves crashing over them, delirious due to dehydration, burnt by the Mediterranean sun, wet and cold as night fell, their skin itchy, flaking, bleeding from the salty sea—they improvised in order to survive: they shared dwindling kola nuts, sang together, and prayed to different gods, keeping at bay urges to throw themselves into the sea. Amidst hopelessness, they strategized: they discovered loose ropes hanging from the tuna pen and used them to secure their bodies to the walkway. They recounted past experiences and future aspirations to make sense of a bewildering present (Kenyon 2009). Their improvisations compelled Italy, Malta, and Libya into particular negotiations and relationships. The actions of these twenty-seven men, and those who followed across the sea, influenced policy discussions within the European Union (EU) over rescue and disembarkation. In these many ways, their actions constituted the border of Europe.

The tuna-pen episode was a harbinger of the political dynamics that would reverberate around the Mediterranean and throughout Europe over the next decade, and of the consequences of building walls and fences around the European Union. Although it captured the imagination of journalists and the public, this was not an isolated incident, but rather one of many where government inaction on both sides of the Mediterranean proved calamitous (e.g. Spindler and Dobbs 2007).[3] In October 2013, around 400 people drowned

---

[3] For example, only a month later, in June 2007, an almost identical incident occurred but did not appear in the international press. Twenty people clambered onto another tuna pen walkway when their boat capsized. The Maltese crew and Icelandic captain defied orders from Maltese authorities to return them to Libya and the subsequent threat of legal action, instead towing them towards Malta. It would still take two days of political negotiations and the death of one woman before the Maltese authorities agreed to rescue the migrants (Interview: President of Fishing Cooperative, Malta 2011; Grech 2007). Similarly, the previous summer, a Spanish trawler rescued fifty-one people, who remained stranded on board for five days while Spain, Malta, and Libya negotiated responsibility for their disembarkation (UNHCR 2006).

in the central Mediterranean, within a mile of the Italian shores of Lampedusa. The following year, the Mediterranean became the deadliest part of the world for migrants: over 3,000 people lost their lives, making up 75 per cent of global migrant deaths. This bleak picture only worsened with deaths soaring to over 5,000 in 2016 and over 3,000 in 2017.[4]

The tuna-pen incident illustrates the issues that sparked the initial ideas of this book, issues that have become starker with time. It prompted me to consider how policies had developed in the European Union and the Mediterranean to a point where transferring responsibility for twenty-seven people to another country took priority over saving their lives. How had migrants become so dehumanized that their lives were considered less valuable than tuna?

This episode also points to the longer history of constructed crises around migration in the Mediterranean that predates the 'migration crisis' of 2015. Indeed, since 2007, EU politicians have continued to frame the arrival of migrants at the edges of Europe as a 'crisis' as if it were an unprecedented event. Although migrants have been crossing the Mediterranean for decades and the death toll has been rising for many years, the response from the EU and its member states continues to be fragmented and short-sighted. In this book, I investigate the following questions that arise in this context: (1) Why has the EU emphasized the need to fortify the external borders when many more unauthorized migrants arrive through legal channels? (2) Why do migrants continue to attempt the Mediterranean crossing, and continue to die at sea, despite the emphasis on fortified external borders? And (3) how have small member states on the southern periphery responded to the sudden spotlight and their new role in border management?

In broader terms, I am interested in how various actors engage in, imagine, and shape the Mediterranean space. It is from the geographic and political edge of Europe that we can appreciate the importance of migrant agency in answering these questions. Migrants continue to negotiate border crossings and longer journeys despite, and because of, the barriers in place. Their continued mobility represents a contestation of migration controls, borders, and sovereignty. Yet, their agency is co-opted and distorted by states in order to justify further migration controls and leverage power. It is also on Europe's edge that we see how a small state, like Malta, helps construct the migration 'crisis' in the Mediterranean and hence the need to fortify the EU's periphery.

---

[4] These figures are collected by the International Organization for Migration in their Missing Migrants Project. See https://missingmigrants.iom.int/mediterranean

Indeed, in answering these questions, the book identifies the Mediterranean as an important space for the contested construction of Europe.

This book is thus about power at the margins: it is about small states, the power they carve out for themselves, and the strategies they adopt. It is about people who are denied the unfettered mobility venerated in discourses of globalization and a new 'borderless world'. It is about men, women, and children sailing across the Mediterranean on rubber dinghies rather than luxury yachts. The book explores the power that these people hold despite their marginalized positions, the spaces of resistance they negotiate within and between states, and the agency they exercise.

This introductory chapter first turns to briefly examine how and why EU migration policies have focused on control at the external border. The following section looks at how these policies encourage dangerous journeys across the Mediterranean and have resulted in an increasing number of migrant deaths at the edge of Europe. In this context, shipwrecks play an important role in the politics of migration and are alternately cast as a humanitarian crisis and an enforcement problem, with migrants reduced to symbols of suffering or criminality and disorder. The next section introduces the central case study of Malta, which EU policies place in the crosshairs of migration flows and migration control. It is from here, the EU's smallest and most southern member state, that I examine migrant experiences as well as Malta's response to its migration gatekeeping role within the EU. Finally, I describe my methods and methodology before turning to map the subsequent chapters of the book.

Bordering Moves: EU Migration Policies and Border Politics

Migration dynamics are contested and shaped within and beyond borders. However, national borders remain a powerful, symbolic site where state sovereignty and citizenship are performed (Brown 2010; Salter 2008). This also holds true at a regional, EU level. Although much public and policy attention centres on migrants who cross the EU's external border without authorization, like the men stranded on the tuna pen, most migrants without status in the EU have not entered the bloc in a clandestine manner. Rather, the majority arrive through legal channels and subsequently overstay or violate the conditions of their visas (e.g. United Nations 2013: 6). Others may lose their status when their asylum claims are denied but are not or cannot be removed by the state. Some are made 'illegal' due to the failures of government bureaucracies to renew residence and work permits or to assess appeals in a timely manner. In 2009, the Clandestino Project (2009) estimated that only 10 per cent of people without status had entered the EU without authorization (cf. Düvell 2011; Düvell and Vollmer 2009). This trend is replicated at the national level: for example, in Italy, the Ministry of Internal Affairs estimated that over two-thirds of people without status had overstayed their visas between 2000 and 2006 (Fasani 2010; cf. Cuttitta 2006: 2–3). In 2015, in the UK, an estimated 80 per cent of people without status had overstayed their visas (Erlanger and De Freytas-Tamura 2015).[5]

Two dozen men on the verge of drowning are not in themselves a threat to nation states. If one considers their limited number in addition to the evidence that 'irregular' immigration in the EU is not constituted primarily by people crossing the border without authorization, the reaction of the states involved appears at the very least disproportionate, if not morally perverse. It suggests that state actions were not based on immediate threats and that other dynamics were at play. Whether in the context of war or migration, politicians have characterized the Mediterranean and, by extension, the EU's southern member states as Europe's 'soft, vulnerable underbelly'.[6] The perceived vulnerability of external borders to the imagined hordes of people waiting to cross into Europe has been a feature of EU policies and politics on migration and asylum for many decades. In response, the EU and its member states have placed discursive and material emphasis on excluding migrants at the southern and eastern external borders. From the Schengen Agreement (1985) to the Dublin Convention (1990), EU policies and politics have moved responsibility for border control and asylum towards the external border and beyond.[7] Along the Mediterranean border, the use of drones, surveillance technology, and other military hardware for the purposes of migration control exemplifies this dynamic (Cuttitta 2006; Lutterbeck 2006).

---

[5] Although there may be sporadic increases in unauthorized entries in the wake of political violence and unrest, as occurred in Europe in 2015 and 2016 with large numbers of Syrians, Iraqis, Afghans, and others arriving, many of these people quickly regularize their status by applying for and being granted refugee status.

[6] Winston Churchill first used the term in World War II during the invasion of Sicily to note where the Axis forces were most vulnerable. More recently, it has been adopted within the EU's discourse on migration (Haynes 1999: 19; Katrougalos and Lazaridis 2003: 169).

[7] Nevertheless, migration controls continue to exist to varying degrees across all member states, such as in airports and through bureaucratic mechanisms that control formal access to labour markets.

Migration controls at the border reflect and reinforce the stark unequal access to mobility in this era of globalization. The facilitation of the movement of goods, capital, and privileged people has become emblematic of today's globalization, while the vast majority of people remain excluded from such feted mobility, unable to travel to most countries without a visa. Even in the case of the EU, where there has been an exceptional increase in the freedom of movement for people within the Union, stricter controls for non-EU citizens, particularly along the external border, arose in conjunction with this internal freedom. Yet, despite the enormous investment in border controls, migrants continue to arrive at the EU's external border, indicating a failed 'fight against illegal immigration' (Andersson 2016). Moreover, the emphasis on border control belies the reality of 'irregular' migration comprised primarily of those who arrive legally. This exclusion of people at external boundaries within the EU and globally is often justified as part of state attempts to 'manage' migration. Calls for more coordinated approaches to migration governance invoke notions of law and order in the face of ostensibly chaotic migration flows and migrant deaths. However, the managed migration paradigm disregards the ways in which migration controls and growing inequalities produce clandestine flows, people without status, and migrant deaths. It also discounts the agency of migrants, understanding them as objects to be governed rather than subjects who challenge sovereignty and affect state relations, as the tuna pen above illustrates.

The increase in restrictive migration controls at and beyond state borders is not unique to Europe. Across Western states there are attempts to restrict particular migration flows through practices such as interdictions at sea and in transit states, the use of offshore and onshore detention centres, and fast-track deportations. Australia's infamous 'Pacific Solution', implemented between 2001 and 2007 and reintroduced in 2012, epitomizes these exclusionary policies and involves the interception of boats at sea, the relocation of asylum seekers to islands such as Papua New Guinea and Nauru, and the legal excision of large parts of Australia's northern coastline for the purposes of asylum (Mountz 2011a; Hodge 2015). These practices reinforce global hierarchies of mobility that privilege few, restrict many, and shrink spaces of protection around the world. They amount to the construction of walls around the West (Andreas and Snyder 2000), an implicit encouragement of dangerous journeys taken by people like the men stranded on a tuna pen in the Mediterranean, and of a growing number of migrant deaths.[8]

---

[8] For visual representations of the walls around the West, see maps by Phillipe Rekacewic (2013).

Shipwrecked Politics: Mediterranean Deaths
and the Construction of 'Europe'

EU external border policies have divided the Mediterranean in manifold ways, separating people, countries, and spaces with intertwined histories. These borders are relatively ineffective and have enormous human costs. People continue to arrive in Europe; many are afforded no alternative route and must thus attempt the perilous Mediterranean crossing. Increasingly restrictive policies encourage more dangerous journeys and have turned the seas between Libya and Italy, Greece and Turkey, and Spain and Morocco into watery graves for thousands of people, despite the proliferation of security actors and technologies deployed along coastlines and at sea. Recent estimates suggest that over 30,000 people died trying to enter the European Union between 2000 and 2015, the majority—over 23,000—in the Mediterranean (see Figure 1.1).[9]

In the context of a rising Mediterranean death toll, migrant shipwrecks have become symbolic of political tension and ambivalence over migration control at the edge of Europe. For many, shipwrecks denote Europe's shame, its indifference towards those needing rescue and refuge (cf. Basaran 2015; Popham 2007a). For others, they are indicative of a migration crisis, of the millions imagined waiting at the edge of Europe for their chance to cross the sea. European politicians and media outlets have frequently repeated this type of sensationalist narrative throughout the twenty-first century, despite evidence that the number of people trying to enter Europe is much more limited.[10]

In October 2013, Europe's political ambivalence came to the fore when over 400 people drowned within 800 metres of the shores of Lampedusa. The

---

[9] This number is compiled using data collected by The Migrants' Files (Journalism++ SAS et al. 2015). Counting the dead is of course a politicized and contested process (Tazzioli 2015). The actual number of deaths is likely to be higher as there are people who die at sea and leave no trace. Such statistics also fail to capture the individual lives that are lost and the families and friends who are left behind.

[10] For example, in August 2015, UK Foreign Secretary, Phillip Hammond, said 'Europe can't protect itself, preserve its standard of living and social infrastructure if it has to absorb millions of migrants from Africa' (Perraudin 2015). For other examples of accounts that invoke the spectre of hordes of people waiting to enter Europe, see Townsend (2008) and Düvell and Vollmer (2009: 8–9). Estimates from academics and organizations are more modest than the millions reported elsewhere. Indeed, academics and NGOs regularly refute the sensationalist numbers, and present evidence that, for example, only a fraction of the migrants in Libya attempted to cross the Mediterranean before 2011 (e.g. Cuttitta 2006; de Haas 2007). The International Centre for Migration Policy Development suggested that around 100,000 migrants crossed the entire Mediterranean each year in the early 2000s, while the EU's border agency, Frontex, reported 90,243 doing so in 2008 (Simon 2006: 26–42; cf. Frontex 2009: 12).

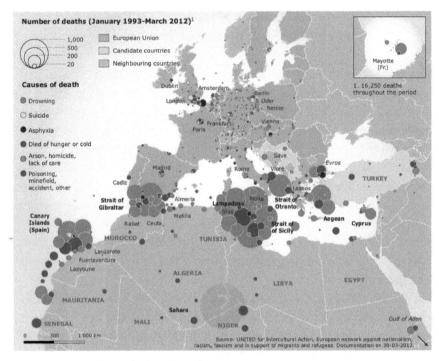

Figure 1.1. Deaths at the borders of Europe

Source: Reprinted by kind permission of New Internationalist. Copyright New Internationalist. www.newint.org

vast majority of the men, women, and children who lost their lives so near to their destination were refugees from Somalia, Eritrea, and Syria. The response by the Italian government exemplifies the politics of shipwreck: it declared a national day of mourning and granted all the deceased posthumous Italian citizenship. The Italian president described the shipwreck as a 'slaughter of innocents' (Davies 2013). Within a year, the government fixed an underwater plaque to the sunken shipwreck to commemorate the 400 dead migrants (Wall Street Journal 2014). However, for the 150 survivors, a different fate awaited. The government branded them 'illegal', fined each individual €5,000 for entering Italy without authorization, and incarcerated them in holding centres housing four times their normal capacity. Migrants thus elicited a humanitarian response only at sea and in death. As Susan Bibler Coutin (2005: 199) notes, 'In death, migrants are at once more human than ever and more realized as an object.'

In contrast to the Lampedusa shipwreck, many migrants leave no physical traces and are swallowed by the sea before maritime rescue centres locate them or before they dispatch rescue vessels. Just days before the tuna pen incident in May 2007, Malta's Armed Forces took an aerial photo of a boat located 150 kilometres south of the island, a three-hour journey for one of Malta's patrol vessels. The fifty-three Eritreans on board appeared to be bailing water out of the vessel. The image, along with a distress call made by satellite phone to relatives in Italy, were the last traces of the boat and most of its passengers. When a Maltese rescue vessel arrived over nine hours later, they found nothing. In the days that followed, a French navy ship recovered twenty-one bodies from the sea. Yet even in death, Malta refused to take responsibility for the migrants. After hours of negotiation between Malta, Libya, and France, the frigate sailed to France still carrying the corpses (Bilefsky 2007a; Popham 2007b).

In such cases, the bodies of the drowned are sometimes retrieved from the sea by fishermen and other mariners or wash up on beaches days later. Brown bodies are bleached white by the sun and sea salt. Eyes are gouged out by seagulls. Where shipwrecks occur closer to European shores, the wreckage is more immediately visible as journalists capture bloated bodies floating amongst splintered planks of wood. Most often it is the scenes of amorphous masses of huddled Africans on rescue vessels that accompany news reports of rescue and death. The media scenes dehumanize migrants into 'hordes' and 'masses' at the gate, imagined as the residue of structural poverty and violence that afflicts the Global South.

Propagated by the media, governments, and NGOs, such images simultaneously reinforce a humanitarian framework. In the Mediterranean, the spectacle of shipwreck renders migrants into helpless victims exploited by unscrupulous smugglers, so desperate that they take unfathomable risks. The scenes of rescue depoliticize: they turn European states and their border guards into heroes that rescue migrants from the clutches of smugglers and the sea, while obscuring how EU policies encourage such journeys. When migrants are not rescued, the dead are commemorated with ceremonies and plaques, and politicians express momentary anguish at the mounting death toll.

The fluctuating spectacles of humanitarianism and enforcement in the Mediterranean not only securitize migrants as a threat to communities, but also make possible the continued social, political, and economic marginalization of these travellers as subhuman or at least as a fully subordinated class. In the context of Southern Europe, Kitty Calavita (2005) has demonstrated how racialized otherness is not just a characteristic that migrants bring with them, but one that is constructed and reproduced legally and materially through state policies and migrants' location in the economy as an underclass of workers, through the economics of altérité.[11] Similarly, the spectacle of shipwrecks, death, and shipwrecked lives makes possible the marginalization of survivors of the sea: it marks them as 'other' and allows for their detention and deportation, their preclusion from integration and citizenship, and their relegation to the socio-economic fringes where few rights are afforded.

In these narratives, migrants remain voiceless, without agency, and less than human, rendered as 'shipwrecked lives'. As Tazzioli (2015: 3) has argued, 'people escaping wars can seek asylum only by first becoming shipwrecked persons to rescue. Humanitarian and security measures are thus two intertwined political technologies of migration governmentality.' Indeed, a security logic quickly trumps any humanitarian concerns after rescue: the same men, women, and children who are voiceless victims become risky bodies when they reach the shores of Lampedusa, Malta, Greece, and other European territories. The security and humanitarian frameworks converge, however, in a logic that demands more migration control at the European Union's external border as a moral measure taken for the common good of saving lives in response to migration 'crises' (Albahari 2006; Perkowski 2016). For example, in reaction to increasing deaths at sea in 2015 and the drowning of over 1,200 in one month, the EU proposed to use military force against 'smuggling vessels' in the Mediterranean. Despite fervent criticism from activists and academics, EU policymakers defended the proposal on humanitarian grounds. In May 2015, the EU's foreign policy chief, Federica Mogherini, sought authorization for the proposal at the United Nations Security Council, stating, 'We need to count on your support to save lives' (BBC 2015a).

The humanitarian and enforcement spectacles depend on the portrayal of the Mediterranean Sea as *mare nullius*, an empty wilderness, where smugglers expose migrants and refugees to the unpredictable elements, dangers from which the EU might rescue them. Removed from the scene are state and non-state actors that regularly populate the sea and that might disrupt the spectacles: coastguards, fishermen and other commercial vessels, military ships, and, more recently, NGO ships. The construction of *mare nullius* obscures the overlapping legal regimes that structure responsibilities, such as rescue and disembarkation, at sea. Gone are the political and legal conflicts that arise between states and result in non-assistance. In this way, the depiction of the Mediterranean as an empty, inhospitable, and ungovernable space provides a moral alibi for EU border guards and politicians when migrants die at sea,

---

[11] Calavita (2005: 207) employs the more commonly used French term for 'alterity', choosing it instead of 'difference' due to its suggestion of 'alteration' and implication of process.

much like the Sonoran Desert does on the US–Mexico border (Albahari 2016: 95–116; Doty 2011: 607). This (neo)colonial strategy of constructing an imagined geography empty of actors, history, and power relations obscures the complicity of EU policies, border guards, fishermen, military ships, and commercial vessels in migrant deaths (cf. Heller et al. 2012; Shaw et al. 2006).

Through the construction of the sea as an empty, uncivilized space and the projection of military-humanitarian spectacles, the migration 'crisis' is located outside of Europe, or at best on its fringes, rather than one in which the EU's migration regime is implicated. 'Europe', in contrast, is constructed as civilized, designated as the problem-solver tasked with resolving the migration issue. This narrative expunges the colonial history of Europe and the European Union and the ways in which this history, alongside contemporary, neocolonial 'interventions' and wars, shape migration today (De Genova and Tazzioli 2016: 12; Gregory 2004; Hansen and Jonsson 2017). The spectacles in the Mediterranean conceptualize Europe as a unified, singular actor with a hard border (enforcement) and a benevolent, democratic, human rights–oriented disposition (humanitarian) (De Genova 2016: 89).

However, as Braudel (1995a: 13) reminds us, 'The Mediterranean speaks with many voices.' Taking migrant experiences more seriously shifts this conceptualization of the Mediterranean and uncovers Europe's contradictions. Migrant narratives call attention to the different actors and overlapping legal regimes at sea, and the ways in which they fail to ensure rescue. Migrants' continued mobility across the Mediterranean, despite the risks and barriers, recalls the sea's long history of movement and the ways different actors have projected their power across it to control mobility throughout history (Braudel 1995a; 1995b). To many migrants, the sea is an unknown terrain that must be crossed in order to reach 'Europe', imagined as a space of refuge and opportunity. Yet, on European shores they are met with violence and marginalization: detained, threatened with deportation, and condemned to the margins of society. 'Europe' is thus both very real and an elusive imaginary for many who arrive on its shores and, dumbfounded at their violent treatment, ask 'is this Europe?'[12]

Bringing migrants to the centre of our analysis demonstrates how the Mediterranean is a contested space that is empirically and theoretically important in the construction of a contested 'Europe', a contradictory and incoherent project in the making. Although this study focuses in large part on

---

[12] A phrase repeated a number of times in discussions with migrants in Malta (Fieldwork, 2006–2015).

the European Union and its policies, it also encompasses other European institutions, such as the European Court of Human Rights, that sometimes mount challenges to the EU. In this way, I seek to problematize the frequent reduction of Europe to EU institutions and the equation of the EU with Europe, as other scholars have done (e.g. Stierl 2018). Even within the European Union, tensions, contradictions, and different interests come to the fore in the migration policy field. Migrants, a permanent feature of Europe throughout history, challenge the EU, its borders, and migration controls. Member states may also be subversive: the EU imposes structures and directives on member states that may defy regional authority and authorities; member states simultaneously exploit their membership by using the EU as a scapegoat.[13]

As will be explored further in this book, locating the migration 'crisis' in the Mediterranean projects an image of unified Europe while also, paradoxically, reinforcing the tension between Europe's 'core' and 'periphery'. Member states on the edge of Europe are sceptically assessed as failing to live up to 'European' standards of border controls, as well as other cultural, economic, and political standards. In the case of Greece, the economic crisis led to threats of withdrawal of EU membership. In this context, member states on the edge must go to greater lengths to perform their 'Europeaness' and thus distinctiveness from their non-EU neighbours with whom they have long histories of association. This is especially true for states like Malta and Cyprus that are former colonies of European powers. The performance is nonetheless an ambivalent one, especially in the realm of migration policies that place disproportionate responsibility on the periphery: politicians may pay lip service to a cohesive Europe while defying EU policies in practice (Mitchell 2002; Mufti 2014).

William Walters (2009: 487) has argued:

We cannot point to a place, state or continent called Europe which readily reveals its borders, edges or divisions to an impartial observer. On the

---

[13] Similar dynamics play out in other policy fields as well. Poland, for instance, defied an EU court order in 2017 to stop logging in a forest protected as a UNECSO world heritage site, despite the threat of hefty fines (Neslen 2017). Indeed, EU law includes infringement proceedings for member states who do not comply with court orders, including the imposition of financial penalties by the European Court of Justice (Chalmers et al. 2010: 315–49). Such conflicting interests and tensions are to be expected in a confederate system; they manifested spectacularly in the Greek debt crisis and the subsequent referendum on an EU bailout, as well as the UK referendum on exiting the European Union. However, the tensions between member states and the EU are particularly clear and unfaltering around migration due to the unequal distribution of responsibility for migration control and asylum and the politicized, symbolic, and sensationalized ways in which migration is associated with and produces anxieties about sovereignty and the nation. These patterns also emerged in the Brexit debate, vote, and continued negotiations.

contrary... debates about the frontiers of Europe are unavoidably political interventions which interject elements of fixture into the fluid and ambiguous space that is Europe.

As with geographies everywhere, the boundaries of Europe are not 'objective' or 'fixed'. Before decolonization in the 1950s, Europe officially stretched into Africa. In contrast, in 1987, the Turkish and the Moroccan governments caused consternation by asking to join the European Community. An anonymous and aghast European diplomat was quoted as saying, 'This is getting out of hand. First Turkey, now Morocco, who will be next to apply to join? Cyprus? Malta? Norway?' (quoted in Haynes 1999: 18). Although Malta's place in the European Union was secured almost twenty years later, the (neo)colonial question of the limits of 'Europe' continues to shape migration policies and practices in the Mediterranean.

Europe's Gatekeeper? The Island Republic of Malta

Malta is the smallest state, and we are carrying a burden that is much bigger than any other country.

Maltese Prime Minister Joseph Muscat, 2013[14]

EU membership has placed Malta and other member states along the Union's southern periphery in the migration spotlight. As dead bodies wash up on Mediterranean beaches and people continue to make perilous voyages, Europe's 'Rio Grande' represents one of the steepest value thresholds in the world where a few hundred kilometres of sea separate stark discrepancies in living standards (Montanari and Cortese 1993; Hadj-Abdou 2014). The discrepancies came into sharp relief in the twenty-first century as migrants on inflatable dinghies paddled by luxury yachts and cruise liners, and holiday-makers on beaches looked on while migrants were rescued from the sea (e.g. Jones 2015). Governments' divergent responses to different migrants was also stark as those seeking refuge were summarily locked up in detention centres, while the super-rich were sold citizenship.[15]

---

[14] Quoted in Freeman and Squires (2013).

[15] Malta launched a controversial Individual Investor Programme in 2014 that grants Maltese and thus EU citizenship to applicants if they contribute €650,000 to a national development fund, invest €150,000 in government stocks or bonds, and own a property worth at least €350,000 in Malta for at least one year. By 2018, the programme had generated €718 million in revenue. Other EU states have similar schemes (Cooper 2016; Peel and Khan 2018).

At this threshold, on the EU's southern periphery, the Republic of Malta acceded to the Union in 2004. Malta is an archipelago made up of three inhabited islands and numerous smaller uninhabited ones. Its geographic position places it at the centre of contemporary migration flows from Libya to Europe and it serves both as a destination and transit point for migrants along the central Mediterranean route. For much of the twenty-first century, Malta also received the greatest number of asylum seekers per capita within the EU. Although these numbers are far less significant when calculated against GDP per capita, the European Parliament echoed government rhetoric in identifying Malta as the EU member state experiencing the greatest migratory pressure 'out of proportion compared with its capacity' in 2010 (European Parliament 2010: 68; UNODC 2011: 14).

Simultaneously sites of mobility and immobility, islands are an interesting vantage point from which to examine patterns of migration. Napoleon's banishment to the island of Elba, the construction of a federal prison on Alcatraz, and the erection of an Australian immigration detention centre on the island of Nauru are examples of islands playing a function based primarily on their insular and isolated character.[16] However, the size and location of islands around the world have also prompted mobility: emigration has followed economic hardship and natural disaster, while immigration has taken the form of military conquest, retirement migration, tourism, and return migration (Braudel 1995a: 158–60; King 2009).

Malta is no exception: the comings and goings of merchants, soldiers, sailors, slaves, noblemen, workers, tourists, and others have been a constant in the archipelago's history due in part to its deep, natural harbours and its geostrategic location as a military and transport hub in the central Mediterranean. Phoenicians first colonized the islands in the seventh century BCE and used them as an outpost to expand exploration and trade in the Mediterranean. They called the islands 'Maleth', meaning shelter or haven. From 1814 to 1964, Malta was a British colony and was used as a shipping waystation and its Mediterranean fleet headquarters.

After the destruction of much of the country during World War II, Malta's migration patterns were defined by large-scale emigration. However, in the early twenty-first century, just prior to its accession to the EU, Malta experienced a significant increase in the arrival of migrants and refugees travelling by boat from Libya. Previously, few people had arrived in this

---

[16] Alison Mountz (2011a) provides an important discussion on the critical role islands play in migration control.

manner: for example, in 2001, only fifty-seven people arrived on the island without authorization. The following year, the number increased to 1,686, an almost 3,000 per cent increase in twelve months. The arrivals remained relatively high over the next decade and peaked in 2008 at 2,775 (NSO 2011). Although these numbers are not large in absolute terms, successive government administrations argued that the arrivals constitute a crisis if one takes Malta's small population of around 420,000 people into account. For example, the 1,250 asylum applications lodged in Malta in 2006 are equivalent to nearly 200,000 applicants in France and the UK if compared per capita. The actual asylum claims made in France and the UK that year were 26,300 and 27,850, respectively.[17] Maltese politicians have also frequently pointed to the fact that Malta's population density is one of the highest in the world, which, they argue, amplifies the effects of arrivals.[18] Maltese officials therefore repeatedly called upon the EU to share responsibility for the migration 'burden' (Crosbie 2007).

Malta's geographic location allowed it to acquire EU membership in the twenty-first century. Although its EU membership ostensibly increases its relative power, this power comes at a price: Malta's permeable maritime borders have been redefined as external EU borders in need of fortification and control. The country now acts as a migration gatekeeper for the EU, with responsibility to rescue those in distress in the central Mediterranean, disembark them on its territory, and process asylum claims. Moreover, Malta's capacity to receive migration flows is conditioned by the fact that it is the smallest country in the Union in terms of population and land area, and one of two autonomous states on the southern periphery separated from the European mainland.[19] Indeed, its geopolitical position between Europe and Africa, at first glance, appears to put it in a structurally weak arrangement within the European Union.

In this book, the Maltese case study grounds the analysis of EU migration policies and their effects in a specific context. Although its status as a small outpost island state shapes some of these dynamics in distinct ways, many

---

[17] The population figure given is for 2016, as estimated by the United Nations (2016). Asylum figures were calculated using the following sources: Malta's National Statistics Office; the UK's Office for National Statistics; and the French National Institute of Statistics and Economic Studies. For political statements to this effect, see, for example, an article written by the former prime minister, Lawrence Gonzi (2007).

[18] Malta's population density is 1,311 people per square kilometre (United Nations 2016). Within the EU, the closest population density is that of the Netherlands at 504. Italy, Spain, and Greece have population densities of 203, 92, and 85 per square kilometre, respectively.

[19] The Republic of Cyprus is the other autonomous island state on the southern periphery. However, it is located in the eastern basin of the Mediterranean, remains outside the Schengen Zone, and has thus far not received such large flows of unauthorized migration (Mainwaring 2014).

parallels exist with other member states along the EU's southern periphery as well as with other Western states that experience increases in immigration and act as migration gatekeepers. Within the EU, the focus on particular migration gatekeepers fluctuates, for example from Spain to Malta and Italy to Greece and back, as migrants respond to new barriers and create new routes or retrace old paths into Europe.

The focus on Malta also fills an empirical gap. Although the literature on other southern EU countries, such as Spain, Italy, and Greece, is plentiful and provides fruitful comparisons, the relevant political and academic discussions have largely neglected Malta and other small states.[20] There are a number of reasons to correct this omission and include Malta in the discussion on the southern periphery. First, the policy response to migration on the island echoes the puzzle at the EU level: the volume is small in absolute terms but has received considerable political attention. Second, Malta lies on a political, economic, and demographic threshold separating Europe, with its ageing and dwindling population, from poorer Africa, with its young burgeoning one. Here on the EU's external border, the negotiations over migration expose the effects of exclusionary logics at play within the Union that are often less obvious at the centre of Europe. Third, Malta's accession into the EU has significantly changed its migration policies, practices, and realities. As an outpost of the EU, it has assumed a much higher responsibility for migration than any other equally small but landlocked EU member state. Malta thus provides an exemplary lens through which to freshly examine the migration policies and realities of the EU.

Centring on the Margins: Power and the Everyday

In this book, I adopt a view from the margins in two ways. First, the tiny island state of Malta is taken as a case study, given its central location in the migration drama unfolding in the Mediterranean. Second, the experiences of migrants are central to my analysis, making them subjects rather than the objects of study. Examining clandestine migration and moving marginalized

---

[20] On other southern EU member states, see, for example: Andersson 2014; Cabot 2014; Calavita 2005; González-Enríquez and Triandafyllidou 2009; Innes 2015; King and Black 1997; Solé 2004. Small states, such as Malta, are underrepresented in the migration literature (with few notable exceptions: e.g. King and Thomson 2008; Lutterbeck 2009; Mainwaring 2014; 2012a; 2012b; Thomson 2006). Even within European studies, research tends to focus on larger states, despite the significant increase in the number of small states involved in the 2004 accession round, which has implications for the nature and function of the Union (Panke 2010).

individuals to the centre of the analysis is, as Noelle Brigden (2016: 3) argues, 'a disruption of the boundaries of politics, in itself a political act' (cf. Aradau and Huysmans 2014; Squire 2011). It allows us to question triumphant proclamations of a new transnational, globalized world, while also challenging declarations of the indomitable power of the nation state. Within critical migration studies, it allows us to move beyond polarizing theories that script migrants either as bare lives or as autonomous beings, reifying the power of the nation state and the power of clandestine migrants, respectively.[21]

Analysing clandestine migration and the everyday negotiations that take place at borders reveals the ways in which migrants question and disrupt but also contribute to conventional conceptualizations of sovereignty, territory, and citizenship. Disruptions may take the form of intentional resistance but may also be a product of less organized action (cf. Mahler 1998: 72; Brigden 2016). Echoing bell hooks (1990), Reece Jones (2012: 687) characterizes this as a 'space of refusal' where 'sovereign state practices interact with alternative ways of seeing, knowing, and being'. It thus includes everyday activities that are not necessarily premeditated challenges to the state, but nevertheless 'refuse to abide by the binary framing of state territorial and identity categories' (Jones 2012: 685; cf. Brigden 2018b).

At Europe's Edge explores these spaces of refusal in the Mediterranean, analysing patterns and agents of exclusion as well as resistance to them. Drawing on ethnographic methods to examine global political questions, the analysis considers the relationships between the regional, the national, and the local. I focus primarily on the years between 2000 and 2017, although it is occasionally necessary to delve further back into history. The research draws on fieldwork I conducted over ten years, between 2006 and 2016, including over 150 interviews with migrants, refugees, policymakers, border guards, NGO representatives, and fishermen. Interviews were conducted primarily in Malta but also in Brussels with policymakers at the EU Commission, Council, and Parliament. I carried out participant and non-participant observation with migrants in communities, immigration detention centres, and open reception centres in Malta.[22] The appendix includes a more extensive discussion of methods and ethics.

The data gathered from migrants serves as a method of triangulation to assess data provided by NGOs and government officials. Migrant experiences are crucial in investigating how migration is constructed as a threat or crisis.

---

[21] See Chapter 2 for further discussion of these positions.
[22] During this time, I also carried out interviews and participant observation in Cyprus. This data informs my analysis but is not drawn on explicitly.

They challenge government assumptions and claims, laying bare policies that produce deaths at sea and marginalization within the EU. The ethnographic data thus exposes conditions at the intersection of global, national, and local processes, and adds to our understanding of the world by not divorcing policy from reality, nor the international from the local (cf. Willen 2007; Desjarlais 1997). More broadly, the book posits that migration is a constitutive component of international relations,[23] rather than an exogenous variable to which states respond.[24] An ethnographic approach that focuses on everyday experiences and practices allows us to explore the dynamic relationship between territory, state, and nation, and challenge traditional notions of sovereignty, borders, and security (cf. Brigden 2016).

The study bridges the micro and macro by examining not only how state power and traditional conceptualizations of borders and sovereignty shape migrant experiences but also how migrants affect and produce state relations at and beyond the border (cf. Mahler 2000). Returning to the tuna pen incident is instructive here. In 2007, twenty-seven individuals braved the Mediterranean crossing, making their way towards Italy, perhaps to continue further north into Europe, perhaps to reunite with family or friends. It was state policies and practices—real and perceived, in Libya and in the EU—that provided, at least in part, the impetus for their voyage. Migrants often cite, for example, the violence they experience at the hands of Libyan authorities and the lack of asylum legislation in Libya as factors that eventually lead to their voyage across the Mediterranean. Similarly, hopes of finding refuge from the violence, better economic opportunities, and family members on the northern shores of the Mediterranean encourage their journeys. Libya's history as a centre of pan-Africanism under Gaddafi and its colonial relationship with Italy structure their migration experiences. Interstate relations and agreements also shape their journey and their reluctant rescue in the Mediterranean. This is a dynamic with which many migration and other scholars are familiar. For example, the ways in which interstate relations influence political, economic, and social landscapes is at the heart of much International Relations scholarship, even if the everyday practices that constitute international relations are only recently receiving wider attention (e.g. Kessler and Guillaume 2012; Acuto 2014; Côté-Boucher et al. 2014).

---

[23] Migrant experiences are therefore included on epistemological and ontological grounds.

[24] Considering its transnational character, it is surprising that international migration has not received more attention within the discipline of International Relations (but see Hollifield 1992; Mahler 2000; Miller and Papademetriou 1983; Mitchell 1989; Teitelbaum 1984; Thiollet 2011; Weiner 1985; Zolberg 1981; 1984; Zolberg et al. 1986). The discipline has focused on 'transnationalism from above', leaving 'transnationalism from below'—the everyday practices that shape place, identity, and our understandings of the world—to anthropologists and other scholars (e.g. Mahler 1998).

What is less frequently considered is the ability of the seemingly powerless, such as the men on the tuna pen, to find and exploit narrow margins of manoeuvrability, to exercise agency, to constitute borders, to challenge sovereignty, and to shape state behaviour and interstate relations—as the tuna pen incident described above illustrates. The power of people on the move to affect state relations was reaffirmed in 2011. During the early months of the year, the arrival of people in Malta and Italy who fled violence in North Africa produced diplomatic stand-offs. For example, Tunisians' northward journeys through Italy prompted France to reinstate border controls along the French-Italian border, discarding the Schengen Agreement that had been central to the EU since 1995 (Campesi 2011).

Individual decisions to move across state boundaries, to refuse to abide by binary categories of identity and territory, thus reverberate beyond the local level and create particular relationships between states and regional bodies. These spaces of refusal do not only occur at the border: migrants engage in protests, legal challenges, and other choreographed forms of resistance within the state, often in concert with non-governmental organizations. More subtle, unchoreographed demonstrations of agency are also present as migrants refuse to be fingerprinted, create spaces of solidarity, and undertake new clandestine journeys. An ethnographic approach allows for the analysis of such power at the margins and remind us that 'all margins are dangerous .... Any structure of ideas is vulnerable at its margins' (Douglas 1966: 150).

Naming the Subject

Unsurprisingly, the language used to describe people who move across borders is politicized. Those who have darker skin and more limited access to wealth are more likely to be called migrants—illegal, undocumented, *klandestini*, unauthorized, irregular, or unskilled depending on the context and geography. On the other hand, those with lighter skin and access to wealth are labelled expats, skilled, entrepreneurs, investors, backpackers, and tourists. The former categories help to construct a narrative of disorder, chaos, and crisis in stark, manufactured opposition to ordered, managed migration flows. They stigmatize and criminalize people who have often only committed an administrative offence in crossing borders without authorization,[25] who

---

[25] In Malta and many other Western countries, crossing territorial borders without state authorization remains an administrative offence akin to paying your taxes late. In recent years, some states have moved towards criminalizing migration: in 2009, Italy decreed that 'illegal immigration' was a

contribute their labour to national economies, and who may quickly regularize their status through asylum claims, marriage, or other processes.

Here, I use the word 'migrant' as an umbrella term in relation to people who move north across the Mediterranean, the EU's southern external border, often in a clandestine manner. Many are refugees. Some will not obtain refugee status, perhaps because they do not meet the Refugee Convention definition of an individual who has faced persecution on the grounds of race, religion, nationality, membership in a particular social group, or political opinion. Others will not be granted refugee status because they do not remember exact dates surrounding their persecution; case officers are more likely to dismiss their asylum claims as inconsistent and therefore not credible (Griffiths 2012). Indeed, migrant status is fluid, created by varying state regulations, rather than an objective reflection of a person's character or behaviour. Migration controls are not just filters that separate the legal traveller from the illegal, or refugees from 'bogus' asylum seekers. Migration controls are productive, constructing the categories between which they aim to distinguish and reinforcing power hierarchies. Thus, where possible, I have tried to speak about people and their experiences without reference to bureaucratic categories that are politicized, vary across geographies and time, and are inherently inadequate in capturing the complexities of lived realities.

Mapping the Book

The following chapters delve deeper into the issues sketched in this introduction and the questions posed at the outset: (1) Why has the EU emphasized the need to fortify the external borders when many more unauthorized migrants arrive through legal channels? (2) Why do migrants continue to attempt the Mediterranean crossing, and continue to die at sea, despite the emphasis on fortified external borders? And (3) how have small member states on the southern periphery responded to the sudden spotlight and responsibility for migration control? In answering these questions, the book adopts a view from the margins, bringing migrant experiences to the centre of its analysis and showing how the Mediterranean is an important space for the contested construction of Europe.

criminal rather than administrative offence, only to abolish the legislation in 2014 and reclassify it as an administrative offence. Nevertheless, many states adopt policies, such as mandatory detention, that de facto criminalize irregular entry.

The next chapter sets out the conceptual building blocks for the book and develops the idea of migrant agency, situating it within the relevant literature. The argument put forth is that power, politics, and people are significant and often neglected elements of migration governance processes. Ignoring their role in migration governance contributes to the unremitting promotion of the migration management paradigm. In contrast, I examine the interplay of actors, practices, and discourses within the realm of migration governance. Here, political power is often drawn from constructed crises based on a discourse of exceptionalism and sovereignty. Migrants are framed as symptomatic of globalization's attack on state sovereignty and constructed as victims or villains.

In this second chapter, I argue that the managed migration paradigm depends on the construction of a migration crisis to which the policy ostensibly responds. Such migration 'crises' obscure the complicity of the state in the production of vulnerability, marginalization, violence, and death through its border regimes, and reify the power of the state to control migration, despite paradoxically being promoted based on imagery of the state as overwhelmed. Within the context of Europe, the chapter demonstrates how the emphasis on migration control at the EU's external border results from constructed crises in the Mediterranean.

The third and fourth chapters make up the bulk of the empirical research and trace migrants' clandestine journeys into Europe. The third chapter follows migrant journeys to the edge of Europe, across the Sahara Desert and Mediterranean Sea. It analyses the fluctuating politics of rescue in the Mediterranean to reveal how the EU has contributed to deaths at sea and simultaneously pointed to these deaths and broader migration flows as a crisis. By following the journeys of migrants into Europe, this chapter demonstrates how state narratives obscure the ways in which migrants negotiate passage and challenge sovereignty. Analysing the changing politics and practices of rescue during the twenty-first century exposes how the Mediterranean is constructed through processes of making (in)visible. Through alternating politics of neglect, security, and humanitarianism, southern EU member states have constructed a migration 'crisis', depicting long-standing migration flows across the Mediterranean as chaotic and unprecedented. Key to the crisis narrative and the subsequent securitized humanitarian politics is the portrayal of migrants either as victims with no agency or as villains endowed with a dangerous, Herculean form of agency. This allows states to render border controls and externalization practices as life-saving measures.

The fourth chapter turns to the policies and practices that migrants encounter once they arrive in Malta and on EU territory. After a review of the history of migration to the island and the contemporary migration situation, it traces migrant journeys from the detention centres that await them upon arrival to possible deportation. By examining the sites and processes where migrants continue to be securitized within the border, the chapter argues that even when rescued from the sea, migrants do not escape political, social, and economic marginalization. The securitization of migration contributes to the construction of a crisis and fuels racism and xenophobia within the host population. Migration becomes an easy scapegoat for uncertainties and inequalities of a twenty-first century society.

Throughout these two chapters, migrant accounts of border crossings and experiences within host states demonstrate their agency and the narrow room for manoeuvre they are sometimes able to exploit. Ignoring this agency reifies the power of the state to 'secure' borders and control migration, and conceals the contested politics of mobility and security evident in negotiations between migrants, borders guards, smugglers, fishermen, and other actors. Such encounters question traditional conceptualizations of sovereignty, security, and citizenship. They illustrate alternative modes of seeking security that move beyond the state and citizenship as the sole frameworks of security and endorse a more nuanced picture of the border as a contested space.

Chapters 3 and 4 propose answers to the second question posed above about why migrants continue to make the Mediterranean crossing and to die at sea, despite the fortified external border. Migrant accounts reveal the longer journey that begins before the Mediterranean shores and demonstrate the room for manoeuvre that migrants find and exploit that renders the EU more sieve than fortress. Their experiences also illustrate how a politics of neglect results in deaths at sea. These chapters contribute to the literature on spectacle by illustrating how both humanitarian and enforcement performances reify the power of the state and construct 'Europe' as a discrete unit, a benevolent actor in control of its borders. In doing so, the spectacles cast the Mediterranean as an empty, marginal space and construct migrants as objects to be governed, as symbols of disorder and chaos. Significantly, the spectacles at sea brand migrants as victims or villains, ultimately as 'others', which allows for their continued marginalization in Europe.

The fifth chapter analyses how in this context Malta constructed a crisis around the issue of migration, and how the small state exploited the crisis to secure more EU funds and support. It thus focuses on the third question posed above about the response by member states on Europe's periphery. The chapter analyses Malta's strategies at the EU level and its lobbying around particular policies. The research demonstrates how Malta exerted an unexpected level of influence on EU migration governance by adopting a number of strategies, including emphasizing its small state status, its gatekeeper role, and the 'crisis'. However, this Lilliputian power has come with an increased responsibility for control of the EU's external border. Moreover, Malta's power to change the system is limited: the EU framework now shapes its interests and strategies. EU structures encourage Malta to frame migration in the Mediterranean as a crisis overwhelming a small country. This portrayal reduces migrants to symbols of disorder and reinforces the need to control migration along the EU's external border.

The concluding chapter returns to the main themes explored in the book and the contestation over borders, migration controls, and mobility at the edge of Europe. It considers the future of Europe and the European Union, its border controls in the Mediterranean, resistance to them, and alternative policy choices. While state policies erode spaces of asylum, undermining refugee protection and access to global mobility, inequality is on the rise and people continue to cross borders, often at great risk.

2

Constructing Crises to Manage

Migration Governance and the Power to Exclude

Managed Migration?

Today, the term 'managed migration' is never far from the lips of bureaucrats, politicians, policymakers, and even academics and activists. The concept first emerged in 1993 at the United Nations' Commission on Global Governance (Ghosh 2000). Over the next decade, it was touted as a more progressive framework than the restrictive immigration policies that many Western states adopted after the 1973 oil crisis. These restrictive migration policies had intensified following the fall of the Berlin Wall, the so-called European asylum 'crisis' in the 1990s, and migration 'crises' in other parts of the world (Van Hear 2012: 4–5; Schuster 2005).

Since the 1990s, initiatives to promote a 'managed' approach to migration proliferated at the global, regional, and national levels, from the United Nations' Global Commission on International Migration launched in 2003 and its Global Forum on Migration and Development in 2007 to the 2014 EU-Horn of Africa Migration Route Initiative, known as the Khartoum Process, and the EU's 2015 Agenda on Migration.[1] In 2016, the United Nations High Commissioner for Refugees confirmed, 'Europe is now also seeing record numbers of refugees, and migrants, arriving on its shores....This emergency does not have to be a crisis, it can be managed.'[2]

Such initiatives are couched in neutral, technocratic language that promises ambitious results: an orderly alternative to the disorder of 'spontaneous' and 'irregular' migrant arrivals at the borders of the Global North that is

---

[1] The 'Agenda' is one of a long line of similar EU initiatives implemented since the turn of the twenty-first century. These include, for example, the Commission's Communication on a 'Community Immigration Policy' (European Commission 2000), its Communication on 'Strengthening the Global Approach to Migration' (European Commission 2008), and the EU Ministers of Justice and Home Affairs' perennial paper 'Action on Migratory Pressures' (European Council 2012b; cf. Salt 2002: 39–42). Outside the EU framework, the Council of Europe (2002) has also championed 'migration management'.

[2] Speech given on International Women's Day to the European Parliament, Strasbourg, 8 March 2016.

economically productive and humane, a 'triple win' for sending states, receiving states, and migrants (Geiger and Pécoud 2010: 9; cf. ILO 2004; GCIM 2005; Taylor 2005). The managed migration discourse thus neatly, if superficially, reconciles tensions between humanitarian and security concerns, epitomized by recent migrant shipwrecks in the Mediterranean. For example, the EU Commission's 'Global Approach to Migration and Mobility' promises to uphold human rights and save lives by increasing surveillance and screening. Measures like the European Border Surveillance System, traditionally associated with deterrence and control, are reframed as 'life-saving instruments' (European Commission 2011a; 2013).

At the heart of the approach is the fundamental idea that migration can and should be managed. Notions of sovereignty loom large in the managed migration discourse, which assumes that states have the capacity to control migration absolutely and that there is a normative imperative to do so in order to reduce forms of unauthorized movement. The paradigm appeals to liberal traditions of the rule of law and harm reduction, where migration controls are a moral good that inhibit exploitative practices of smugglers and traffickers, reducing violence and death, while also protecting citizens from unsavoury foreigners who would threaten their welfare, livelihoods, and security (Anderson 2012; Inder 2010). For example, the UK's 2002 white paper, 'Secure Borders, Safe Haven', pledged to:

> manage flows through legitimate entry routes, developing managed migration policies to attract the people we need to compete and prosper in the global economy in a manner consistent with our international commitment to eliminate world poverty and domestic commitment to achieve employment opportunities for all. We will develop our methods to counteract organised immigration crime and illegal working and crack down on those who undermine and abuse our system. And fundamental to our moral and humanitarian objectives we will develop a seamless asylum process which is clear from induction to integration or return.   (Home Office 2002: 20)

Here, 'managed migration' not only promises to combat organized crime and ensure competitiveness in the global economy but to also eliminate world poverty and create employment for all! Central to the discourse is the neoliberal goal of a 'flexible' labour force, where migrants become the perfect labourers: able to fill gaps in the market to enhance a state's global competitiveness and easily returned 'home' within circular migration flows in times of economic recession. Indeed, across Europe, North America, and the Middle East, many states have expanded their temporary migrant worker programmes in the twenty-first century (Castles 2006; Preibisch 2010). The technocratic language that frames managed migration as mutually beneficial to all depoliticizes the policymaking process and disregards economic, political, and social inequalities in the world that prompt various forms of migration and reinforce a global hierarchy of mobility. The framework overlooks asymmetries of power and divergent interests within and between countries.

As Boucher (2008: 1462) argues, in the global policy discourse on international migration, 'the structure of the global capitalist system in its neoliberal form is taken for granted, and not taken as part of the problem.' In this depoliticized space, 'best practices' can be deployed and shared in order to manage migration without real-world complexities and complications. Migration is once again imagined as a water spigot that can be turned on and off, a debunked idea propagated in the context of large guest worker programmes in the US and Europe after World War II that ignores the fact that migration involves humans with their own agency (Cornelius 2001; Castles 2005).

More than two decades after the UN's Commission on Global Governance, it is also increasingly clear that although the language of migration governance may have become more sanitized and optimistic, the migration practices of most Western governments remain restrictive, with enforcement and deterrence at their core, especially with regard to those illegalized by state policies: the unauthorized entrant, the asylum seeker, and the victim of trafficking. The division of individuals into these categories and the attempts to 'manage' their mobility are politicized processes that 'track historic grooves of colonial and geopolitical subjecthood, acting as forms of administrative violence' (Loyd and Mountz 2014: 34).

Scholars have demonstrated how, despite the language of law and order and harm reduction, the build-up of enforcement practices at and increasingly beyond the border contribute to the vulnerability, violence, and death seen during migrant journeys, increase the need for many to use smugglers and enter states illicitly, as well as increase precarious employment conditions and legal statuses in countries of destination (e.g. Anderson 2010; Cornelius 2001; Mainwaring and Brigden 2016). The focus on migration controls at and beyond the border thus arguably increases the 'disorder' to which such controls purportedly respond.

In this chapter, I argue that the managed migration paradigm depends on the construction of a migration crisis to which the policy ostensibly responds. Such migration 'crises' obscure the complicity of the state in the production of vulnerability, marginalization, violence, and death through its border regimes, and reify the power of the state to control migration, despite paradoxically being promoted based on imagery of an overwhelmed state. To complete this sleight of hand, policy discussions on migration governance ignore the role of migrants themselves. The absence of migrant experiences and voices in scholarship on migration governance reinforces the orientalist logic and assumptions within policy discourse that migrants are objects to be governed, not subjects who engage in decision-making, resist, and ultimately constitute international relations (Calavita 2005: 150–1; Rother 2013; cf. Hage 2000).

The chapter first examines how crises are constructed through a narrative that frames migrant arrivals, and by extension the nation state, as exceptional. It then analyses how the construction of migration crises led to an emphasis on migration controls at the EU's external borders, through in particular the Schengen Agreement and Dublin Regulation. Finally, it turns to the question of migrant agency and argues that casting migrants as objects to be governed, often villains or victims, is fundamental to the construction of a crisis and the migration management paradigm.

Migration Crises: State Sovereignty and Myths of Exceptionalism

Migration crises seem to be on the rise. From Syrian families crossing the Aegean and other parts of the Mediterranean, to Central Americans travelling north towards the US–Mexico border, Rohingya stranded in the Andaman Sea, and trafficked labourers working on Thai fishing vessels, the strained expressions of migrants and refugees are splashed across newspapers under headlines that read crisis in big, bold letters. The global migration policy arena echoes these pronunciations of crisis, as does some of the scholarly literature on migration (e.g. Martin 2014; cf. McAdam 2014).

A crisis can be defined as a sudden change that causes alarm (Mountz and Hiemstra 2014: 383). If crises are a disruption to the norm of presumed stability (Roitman 2013: 4), migration crises appear to be a permanent feature of governance in Europe, albeit with peaks and troughs of intensity. As the New Keywords Collective have argued, 'regarding illegalized migration into and across Europe—the very distinction between (and separation of) what is ostensibly "stable" and "in crisis" is altogether tenuous, indeed, dubious' (Heller et al. 2016: 10). While some scholars have critically assessed the current moment as a crisis of governance, rather than of migration (e.g. Crawley et al. 2017; cf. Vincenti 2018), here I am more interested in how crises are a tool of governance. As Giorgio Agamben (2013) reminds us:

> [t]he concept 'crisis' has indeed become a motto of modern politics, and for a long time it has been part of normality in any segment of social life .... Today crisis has become an instrument of rule. It serves to legitimize political and economic decisions that in fact dispossess citizens and deprive them of any possibility of decision.

Invoking a crisis charges political debates with a sense of urgency and in doing so enables new political possibilities, while foreclosing others. Although references to migration crises abound, they have not been the subject of extensive critical scholarship (but see De Genova and Tazzioli 2016; Mainwaring 2012b; Mountz and Hiemstra 2014; Vaughan-Williams 2015). Yet, they are important in laying the foundation for logics that assume the need to manage migration, to order the disordered. For instance, in 2012, the International Organization for Migration (IOM) chose the theme 'managing migration in crisis situations' for its International Dialogue on Migration. Indeed, the IOM has played a central role in promoting the managed migration paradigm. A creative public relations effort centred on humane and orderly migration obscures the fact that the IOM engages in coercive practices, such as interdiction, detention, and deportation, at the behest of states who are unable or unwilling to do so directly. These practices effectively reduce access to asylum for most of the world's population and ultimately encourage 'unauthorized' forms of migration (Ashutosh and Mountz 2011; cf. IOM 2005).

　Why is mobility, a long-standing feature of human history, framed as a crisis when particular people engage in it or when those people cross particular borders? What space does crisis rhetoric create for state and non-state actors operating in the realm of migration? And what questions, understandings, and actions does it foreclose? State actors and the media frame particular forms of mobility across particular economic, political, legal, and cultural thresholds as chaotic and exceptional. Clandestine journeys and border crossings, especially from poorer to richer countries, are constructed as threats to sovereignty, the economy, and national identity. The seemingly contradictory enforcement and humanitarian spectacles around migration both contribute to the sense of crisis and also provoke fear and anxiety about order and the waning power of the nation state in a fast changing, globalized word. In turn, the constructed migration crisis serves to corroborate the state narrative that it faces an exceptional situation, reinforce state legitimacy and sovereign power, and justify the implementation of exceptional policies.

Exceptional Moments?

In constructing a migration crisis, politicians, the media, and others frame migration flows, and by extension the nation state, as exceptional and ahistorical. Long-standing mobility as well as complex historical and contemporary ties between countries are erased. The source of the 'crisis' is positioned externally to the state and its policies, neatly fixed on 'foreign' bodies. The number of arrivals, within an arbitrary length of time and geographical space, is produced as evidence of the crisis: charts are drawn up and temporal comparisons made to demonstrate the 'unprecedented' and 'alarming' levels of migration. For example, in 2016, one newspaper repeated a common refrain about the migration 'crisis' that has seen the number of Syrian and other refugees arriving at Europe's borders increase: 'More than 100,000 refugees and migrants have arrived in Europe so far this year—more than eight times the rate seen during the same period in 2015' (Dearden 2016a). Similar foreboding comparisons were made in the context of arrivals in the Canary Islands and in the central Mediterranean earlier in the twenty-first century and were accompanied by references to the 'millions' in Libya and elsewhere waiting for an opportunity to make their way to Europe (e.g. Poutignat and Streiff-Fénart 2010: 207; de Haas 2008).

Scholars have frequently questioned these statistics pointing to a 'myth of invasion' (de Haas 2008), and a politics of counting (Tazzioli 2015; cf. Martin and Lynch 2009). For example, the Clandestino (2009) research project reveals that the majority of migrants without status do not enter the EU clandestinely but overstay visas after arriving through formal channels. The project also estimated the overall number of 'irregular migrants' in the European Union to be between 1.9 and 3.8 million in 2008, making up less than 1 per cent of the total EU population and significantly lower than the previously touted estimates of up to 8 million. More recently, Nando Sigona (2015) has noted how Frontex, the EU's border agency, double counts migrants and refugees as they cross over multiple borders within the European Union, adding to the sense of crisis.

Significantly, crises are constructed around migration even when the number of arrivals is limited. This is accomplished through a politicized counting and racialized imagery of 'floods' of migrants, but also through a sensationalism around the effects of arrivals as a threat to a nation's culture, security, and economy. For example, despite the relatively small number of asylum seekers involved, Australia constructed a crisis around boat arrivals in the 1990s and 2000s that was deployed to justify the implementation of the 'Pacific Solution', a policy that included the offshore interdiction of boats and the transfer of asylum seekers to detention centres on remote islands such as Nauru, Manus, and Christmas Island (Hyndman and Mountz 2008: 256–62; Phillips 2014).

Here, as elsewhere, the construction of a crisis involved the othering of asylum seekers as masses of unknowable bodies with barbaric practices and terrorist intentions (Mares 2002: 134–5). In 2001, a boat carrying 223 people, including seventy-six children, sank as the Australian navy attempted to tow it back to Indonesia. In the weeks before a national election, Prime Minister John Howard demonized the asylum seekers, claiming that they had tried to toss their children overboard to provoke rescue and disembarkation in Australia. The 'children overboard' story spread rapidly and propagated the portrayal of people travelling in such a manner as uncivilized and unwelcome, contributing to the sense of crisis around boat arrivals. On the radio, Prime Minister Howard declared, 'I can't comprehend how genuine refugees would throw their children overboard....I certainly don't want people of that type in Australia' (Marr and Wilkinson 2001). It was only the following year, after Howard had been re-elected, that a senate inquiry into the incident confirmed that no children had been thrown into the water (Commonwealth of Australia 2002).

Similarly, in 1999, the Canadian government framed the arrival of 599 Chinese asylum seekers on four boats as a crisis and used it to support new, more restrictive immigration legislation including the expansion of immigration detention (Mountz 2010: 13–17). A decade later, the arrival of two boats, the *Ocean Lady* carrying seventy-six Sri Lankan Tamils and the *Sun Sea* carrying 492, prompted the Canadian government to introduce Bill C-31. The 2012 bill expanded the Immigration Minister's power to deny access to refugee protection based on a 'safe' country list. Hours after the arrival of the *Sun Sea*, the Public Safety Minister Vic Toews stated the government 'must ensure that our refugee system is not hijacked by criminals or terrorists' (Derosa 2012). A decade apart, the arrivals were framed as exceptional and as requiring exceptional policy responses, obscuring the fact that many more asylum seekers arrived in Canada via other routes.

In New Zealand, constructing a crisis has not even required any arrivals: as of 2017, no asylum seekers had arrived by boat to the country (Global Detention Project 2014a). Nonetheless, reportedly worried about New Zealand's relatively relaxed policies, former Prime Minister John Key warned of the need to develop harsher detention policies, including offshore processing for boat arrivals, due to an 'ongoing threat' of mass arrivals (Ghezelbash 2014: 149; Flynn 2014: 185). Referring to the Sri Lankans who arrived in Canada in

2010, Key said, 'If they can get to Canada they can get to New Zealand so we are looking at our own legislation and our response to this issue' (Vance 2010). As a result, New Zealand amended its legislation in 2013 to permit the indefinite detention of non-citizens who arrive by boat, despite the complete absence of boat arrivals (Global Detention Project 2014a).

Expanding Sovereign Power and Introducing Exceptional Policies

Such migration 'crises' reinforce the modern geopolitical imaginary of state borders as territorial markers of the limits of sovereign authority that neatly encompass the polity (Agnew 1994; cf. Vaughan-Williams 2009). Indeed, as inherently unstable formations, nation states must be constantly reaffirmed (Hall et al. 2013; Loyd and Mountz 2014: 28). Moreover, the symbolic and material reinforcement of territorial borders is politically useful in a globalized, 'borderless' world that has seen premature predictions of the end of the nation state and deep anxiety about a waning of state sovereignty (Ohmae 1994; cf. Brown 2010). Within a rhetoric of crisis, the interplay between chaos and order and between vulnerability and superiority promotes sovereign power as a force of stability where chaos emanates from outside the state and its borders.

In this context, nationalism plays an important role: it reaffirms a sense of exceptionalism and conveys security and unity in a time of 'crisis'. National myths and nationalist narratives often rest on an assumption of the exceptional nature of the nation state and its people. For example, in the seventeenth century, the British believed they were exceptionally rational and scientific, while Americans today believe that the historical origins of their nation state have endowed them with exceptional political and social ideals (Merom 1999: 409–10). Crisis rhetoric can bolster this sense of exceptionalism by framing a current moment or event as unique, but also by reinscribing imagined and acquired senses of national identity. In particular, migration crises reinforce an exceptional nationalism by emphasizing differences between 'us' and 'them' that constructs migrants as 'marauding' masses and an easy scapegoat for society's ills (Perraudin 2015). While reinforcing a sense of superior exceptionalism, the construction of migration crises also calls attention to the exceptional vulnerability of a nation state to the 'threat' of migration flows. In doing so, politicians, the media, and others rely on narratives and racialized imagery that recall unique historical moments, often other historical 'crises' faced by the state (Hier and Greenberg 2002). For example, in Malta and

Italy, parallels have been drawn between current migrant arrivals and Ottoman invasions in the fifteenth and sixteenth centuries (Albahari 2006: 5; Pisani 2011: 30–2).

Migration 'crises' thus serve to justify the fortification of borders. Despite pronunciations of a borderless world, scholars have demonstrated the absence of an erosion of borders after the end of the Cold War. Instead, Western governments introduced a host of new migration and border policies that simultaneously thickened, thinned, and delocalized the border (e.g. Andreas 2003; Mountz 2010; Salter 2004). As the focus of border security shifted from interstate military invaders to transnational law evaders, migration regimes were restructured through the introduction of restrictive immigration policies— including lengthy detention periods, the denial of asylum claims, and increased deportations—the geographic extension of policing away from borders, increased surveillance across and within nation states, and international security cooperation (Andreas 2003: 82). At the same time, state borders became more permeable for goods, capital, and the wealthy. As Etienne Balibar (1998: 220) observes, borders are now 'vacillating...multiplied and reduced in their localization...thinned out and doubled...no longer the shores of politics but...the space of the political itself'.

Although processes of inclusion and exclusion are conducted within and beyond national boundaries, borders continue to act as particularly salient symbols and locations of exclusion. Around the world, states build walls, raise barbed wire, and lay landmines as demarcations of who is inside and a member and who remains outside, subject to the political contingencies that will determine whether they are desirable migrants. While such bordering processes have practical ramifications for those crossing borders, power lies also in their symbolic significance: borders are not only a site of control but also a site of the spectacle of sovereign control, and as such symbols of identity (Brown 2010). A national border projects an image of a powerful and cohesive nation state, ostensibly functioning as a barrier to 'manage' migration and intercept flows of 'illegal' migrants. Borders obscure complex histories and relationships by creating symbolic divisions between states and people. A fundamental component of the nationalist myth is the border framed as an enduring, objective feature of the state, rather than a historically contingent and unstable artefact of power struggles and war, a fact that maps of the Middle East or divided islands such as Cyprus and Ireland make more obvious. As Mike Haynes (1999: 22) urges, we must 'reject the idea that there is an objective geographical, cultural, linguistic, economic, ethnic or any other component that distinguishes not only national groups from one another but the European from anyone else'.

Migrant crisis rhetoric that at once emphasizes the idea of sovereign control demarcated by clear territorial borders has also been used to extend sovereign power beyond the border. This expansion of sovereign power in moments of migration 'crises' involves for instance the externalization of migration controls and asylum processing, offshore interception, as well as the internal expansion of policing power (cf. Mountz and Hiemstra 2014). At and beyond the border, state immigration practices that are justified by the crisis simultaneously reinforce the crisis: for example, offshore interdiction, immigration detention, and highly visible immigration controls at and within the border contribute to the sense of emergency and the construction of migrants as criminals (Brown 2010; Coleman 2007; De Genova 2013; Mainwaring and Silverman 2017; Mountz 2011a).

The crisis depends not only on the material power of the state—the resources to build walls and launch militarized operations against migrants at sea and on land—but also on its non-material power, the arguments made and narratives told about the exceptional nature of the 'crisis'.[3] The emergency nature of the migration crisis needs a visual frame and its success rests on the politicized interplay between visibility and invisibility (Butler 2009: 6; Andersson 2014: 150). For instance, humanitarian rescue and border enforcement are made hypervisible and spectacular. The role of exploitative, violent smugglers is likewise sensationalized. Simultaneously, the role of the state in creating unauthorized migration flows is obscured, as is the violence it inflicts through practices, policies, and neglect. Concealed also are the daily contestations of sovereignty that occur at the border as those who are deemed 'unwanted' enter in a clandestine manner, negotiating with border guards, smugglers, fishermen, and other mariners. Similarly, the ways in which migrants and refugees integrate and contribute within societies after arrival is hidden behind prominent narratives of waves of 'illegal' migrants. Migrants as subjects, in all their complexity, are erased and replaced with flat objects as victims or villains.

Complicity in the Crisis

A crisis narrative takes arrivals out of a broader historical and political context in order to create a sense of disorder. Susan Bibler Coutin (2005: 195)

---

[3] A state derives material power from resources such as its military, economy, territory, or population; whereas non-material power is based on resources such as knowledge, networks, moral authority, or symbolic capital. Non-material power is thus often exercised through discursive practices (Mainwaring 2014).

argues that many clandestine migration flows and routes are a 'hidden, yet known, dimension of social reality'. Moreover, 'spontaneous' arrivals are often predictable, the result of military invasions or an increase in migration controls elsewhere. For instance, the eastward shift of migration flows across the EU's southern periphery since 2005 was a foreseeable result of an increase in migration controls at particular thresholds, despite being repeatedly characterized as a crisis.

In 2006, the 'cayucos crisis' erupted in the Canary Islands when around 30,000 people arrived, having departed from the West African coast on small fishing boats known as *cayucos*. The increase in migration flows to the Canary Islands was in part a response to the intensification of controls around the Spanish enclaves of Ceuta and Melilla in 2005. Likewise, the preceding increase in controls across the Strait of Gibraltar had diverted flows towards the Spanish enclaves (Ferrer-Gallardo 2008).

In response to the arrivals in the Canary Islands in 2006, Spain and the EU deployed Frontex patrols around the Islands while Spain began to formalize cooperation and sign readmission agreements with West African states under its Action Plan for sub-Saharan Africa.[4] These measures first caused migrant embarkation points to shift southward from Morocco to Western Sahara to Mauritania and finally to Senegal. Boat journeys across the Atlantic became longer and more dangerous. Eventually, as Spain signed cooperation agreements with these countries, more people began to travel through central Africa towards Libya, making their way to Europe across the central Mediterranean (de Haas 2008; Godenau 2014). By 2008, the sense of crisis in the central Mediterranean was palpable. Government and media accounts claimed that '[u]p to a million migrants have gathered in Libya, from where they will attempt to sail across the Mediterranean for Europe and, ultimately, the UK' (Townsend 2008). These claims persisted despite evidence from academics and international organizations that indicated that most migrants in Libya, a country with a long history of labour migration, did not intend to cross the

---

[4] Spain's Action Plan for sub-Saharan Africa involved cooperation and readmission agreements with Guinea Conakry (2007), Guinea Bissau (2008), the Gambia (2008), Senegal (2008), Cape Verde (2008), Niger (2008), Mali (2009), and Cameroon (2011). It already had readmission agreements in place with Morocco (1991) and Mauritania (2003/2006). Although the agreement with Morocco ostensibly allowed Spain to return Moroccans and third-country nationals who had transited Morocco, in practice, Morocco refused to readmit third-country nationals, claiming that there was no proof of their transit through Morocco. Since 2003, however, third-country nationals were readmitted to Morocco if they had travelled by boat to Spain or the Canary Islands under the captaincy of a Moroccan national (Carling 2007; Cassarino 2010; see also 'Inventory of the agreements linked to readmission' by Jean-Pierre Cassarino, European Union Institute. Available here: http://www. jeanpierrecassarino.com/datasets/ra/).

Mediterranean. It was not until 2011 that the Libyan Revolution and NATO intervention caused many more people to flee the country.[5]

Framing migration as a crisis conceals how the state and its policies encourage dangerous and clandestine migrant journeys. For example, the 1990 Martelli Law in Italy introduced visas for North Africans and sanctions for airlines and ferries that transported passengers without proper entry documents. In doing so, it effectively created 'illegal' migration across the central Mediterranean (Dines et al. 2015: 432). The crisis discourse also obscures historical and structural factors that shape decisions to migrate: colonial histories and contemporary policies that continue to produce inequality, poverty, and violence (De Genova and Tazzioli 2016: 10, 21). Policy debates over migration rarely take into serious consideration how contemporary and historical subjugation and exploitation by the West, alongside the border regimes established at its edges, encourage migration. As De Genova (2017: 18) has incisively observed, 'it is a new Europe, fortified by very old and morbid cruelties.' Framing migration as a crisis also disregards migrant agency and reduces migrants to flotsam and jetsam pushed and pulled by forces beyond their control. Within the crisis narrative, migrants become irrational victims taking unfathomable risks, coerced by ruthless smugglers, and enticed by pull factors, such as rescue missions and high standards of living on the northern edges of the Mediterranean.

Such crises are productive moments: logics of exceptionalism validate the nation state and create space for the expansion of sovereign power and the implementation of exceptional policies. Non-state actors also benefit politically and financially through the mobilization of a crisis narrative, the exploitation of uncertainty, and the promotion of more punitive immigration policies. For instance, security actors—private security companies, border guards, and the military—profit from expanding immigration detention regimes and other immigration controls (Doty and Wheatley 2013; Mainwaring and Silverman 2017). Advocacy organizations may benefit as their work is rendered more essential and they are able to attract more funds (Agustín 2007). Migration scholars are also suddenly in high demand: policymakers, journalists, and politicians want quick-fix solutions to the 'crisis'; and new streams

---

[5] In 2016, the central Mediterranean was once again the focus of crisis rhetoric. The agreement struck between the EU and Turkey in March 2016 increased migration controls along the Turkish border and allowed the EU to return people from Greece to Turkey. Shortly after, there was an increase in migrants using the central Mediterranean route from Libya to Italy. Although evidence later showed that the increase was not made up of people redirected by the EU–Turkey deal but included a large increase in Nigerians (UNHCR 2017b), politicians took the opportunity to warn of the crisis that was looming in the central Mediterranean (e.g. Leone-Ganado 2017).

of 'emergency' funding are created for academics to study the 'problem' (Andersson 2018). Even critical scholars build careers on moments when migration research is sexy and lucrative, and they can easily demonstrate 'impact'. Naomi Klein (2007) argues that in our neoliberal era, a variety of private and public actors mobilize crisis narratives and exploit man-made and natural disasters to advance neoliberal policies and turn a profit. Man-made and natural disasters converge in the discourse around migration crises which points to exploitative smugglers as the drivers of 'floods', 'avalanches', and 'tidal waves' of migrants. The next section explores how such migration 'crises' have been constructed on the edge of Europe, locating the 'problem' and responsibility for migration control at the external border. It also examines how this displacement creates a perverse incentive for member states on the periphery to reproduce the crisis and to marginalize migrants.

Crises at the Edge of Europe

Migration crises have a long history in Europe. Constructed and exploited by member states, they precipitated the emphasis on migrant arrivals at the external borders of the European Union. Initially, the Schengen Agreement (1995) noted the need 'to take complementary measures to safeguard internal security and prevent illegal immigration' (European Union 2000). Thus, the EU linked the reduction of internal border controls to increased controls at the external border. More freedom of movement within the Schengen area would be coupled with further restrictions on mobility. The EU operational-ized the emphasis on migration control at the external borders through the transfer of funds to peripheral member states and the creation of an EU agency for external border security, Frontex, in 2005.[6] Cooperation between

---

[6] The agency is tasked with the operational application of the Schengen Borders Code and is the institutional manifestation of the EU's 'Integrated Border Management'. As such, it is responsible for external border security, it coordinates the activities of national border guards, and it carries out risk analysis on borders (European Council 2006; 2004). The conception of border management envisaged in Frontex's mandate gives priority to the understanding of the border as a demarcating line between what is inside and what is outside (Carrera 2007: 2–8). Moreover, an essential aspect of the Integrated Border Management approach is the particular focus on the southern maritime border. Although Frontex is headquartered in Warsaw on the EU's eastern border, so many of its activities have taken place on Europe's southern periphery that opening a separate Frontex branch in the Mediterranean was proposed in 2006 (European Commission 2006; Interview: Research Fellow, Centre for European Reform, July 2010). Officially a Community organization, Frontex remains highly dependent on member states, financially and politically, and is thus susceptible to focusing on 'emergency-driven situations as politically constructed in the national arena' (Carrera 2007: 27). Indeed, the Agency first launched its European Patrol Network in the Canary Islands in 2007 in response to the 'migration crisis' there. Since then, Frontex's missions have expanded eastward across the Mediterranean. As Frontex extended its geographic sphere across the Mediterranean, as well as along the EU's eastern land borders, it also expanded the type of activities in which it engaged. For example, it developed Rapid

customs and police authorities in member states, alongside the collection and exchange of information on migrants entering the EU, continues to be critical to control of the external border and attempts to create common rules for access to EU territory.

The task of fleshing out the compensatory measures called for in the Schengen Agreement also led the Ad Hoc Group on Immigration to draft the Dublin Convention (1990), which established responsibility for asylum applications (Brouwer 2008: 13–46; Karyotis 2007).[7] Echoing the Schengen Agreement, the Dublin Convention restricted the right of asylum seekers to determine where to lodge a claim. The Convention entered into force in 1997 and, with the exception of spouses and children, designated the first member state through which an asylum seeker had entered the EU responsible for their subsequent claim. It also allowed for 'Dublin returns', whereby member states could deport asylum seekers found to be residing within their borders to the member state where initial entry into the EU took place (European Union 1997).

Northern EU states' mistrust of southern member states, especially in terms of their capacity and willingness to limit migration, spurred the displacement of responsibility for asylum and immigration controls to the external border.[8] After the 1973 oil crisis, economic recession swept across Europe and prompted governments to close off labour migration routes into Northern Europe. Labour migration that had previously been encouraged became unwanted 'illegal immigration'. Alongside this change in policies, civil wars and foreign interventions in Iran, Iraq, Lebanon, Sri Lanka, and elsewhere caused asylum applications in Europe to increase: from 13,000 in 1972 to 158,500 in 1980 to 425,100 in 1990. Moreover, the majority of asylum claims were lodged in Northern Europe. For instance, between 1988 and 1990, 60 per cent of asylum applications in the EU were made in Germany and 20 per cent in France (Joly 1994: 162–3; cf. Martin and Widgren 2002: 19–20).

Intervention Border Teams to react to 'emergency' situations. The first of these was deployed along the Greek-Turkish border in 2010 (European Parliament and Council 2007: 30–9; Human Rights Watch 2011). Frontex involvement in return activities also garnered criticism as its role in deporting migrants lacked a legal basis and remained undefined in its mandate (Carrera 2007: 17–18). In parallel with the Agency's expanding activities, the subsidy it receives from the European Community more than quadrupled during its first four years, from €18.9 million in 2006 to €77.3 million in 2009 (Frontex 2010b; 2007). In 2016, the agency's mandate was again significantly expanded when it rebranded as the European Border and Coast Guard Agency.

[7] The Dublin Convention was replaced by the Dublin II Regulation in 2003 and by the Dublin III Regulation in 2013. A proposal for a fourth version of the regulation is currently being considered.

[8] Elsewhere, I have written about the movement of immigration controls *towards* the EU's external borders, which I call 'distalization' in order to distinguish it from 'externalization', the movement of immigration controls *beyond* the EU's external border, which many other scholars have written about (Mainwaring 2012a; cf. Boswell 2003; Geddes 2005; Lavenex 2006; Noll 2003).

Northern states suspected that asylum seekers entered the Union through southern states and then travelled north, lured by higher standards of living. The mistrust that continues to characterize much of the relationship between northern and southern states vis-à-vis migration was already evident. In response, the Schengen Agreement and the Dublin Convention established measures emphasizing control at the external border. This in turn located the migration 'problem' outside or, at best, on the edge of Europe.

A major aim of the Dublin Convention was to hinder so-called 'asylum shopping': asylum seekers making multiple applications in different EU countries or moving beyond the initial state in which they arrived to make an application in a different member state. To achieve this aim, the EU created the European dactylographic system, or Eurodac. The Eurodac was originally designed as a database that would hold the fingerprints of asylum seekers in order to allow member states to ascertain whether previous applications had been made in other EU states. In 1993, the Council's Legal Services advised that the database should not be used for 'the functioning of other international instruments' or 'starting criminal investigations against asylum seekers' (Legal Service of the Council 1993; Brouwer 2008: 119). Nevertheless, over the 1990s, the Eurodac took on a secondary role of preventing 'irregular' immigration. In 1997, the Schengen Executive Committee noted 'that it could be necessary to take the fingerprints of every irregular migrant whose identity could not be established without doubt, and to store this information for the exchange with other member states' (quoted in Broeders 2007: 82).

In the late 1990s, the arrival of a relatively large number of primarily Kurdish refugees from northern Iraq and the framing of the arrivals as a crisis accelerated the expansion of the Eurodac. Many of the refugees arrived in Italy and other Southern European countries before travelling northwards to Germany, France, the Netherlands, and Scandinavia, unhindered by the Italian authorities (Aus 2006: 7; Puggioni 2005: 327). In response, the Schengen Executive Committee created a Task Force made up of officials from both European transit countries (Italy and Greece) and destination countries (Germany, France, the Netherlands, and Sweden) to coordinate measures to curb this migration. During its first meeting in early 1998, the German government exerted formidable pressure on its southern partners to interpret the situation as an 'illegal immigration' problem rather than one of international protection (Aus 2006).

Political tension heightened over the first half of 1998. Austria reintroduced immigration controls on the Austro-Italian border, compromising the Schengen Agreement. Germany also threatened to veto the Eurodac proposal on the table if its *ratione personae* did not include 'illegal immigrants' as well as asylum seekers (Aus 2006; EU Council 1998). By April 1998, the Schengen Executive Committee (2000: 191) had concluded that the Eurodac would hold the fingerprints of 'every foreign national entering the Schengen area illegally'. Moreover, the rationale for broadening the scope of the database was explicitly linked to the 'increase in the number of foreign nationals immigrating into the Schengen States, in particular nationals of Iraq and other States' (Schengen Executive Committee 2000: 191). Due to the interpretation and political exploitation of migrant and refugee arrivals in the late 1990s as a crisis (e.g. Tagliabue 1998), the Eurodac, which came into operation in January 2003, today holds the fingerprints of all asylum seekers over the age of fourteen, as well as migrants who enter the EU without authorization (European Union 2000).[9]

The arrival of Kurdish refugees by boat on Italian shores in the late 1990s underscores the long history of migrant journeys across the Mediterranean. Equally, the response by EU states reveals the history of interpreting migration as a crisis in order to realize the interests of particular member states and to push migration controls beyond territorial borders. It was also an early indication of the fragility of the Schengen Agreement and a harbinger of the reintroduction of border controls that would occur in the twenty-first century.

The Eurodac system and the Dublin Convention were unambiguous and deliberate steps towards the movement of migration controls towards the EU's periphery. They were also initially successful: the percentage of asylum applications made along the external border increased after 1997 and decreased in France and Germany (see Graph 2.1).[10] Although the Convention ensured that asylum applications would be assessed in at least one country, it also placed an arguably disproportionate responsibility on peripheral

---

[9] In the end, the Council (1999) decided that in addition to the fingerprints of asylum seekers and those migrants crossing external borders without authorization, the Eurodac would hold the fingerprints of every 'alien [who] is apprehended beyond the external border, where he/she is still en route' (cf. Aus 2006).

[10] This trend reversed in 2008. There are a number of reasons why this might have occurred. Italy negotiated a bilateral deal with Libya in 2008 which effectively shut down the central Mediterranean migration route for a few years. Between 2013 and 2015, Italy also did not fingerprint all arrivals, allowing migrants to travel to and make asylum claims in other EU member states. In part, this was the government's informal response to what it considered a disproportionate burden. Indeed, some officials reported that Italy struck an informal deal with other EU member states to turn a blind eye to people moving north as a quid pro quo for Italy's extensive search and rescue efforts at sea (Interview: anonymous senior government official, Malta, 2015). The practice also aligned with the interests of migrants, who at the time refused to be fingerprinted in larger numbers. However, in 2015, the EU opened infringement proceedings against Italy for not complying with Eurodac regulations and encouraged the country to 'allow the use of force' in order to carry out fingerprinting. As a result, observers documented extensive violence, and even torture, inflicted upon migrants during the fingerprinting process by Italian officials (Amnesty International 2016: 13–26; Yardley and Pianigiani 2013; cf. Heller and Pezzani 2016b).

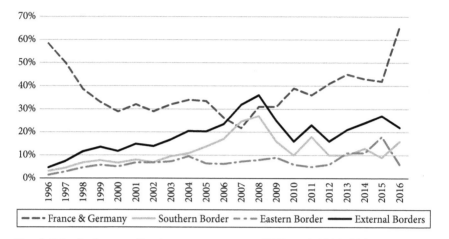

Graph 2.1. Asylum applications as percentage of EU total, 1996–2016

Source: Compiled using Eurostat data. Applications made at the 'Southern Border' include those in: Cyprus, Greece, Italy, Malta, Portugal, and Spain. Applications made at the 'Eastern Border' include those in: Bulgaria, Estonia, Finland, Hungary, Latvia, Lithuania, Poland, Romania, and Slovakia. The 'External Border' is an aggregate of the two former categories.

member states and those with large ports and airports. The Dublin system thus reinforced friction between core and peripheral member states, as well as between member states on the external border and their non-EU neighbours (Koslowski 1998; cf. Grabbe 2000). Alongside the increase in responsibility placed on peripheral states, the EU's priority of moving immigration controls towards and increasingly beyond the external border reduces legal channels into Europe and forces the vast majority of asylum seekers to enter the EU in an irregular manner.[11] It simultaneously positions migration 'crises' at Europe's edge, where arrivals are counted and where the theatre of enforcement and humanitarianism takes spectacular form.

Organizations such as the European Council on Refugees and Exiles (2006) disapprove of the link made between the allocation of asylum responsibility and entry controls due to the disproportionate responsibility it places on particular states, as well as the false assumption that standards of reception and access to protection are comparable and adequate across member states. In reality, the significant discrepancies in recognition rates between member states means that the Dublin system undermines asylum seekers' ability to access refugee protection and limits their ability to join family members and friends (ESI 2017: 21). The Dublin Regulation extends the borders of Malta,

---

[11] Exact figures are, for obvious reasons, difficult to ascertain. Nevertheless, in 2004, the European Council on Refugees and Exiles (2004) estimated that 90 percent of asylum seekers enter irregularly (cf. Oxfam 2005). More recently, the European Parliament (2016) explicitly stated that: 'EU law does not allow for the regulated arrival of asylum-seekers, so their entry into EU territory is usually irregular due to a lack of necessary documentation and/or the use of unauthorised border-crossing points.'

Greece, Italy, and other peripheral member states into the European Union, creating barriers to migrants' onward mobility. With their fingerprints lodged in the Eurodac database, the external border follows migrants throughout Europe, threatening return to their original entry point. Once in another member state, the Regulation relegates migrants to the margins of society, as to enter official bureaucratic channels, such as asylum processes, involves the risk of apprehension and return to the edges of Europe.

Despite the EU's emphasis on returning migrants and asylums seekers to the original state of entry, the number of Dublin 'transfers' carried out between member states is a fraction of the initial requests: for instance, in 2013, states only completed 16,000 transfers out of 76,000 requests (Frantze 2015: 11). This trend is replicated in Malta: between 2008 and 2015, an average of 250 people were returned to the island every year, out of an average of 900 requests.[12] There are a number of reasons for the ineffectiveness of Dublin returns: applicants may appeal a transfer decisions or refuse to cooperate in the return; the receiving member state may also not cooperate with the return either through inaction or on the basis of a lack of evidence that the applicant was initially in that country; and finally, courts have blocked transfers to particular countries, including Malta, due to systemic deficiencies in their asylum procedures (Garcés-Mascareñas 2015).[13] Member states also often transfer similar numbers between each other, raising further questions about the effectiveness of the system (European Commission 2016b: 56; 2007).

Nevertheless, the possibility of being returned remains a powerful reality in the lives of migrants and refugees. Some are returned multiple times from other EU countries. Others, aware of the risk of being forcibly returned under the Dublin Regulation, lament the fact that the EU holds their fingerprints in the Eurodac database to control their mobility. Hassana, a young Somali mother, maintained that 'if Malta gives me my finger, I would go to another [EU] country' (Interview, 2009). Hassana's interpretation draws attention to how migration controls and their biometric technologies contain the body: it is no longer just her fingerprint stored in a Maltese database but her entire finger captured by the state to hold her in place.

Despite celebrations of a Common European Asylum System, discrepancies in reception conditions and recognition rates between EU member states

---

[12] Figures calculated using Eurostat data on 'Incoming "Dublin" requests by submitting country' and 'Incoming "Dublin" transfers by submitting country'.

[13] Indeed, the third recast of the Dublin Regulation, adopted in 2014, made it more difficult to carry out returns by enhancing protection safeguard for migrants and asylum seekers. For instance, states cannot now return migrants who have appealed the court's decision or migrants who risk being subjected to inhumane or degrading treatment in the receiving member state (European Parliament and Council 2013b; cf. United Nations 2015: 8).

also reveal the failings of the Dublin Regulation and the politicized nature of asylum (European Parliament 2009; Schuster 2011). The European Court of Justice (2011) confirmed this when they ruled that the UK could not return an Afghan national to Greece under the Dublin Regulation. The court maintained that member states

> may not transfer asylum seekers…where they cannot be unaware that systemic deficiencies in the asylum procedure and in the reception conditions of asylum seekers in that Member State amount to substantial grounds for believing that the asylum seeker would face a real risk of being subjected to inhuman or degrading treatment.

In cases of particularly vulnerable people, other member states have also suspended Dublin returns to Malta and Italy, as well as Greece (e.g. ECRE 2017; EDAL 2015; 2016). Germany suspended returns to Malta based on inhumane conditions in reception facilities, the overstretched Maltese asylum system, and the need to show solidarity with Malta (UNHCR 2010a: 2). The German rationale establishes an explicit connection between inhumane reception conditions and the need to show solidarity. In doing so, it reinforces the incentive for states on the periphery to emphasize their vulnerability and inability to cope with migrant arrivals; and it perversely creates an incentive to neglect detention conditions and other migrant and refugee rights in order to complete the image of an overwhelmed state.

Overall, the Dublin Regulation falls short of even its own objectives. For instance, despite the regulation, 24 per cent of asylum applicants in the EU in 2014 had previously applied for asylum in another member state. The Commission concluded that 'the Regulation has had little or no effect' on deterring secondary movements (European Commission 2016a). In fact, the number is likely to be higher as there is an indication that some southern EU member states find it expedient to forgo fingerprinting people in order to sidestep their responsibilities under the Dublin Regulation. Despite the use of violence and threats to ensure compliance, migrants also resist being fingerprinted in the knowledge that it reduces their chances of reaching and remaining in their preferred destination (Politi 2015; Politi and Ghiglione 2016; United Nations 2015: 9).

The inadequacies and failings of the Dublin Regulation were once again laid bare in the summer of 2015. In the first six months, Greece overtook Italy as the main entry point into Europe for migrants and refugees. By September, over 200,000 people had arrived in Greece, the majority refugees from Syria, Afghanistan, and Iraq. With Greece in financial crisis and with no legal route into the EU, many refugees embarked on yet another clandestine journey north into Europe. Rather than show solidarity and support the fledgling scheme to relocate refugees from Greece and Italy, member states rushed to seal their borders. In this context and in an unprecedented move, Chancellor Angela Merkel temporarily suspended Dublin returns in relation to all Syrian refugees arriving at Germany's borders.

Over the last thirty years, the Dublin and Schengen Agreements placed migration control and responsibility for asylum along the EU's external border. In this manner, the migration 'problem' was located at the edge of Europe, removed from the core of Europe and the 'civilized' nation states shaping these agreements. Perversely, EU structures have encouraged member states along the periphery to reproduce the migration 'crisis' in order to attract funds and other support. In the next section, we turn to look at how the experiences and voices of migrants are missing in the governance of migration and how their absence is critical to the reproduction of crisis at the edge of Europe.

Migration Governance: Bringing Power and People Back In

Calls for more managed migration are now a routine response to migration 'crises'. However, the individual experiences and voices of migrants and refugees remain habitually absent in policy, media, and NGO discussions (Cabot 2016; Johnson 2011).[14] Recent academic literature on migration governance also largely omits the experiences of migrants and refugees (Betts 2011; Geiger and Pécoud 2010; Koslowski 2011; cf. Rother 2013). In much of these discussions, there is an assumption that migrants are merely objects to be governed and that (Western) policymakers and other global elites should be directing traffic (cf. Hage 2000). The prevalence of this assumption explains in part the hostility and anxiety aroused by 'uncontrolled' migration (Calavita 2005: 150–1).

The absence of migrant experiences in discussions around migration governance also encourages a false sense of optimism about the ability of a global approach to migration to overcome power discrepancies. Policymakers and scholars promote global governance as a less hierarchical form of steering, based on horizontal partnerships. In principle, this type of arrangement would stop powerful states from forum shopping, choosing the regulatory frameworks and institutions that serve their interests, while excluding relatively weak actors, such as sending countries in the Global South (e.g. Betts 2011). Less

---

[14] On the exploitation of refugee voices by NGOs and academics, see Cabot 2016.

than optimal outcomes, such as a rising migrant death toll at the borders of the Global North, are explained as unintended effects and inefficiencies or gaps between migration policies and practices (United Nations 2013: 9; Czaika and De Haas 2013; Boswell 2011; Morawska 2004; cf. Vaughan-Williams 2015: 3).

In the chapters that follow, I demonstrate how deaths at sea are not a product of 'gaps' or inefficiencies, but rather a product of EU policies. Humanitarian and enforcement approaches are two sides of the same coin, often operating in the same geographic spaces (Pallister-Wilkins 2015; 2017). Humanitarian language has been co-opted by elites to justify their enforcement policies. Moreover, the humanitarian space easily contracts and gives way to a securitized approach when political contingencies require.[15] Nick Vaughan-Williams (2015: 3) has argued that 'the inherent ambiguity within EU border security and migration management policies and practices...(re)produces the "irregular" migrant as potentially both a life to be protected and a security threat to protect against.' Moving migrant experiences to the centre of the analysis reveals these dynamics, illustrates the importance of migrant agency, and defines migrants as a constituent force of European policies and polities, rather than an object to be classified and controlled.

The Role of Migrant Agency

Different understandings of migrant agency inform how academics, policy-makers, and activists frame and interpret international migration. They shape how academics theorize migration, how government officials design policies, and how activists devise campaigns. In public and policy discourse, migrants are often characterized in the extreme, endowed with either a dangerous agency as unknowable, risky bodies, criminals, and potential terrorists; an immoral agency as fraudsters, queue jumpers, and welfare scroungers; or no agency at all as refugees, victims of trafficking, and forced migrants more broadly (cf. Nyers 2003; Anderson 2008).[16] The simplistic division between forced

---

[15] For instance, in 2017, NGOs operating at sea and contributing to the rescue of thousands of people in the Mediterranean came under attack, accused of 'colluding' with smugglers and acting as a 'pull factor' for people crossing the Mediterranean. High-level politicians, EU agencies such as Frontex, and the media all contributed to the campaign aimed to criminalize and delegitimize humanitarian work carried out by NGOs (Heller and Pezzani 2017; see Chapter 1 for further discussion).

[16] These depictions are also gendered. Advocacy organizations such as the UNHCR adopt the voiceless, female refugee for their posters, while the spectre of a male, economic migrant haunts the borders of the Global North (Johnson 2011).

and voluntary migration in scholarly, policy, and media rhetoric reinforces a binary understanding of agency.

Moreover, understanding migrant agency in this polarized manner bolsters the refrain for managed migration and has other far-reaching consequences. For instance, developed nations have adopted externalization practices and deterrent non-entrée policies, explicitly indicating their preference to resettle (limited) refugees from areas of conflict rather than accept those who demonstrate agency by arriving 'spontaneously' at their borders (Mountz 2010).

The question of agency also remains pertinent to policies, lived experiences, and rights after migrants cross borders. Any evidence of agency during a clandestine journey can undermine an asylum seeker's 'victimhood' and thus her claim to refugee status (e.g. Oxford 2005: 31–3). Migrants must perform as the depoliticized suffering subject incapable of action and necessitating rescue. Those who do not conform and demonstrate agency, especially those who thwart state controls in order to enter a country, are likely to be securitized and depicted as villains who undermine a nation's security, labour markets, and identity. As such, the victim–villain binary aids in the construction of the 'good' versus 'bad' migrant (Anderson 2008).

Even when constructed as victims, migrants are not seen as victims of the state and its border policies. Migrants are not victims of global capitalist labour markets nor of colonial histories. Rather, migrants are constructed as victims of other villainous forces, generally personified as an exploitative and cruel trafficker or smuggler. Moreover, migrants are also only portrayed as victims within limited physical and temporal spaces. In the Mediterranean, migrants are rendered victims at sea, during rescues, and in death, where they can be pitied, rescued, and mourned as 'good' migrants. However, once ashore on EU territory, they quickly become risky, securitized bodies, possible villains, who must be detained. In both policy and advocacy efforts, these binaries limit the scope of 'appropriate' policy responses to a narrow humanitarian or security framework and contribute to the related humanitarian and security spectacles produced at the border (Sharma 2005; Andersson 2014).

In her scholarship on frames of violence and war, Judith Butler (2004: 20) asks 'Who counts as human? Whose lives count as lives? And finally, what makes for a grievable life?' She argues that 'grievability is a presupposition for the life that matters' and lives that are framed as less valuable are by extension not grievable in death (Butler 2009: 14). These are pertinent questions in the field of migration explored by a number of scholars (e.g. Hodge 2015; Kovras and Robins 2016; Mountz 2015; Stierl 2016b; cf. Danewid 2017). The Mediterranean bears out Butler's thesis to some extent: the deaths of thousands of people go largely unnoticed. These lives matter so little that collectively we do not even grieve them. However, migration politics in the Mediterranean also reveal instances where migrant lives are grievable at sea and in death, when for example large shipwrecks occur close to European shores. Yet, this grief does not translate into these lives being valued and worthy of dignity and rights on land. Fellow passengers who survive the shipwrecks are securitized, detained, and deported, valued less in life than in death. In this manner, brief outpourings of grief become a feature of the humanitarian spectacle.

Within critical migration scholarship, the approach to migrant agency has developed in a bifurcated manner. On one side, scholars influenced by the work of Giorgio Agamben (1998; 2005) have analysed how sovereign power creates states of exception—in the camp, detention centres, at sea, and at the border. Here migrants are reduced to bare life, to a biological existence stripped of political subjectivity, at once subject to the law but having no rights under it (e.g. Hanafi and Long 2010; Rajaram and Grundy-Warr 2004; Salter 2008; Vaughan-Williams 2008; 2009; cf. Dines et al. 2015). Critics have responded that this approach privileges the state's ability to control migration and its borders, and overlooks acts of resistance and migrant agency more broadly (e.g. Johnson 2013; Mainwaring 2016a; McNevin 2013; Nyers 2010; Papadopoulos et al. 2008; Squire 2011).

In contrast, the autonomy of migration literature has theorized migration as a creative force that exceeds or precedes migration control. For example, Maurice Stierl (2017: 210) notes that 'there is an unpredictability of migration, a stubbornness, an inherent recalcitrance that subverts, mocks, or overcomes attempts of (border) control.' Thus, in crossing borders, especially without authorization, migrants are seen to subvert the sovereign order. Migration is understood as a social movement made up of political relations that resists incorporation into categories and systems within the modern state system. These accounts give primacy to mobility and migrants' capacity to escape 'capture' by the state and its migration controls into particular categories (e.g. Mezzadra 2011; Papadopoulos and Tsianos 2013; Papadopoulos et al. 2008).

My aim here is not to endorse the primacy of sovereign power over the lives of migrants or the primacy of human mobility over state control. Rather, I wish to explore the intersection between migrant agency and sovereign power, where contestation and ambivalence prevail. Rather than objects to be governed, migrants, like all of us, remain subjects, both 'subjected by power and…imbued with the power to transcend the processes of subjection that have shaped [them]' (Casas-Cortes et al. 2015: 83–4). Indeed, a grounded, ethnographic analysis reveals more fragmented, contingent processes of governance than state narratives acknowledge where border guards and other agents of sovereign power have a significant degree of discretion, where migrants employ agency to negotiate mobility, and where the negotiation between control and contestation are co-constitutive (Mainwaring 2016a; cf. McNevin 2013; Squire 2011; Vaughan-Williams 2015). As McNevin (2013: 189) has argued, 'The results of this interplay between power and resistance are...far more relational and far less predictable than Agamben and his followers suggest.'

This analysis puts migrants at its centre and examines agency in in-between spaces that might be considered hard cases: within borderzones where sovereign power is thought to create a state of exception leaving only 'bare life' and very little room for agency (Agamben 1998; cf. Mountz 2011b). Although the analysis prioritizes agency, I do not wish to discount the significant challenges, structural constraints, and barriers to mobility, rights, and equality that migrants travelling in an unauthorized manner face. I do not wish to suggest that structural inequalities do not significantly condition their journeys and negotiations. One need not be a discerning scholar to see that access to mobility, asylum, and rights are increasingly out of reach for most of the world's population. Moreover, I reject the idea of particular (subversive) outcomes being a necessary condition for the existence of agency: people's actions may transform or reproduce structures.

Neither do I find it necessary to reduce agency to choice. As other feminist scholars have argued, adopting a neoliberal framework of a unified, rational actor faced with choices in this context is problematic and ignores how 'power works in and through subjects, not in terms of crude manipulation, but by structuring our sense of self, by constructing particular kinds of subjectivity' (Gill 2007: 76). Bridget Anderson and Martin Ruhs (2010: 178) remind us that migrant agency is not simply about 'choice' as is often portrayed in policy debates, but rather about 'understanding decision making, the room for manoeuvre, opportunity structures and migration trajectories' within the context of modern nation states and the global capitalist system. The issue at hand is not about choice or free will, but rather how even on the edges of states and societies, faced with formidable marginalization, people continue to resist, find room for negotiation, and exploit these narrow margins (cf. Andrijasevic 2010; Choi and Holroyd 2007: 491; De Genova 2017: 9).

Following Emirbayer and Mische (1998: 970; cf. Hay 2002: 132), I define agency as an actor's strategic engagement within a specific environment through the interplay of habit, imagination, and judgement. Habit, imagination, and judgement correspond to an iterative element of agency informed by the past (habit), a projective element oriented towards the future (imagination), and a practical-evaluative element that mediates the interaction between past habits and future projects within specific temporal contingencies of the present (judgement) (cf. Sewell 1992: 20; Bakewell 2010). This definition emphasizes the relational and social properties of agency. As Emirbayer and Mische (1998: 970) contend, 'By differentiating between the different dimension of agency, we can help to account for variability and change in actors' capacities for imaginative and critical intervention in the diverse contexts within which they act.'

The focus on judgement as the central pillar that connects the present to the past and future allows us to consider agency in moments where migrants consciously create space for manoeuvre within state structures and in negotiation with non-state and state actors, such as border guards, smugglers, and other migrants. This practical-evaluative element of agency draws on past experiences to characterize a situation as problematic or unresolved, and involves deliberation with others and/or oneself over possible trajectories of action (Emirbayer and Mische 1998: 994–1000). This process is premised on 'reflexivity' or a person's capacity to reflect and monitor their social environment (Giddens 1984: 3).

Such a conceptualization moves away from theorizing agency as 'acts of citizenship' that may be made without judgement, acts that 'can be authored or anonymous, intended or accidental, individual or collective' (Nyers 2010: 130; cf. Isin 2008: 23). Although the acts of citizenship literature continues to produce many important works and insights that this study draws on (e.g. Squire 2017), the conceptual framework reinforces the focus on the relationship between migrants and the sovereign. In contrast, I analyse agency more generally in micro-level negotiations between state actors and migrants, but also between migrants, and between smugglers and migrants.

Examining questions of agency raises the question of how to delimit it. Do all actions constitute agency? Is agency dependent on outcomes? How do we know agency when we see it? The aim of this book is not to give definitive answers to these questions but rather to demonstrate that migrants are not the victims or villains often portrayed in the media, politics, and scholarship. Thus, for the purposes of this book, I take an encompassing view of 'agency'. When, in interviews, people reported strategic engagement or negotiation with actors or their environment, I coded this as agency and explored how these were ambivalent moments of disempowerment and empowerment.

I therefore conceive of this agency as political, as a contestation of bordering regimes. Such acts may be imagined as 'ruptures' to established scripts and subjectivities (Isin 2008) that create spaces of refusal (Jones 2012: 687) but also have the possibility of being transformative to the structures they operate within. Revealing how migrants on the edges of states and societies negotiate agency in familiar ways challenges the 'myth of difference' between historical refugee flows within Europe and contemporary flows from the Global South (Chimni 1998; cf. Johnson 2011), but also between citizens and non-citizens, and between 'good' and 'bad' citizens—the welfare scrounger, the criminal, and the teenage mother (Anderson and Hughes 2015). Indeed, while the agency of wealthy Westerners is often assumed, that of the poor, migrants, slum dwellers, refugees, and minorities is habitually discounted (Cumbers et al. 2010; Scott 1985).

Framing the Migrant

The European Union endeavours to 'manage' migration by fortifying the external border. In doing so, it has located the migration 'crisis' at the edge of Europe in the Mediterranean region. Here, the crisis is attached to the very bodies of migrants, who become a threat, even in death, emblematic of disorder and unstoppable flows. Europe's historical and contemporary responsibility for migration flows and migrant deaths is obscured. The agency migrants employ to negotiate borders is also alternately discounted and reified. Echoing the managed migration rhetoric, migrants are framed as objects to be governed by Western elites rather than subjects who creatively and persistently challenge borders and state sovereignty.

The humanitarian and enforcement spectacles performed around shipwrecks in the Mediterranean work to mark migrants as 'others', laying the groundwork for their continued marginalization. Expressions of agency are not only distorted and exploited to justify further border controls but also used to disqualify people from rights and international protection once they arrive in Europe. The ubiquitous discourse of migrants as victims or villains defines them as either good/passive or bad/active. Those who express agency, especially in crossing borders without authorization, are scripted as untrustworthy and undeserving of rights and protection. By turning to migrant journeys across the Mediterranean, Chapter 3 demonstrates how migrant experiences belie these framings, how agency is not only evident but necessary in order to overcome the barriers to mobility that so many people face in an increasingly unequal world where unfettered mobility is still reserved for the privileged few.

3

Limits of Migration Management

Clandestine Journeys to Europe

no one leaves home unless
home is the mouth of a shark
you only run for the border
when you see the whole city running as well
[...]
you have to understand,
that no one puts their children in a boat
unless the water is safer than the land
no one burns their palms
under trains
beneath carriages
no one spends days and nights in the stomach of a truck
feeding on newspaper unless the miles travelled
means something more than journey.
no one crawls under fences
no one wants to be beaten
pitied
[...]
no one leaves home until home is a sweaty voice in your ear
saying—
leave,
run away from me now
i dont know what i've become
but i know that anywhere
is safer than here

'Home' by the poet, Warsan Shire

Shire's words are one response to the vilification of the migrant and the refugee, an impassioned plea to remember the dignity of those who decide to leave home, the violence they face there and during their journeys. These journeys have become longer, more circuitous, and more dangerous as migration controls have proliferated along and beyond national borders over the last forty years. For much of the world's population, formal migration channels into the Global North have disappeared. Today, those on the losing end of the global hierarchy of citizenship must thus take greater risks, often with the aid of smugglers. Despite still being misrepresented as linear jaunts from point A to B in policy discourse and as menacing arrows pointing northward on maps, their fragmented journeys increasingly involve long periods of waiting or settlement interspersed with short bursts of mobility (Collyer 2010; Mainwaring and Brigden 2016).

The material and discursive emphasis on migration control at the border, and in particular at the edges of the Global North, shifts our attention away from the migrant journey in its entirety, one that begins long before the Mediterranean or the US–Mexican border and continues even when one is successful in crossing these particular thresholds (Mainwaring and Brigden 2016). Disregarding the longer journey allows politicians to speak of saving lives and building walls in the same breath, to mobilize a humanitarian and security discourse simultaneously (Perkowski 2016; Vaughan-Williams 2015). It allows policymakers to maintain that migration deals aimed at deterrence and increased border controls are meant to 'send a strong signal that genuine refugees are welcome', as EU leaders did in 2017 (Grech, Helena 2017).

By following people's journeys into Europe, this chapter unearths how state narratives obscure the ways in which migrants negotiate passage and challenge sovereignty, and the ways in which state practices and policies contribute to migrant deaths. Through an alternating politics of neglect, security, and humanitarianism, southern EU member states have constructed a migration crisis and depicted long-standing migration flows across the Mediterranean as chaotic and unprecedented. Key to the crisis narrative and the subsequent securitized humanitarian politics is the portrayal of the Mediterranean Sea as an empty space and of migrants as either victims with no agency or villains endowed with a dangerous, Herculean form of agency. In this chapter, I trace the journeys of migrants into Europe, and analyse the fluctuating politics of rescue in the Mediterranean, to reveal how the EU is responsible for deaths at sea and simultaneously points to these deaths and broader migration flows as a crisis.

Across the Sahara

When you're in the [Sahara] desert, you see people, the dead ones. You see skeletons of people....Even the ones sitting with you, some end up there because [there is] no food, no water, you don't know where you go, you don't know where you're coming from, and the heavy sun...if you're not strong, you lose your life.

(Interview: April 2009)

Upon reaching the southern edge of the Mediterranean, people from Somalia, Ethiopia, Mali, and other sub-Saharan countries have already survived multiple journeys, violence at the hands of smugglers, recurring distress, and long bouts of forced immobility. Amiin left Janale in southern Somalia in 2011 at the age of fourteen, fleeing at his mother's insistence after being kidnapped by al-Shabaab and escaping only to discover his father had been murdered. Initially, he hitched a ride with a family friend who took him to Ethiopia. The longer journey to Libya took three years during which he travelled hidden in trucks across multiple borders and on foot for two days through a forest, snaking his way through Ethiopia, Sudan, and the vast Sahara into southern Libya (Interview: March 2015).[1]

Amiin's journey, like that of many others travelling towards Europe, was one of longer periods of settlement interspersed with short bursts of mobility. In order to facilitate mobility and in the face of border controls, migrants may choose to immobilize themselves—in the back of Toyota Land Cruisers, inside container lorries, in overcrowded boats, in fake ambulances, and in safe houses. Examining these migrant journeys destabilizes traditional concepts of transit and settlement and of 'push' and 'pull' factors. They also challenge simplified and politicized portrayals of smugglers as highly organized criminals and migrants as victims with little or no agency (Interview: March 2015; Mainwaring and Brigden 2016).

Amiin's journey was one of violence and extortion but also one where he encountered kindness and solidarity and demonstrated agency (Mainwaring 2016a). Ultimately, his journey is one of improvisation in the face of hardships, barriers, and opportunities (Brigden 2016). He recounted his experiences in Khader's, a bustling Somali restaurant in Malta. At just eighteen, his command of English is impressive. Over two hours, he described travelling through Africa with very little cash but working as a porter in Sudan for four months and washing cars for longer periods in Ethiopia and Libya in order to afford the next leg of his journey. He was imprisoned in Ethiopia for being 'illegal', escaped his smugglers in Khartoum to avoid payment, and was twice forcibly detained by smugglers in Libya (Interview: March 2015).

---

[1] Daniel Mainwaring conducted this interview with Amiin, as well as the one below with Saad, for a project we collaborated on for the European Commission (2016c; 2015a).

In a matter-of-fact manner, Amiin recounts how Libyan smugglers detained him 'between two large mountains' in southern Libya at a Saharan camp and repeatedly tortured him in an attempt to extort more money. Without success, they set him to work, collecting firewood and eventually using him as a translator because he spoke Arabic and Somali. After two months, Amiin's captors give him passage north. Arriving in the town of Ajdabiya on Libya's eastern coast, he was once again detained for seven months and tortured. Without access to money to satisfy his jailors' demands, he laughs softly as he recalls imploring them to 'kill me or leave me'. He seized his chance to escape when the detention centre was attacked by a rival militia.

Recognizing him as a fellow Muslim, a farmer offered him work and a place to stay for a few days, before giving him a lift to Tripoli. There, Amiin again faced a long period of settlement during which he washed cars in order to save money for passage across the Mediterranean. He recollects how he had 'the worst trouble' in Tripoli and how a perpetual fear of being kidnapped, detained, and extorted plagued his eight months in the city. He had saved 300 dinars for his onward journey when he was mugged at knifepoint by Libyans. Eventually, a Somali involved in smuggling heard of his plight and, in a compassionate gesture, arranged his free passage across the Mediterranean (Interview: March 2015).

Although most migrants suffer violence during their journey, they also speak of negotiations with their smugglers over prices and conditions of passage. Their room for manoeuvre and negotiation is most obvious where smuggling is characterized by chains of more informal, local networks. Smuggling in the Horn of Africa, between Somalia and Sudan for instance, occurs in this manner, with migrants relying on friends, acquaintances, and co-nationals to make jaunts. The risk of violence increases in areas where smuggling networks are more well-organized and hierarchical, and where migrants are transferred from one smuggling organization to another. At these transfer points, smugglers may inflict violence to extort more money from migrants. Along routes from the Horn of Africa to Libya, people most often note their experiences of violence and torture in the Sahara Desert between Sudan and Libya, and in the southern Libyan cities of Sabha and al-Kufrah. Notably, smuggling networks appear well organized, professional, and highly profitable in this region, especially when compared to smuggling networks used by migrants between Sudan and the Horn of Africa. There is also evidence of a degree of cooperation between Sudanese and Libyan smuggling networks to arrange transfers at prearranged points (Interviews: 2006–15; cf. European Commission 2015a; 2016c).

Physical geography shapes these journeys. The conditions of the roads and the elements increase the risks of passage across the Sahara (Interviews: 2006–15; cf. European Commission 2015a; 2016c). Like Amiin, Saad also faced violence and death during his journey into southern Libya. From an affluent family, he left his home in Kismayo in southern Somalia after repeatedly being approached and pressured by al-Shabaab to join the local militia. Seventeen years old, he took a bus to Kenya and, a few months later, arranged for a Somali smuggler to take him to Uganda in a car. Identified by al-Shabaab elements in Kampala, he quickly decided to leave. He travelled to Juba in South Sudan with sixteen other people immobilized in the back of a container truck. Crammed into small, awkward spaces for five days with inadequate food and water, panic spread amongst the travellers as they realized that the lack of ventilation was causing people to asphyxiate. They banged on the cab, but the driver ignored their pleas. Two women died trapped in the container over those five days (Interview: April 2015).

Unable to find work in Juba, Saad bought a Sudanese passport and plane ticket to Khartoum from one of the many smugglers operating openly on the streets like 'travel agencies'. In Khartoum, the authorities imprisoned him for four months for travelling on false papers, and then transferred him to a United Nations High Commissioner for Refugees (UNHCR) camp in Kassala, on the border with Eritrea. From there, he made his way back to Khartoum with the help of a smuggler and stayed with a Somali friend in university housing for five months. Finding there was 'no possibility for temporary asylum', he decided only then that he must try to get to Europe (Interview: April 2015).

From Khartoum, Saad travelled across the Sahara in a convoy of four or five Toyota Land Cruisers. Sudanese smugglers drove the trucks, which each transported around thirty people from Somalia, Eritrea, Sudan, and even Bangladesh. After just one day, the truck Saad was in broke down and he was abandoned in the desert with thirty-two other people while the rest of the convoy proceeded north. The group remained stranded for three weeks with very few provisions, while they waited for another convoy to pick them up. Saad built a small shelter out of blankets and eventually resorted to drinking his own urine to survive. Twenty-four people died before another Sudanese convoy travelling north picked up the dwindling group (Interview: April 2015).

After Saad and his fellow travellers were transferred to Libyan smugglers, they arrived in Sabha where he was detained and tortured as smugglers demanded a further payment of $2,000. He was beaten with a horsewhip and a metal rebar, water-boarded, and shocked in his genitals with an electric cattle prod. He believes the smugglers grew weary of beating him daily as he was unable to procure more money, and they eventually transferred him to police custody. Despite threats from some policemen, he developed a rapport with the police commander, a 'good man' who eventually transferred him to the Sabha hospital where he recuperated for two months from his abuse and desert crossing (Interview: April 2015).

These experiences reveal the starts and stops of fragmented journeys towards Europe, the risks taken, and the violence endured. They belie politically convenient depictions of linear journeys from A to B and of smugglers as uniformly cruel and exploitative. They reveal a longer journey that begins long before the Mediterranean crossing and is shaped by a lack of opportunities to settle and work along the route and a lack of legal avenues into Europe. Along these well-worn paths that have historically carried people and goods across the Sahara, travellers now improvise to make the next leg of their journey, relying on friends, family, and strangers, working to earn money, gathering knowledge, and seizing opportunities. The journey is therefore dynamic: it is filled with fear and kindness, with periods of settlement, imprisonment, and bursts of mobility; it shifts, side-stepping new barriers and dangers; its destination is not constant or pre-determined, but evolves en route; it shapes those who take it as they shape the places they move through.

Across the Mediterranean

The enduring nature of migration across the Mediterranean Sea reveals the limits of migration management and the failure of the 'fight against illegal migration': border controls have not deterred migrants, rather they have made their journeys longer and more dangerous, and thus contributed to an increase in migrant deaths at Sea and in the Sahara Desert. This section analyses how political developments on both sides of the Mediterranean, as well as further afield, have shaped migration and how migrants and smugglers respond to barriers with new strategies and routes. Indeed, as with the longer journey, there is a dynamism here that is rarely captured in political rhetoric on migration.

Almost all migrants who arrived by boat in Malta and Italy in the twenty-first century travelled through Libya and embarked from its shores. In Libya, sub-Saharans face high levels of insecurity: violence against migrants worsened as the conflict intensified, especially in the aftermath of the NATO intervention in 2011. Years after the start of the civil war, there is no sign of an end to the violence and Libya is now a 'failed state' with hundreds of thousands of Libyans still internally displaced. Armed militias vie for power and territory, detaining, torturing, and killing with impunity (Amnesty International 2015b; Human Rights Watch 2017; UNICEF 2017). The violence and uncertainty in Libya have encouraged more people to embark on the voyage across the Mediterranean (Interviews: 2006–15).

For many decades, Libya was a destination for Africans, as well as an embarkation point for Maghrebis moving across the Mediterranean into Europe. With a population of only 6 million, it was vital for Libya to import labour to maintain its economic growth, especially in sectors such as construction and agriculture. The profits acquired in the wake of the 1973 oil crisis prompted the government to recruit foreign nationals in order to bring ambitious infrastructure projects to fruition. Moreover, in the 1990s, in reaction to the United Nations arms and air embargo, Colonel Muammar al-Gaddafi, who ruled Libya for forty years from 1969 to 2011, adopted pan-African political rhetoric, which in practice included an open-door migration policy to the south. By 2005, the Libyan government estimated that there were up to 1.2 million 'illegal' migrants residing in the country, as well as 600,000 'legal' migrants (de Haas 2007: 11–16; Human Rights Watch 2006: 12–19).

Alongside these migration flows into Libya, the early 1990s saw the emigration of Maghrebis from Libya and other North African states across the Mediterranean. The introduction of new visa requirements in Southern European countries, such as Italy and Spain, shut down legal channels previously used by Maghrebis and encouraged the emergence of smuggling operations to facilitate the journey across the Mediterranean on small fishing boats. In the late 1990s, these patterns of mobility into and out of Libya converged when sub-Saharan Africans joined and eventually surpassed the number of Maghrebis migrating from Libya to Europe. Nevertheless, Libya remained a destination country, as well as a transit hub, and, until the outbreak of the civil war, the vast majority of migrants who reached Libya did not make the trip across the Mediterranean, as many remained to work or returned to their countries of origin (de Haas 2007; Dines et al 2015; Herbert 2016).

At the turn of the twenty-first century, as EU patrols increased around the Canary Islands and western Africa, more migrants began to travel along the central Mediterranean route from Libya into Europe (Lutterbeck 2006). In Malta, for instance, there was a thirty-fold increase in arrivals between 2001 and 2002 as migration flows that once favoured West African routes into Europe shifted eastward. Throughout the late 1990s, controls were tightened over the Strait of Gibraltar and around the Spanish enclaves of Ceuta and Melilla, initially diverting migration flows towards the Canary Islands. In 2004, joint Spanish-Moroccan operations were launched to patrol the waters between Morocco and the Canary Islands, as well as the Strait of Gibraltar (Cuttitta 2006; Interviews: Maltese government officials, 2008–9). The EU also dispatched its border agency, Frontex, to patrol in the region from 2006 onwards.[2] Such migration controls along the West African coast caused embarkation points for the Canary Islands to gradually shift southward from Morocco towards Senegal. As these West African routes became longer and more dangerous, trans-Saharan routes towards Libya became more popular.

Tunisian ports, such as La Goulette (Tunis), El Kantaoui (Sousse), and Sfax, are in fact closer in proximity to Malta and Italy than Libyan ports and had previously been used as departure points for people travelling across the Mediterranean. However, Italy and Tunisia signed a readmission agreement in 1998, as well as an agreement detailing police cooperation on border surveillance in 2003. Moreover, in 2004, Tunisia implemented new laws introducing stricter surveillance of vessels in its waters, and much larger penalties—up to twenty years in prison and fines over €65,000—for people smuggling (Boubakri 2004: 22–3; de Haas 2007: 15, 19). Thus, people arriving by boat in Malta and Italy now generally embark from Libyan shores.

Many of those who make the journey across the Mediterranean have spent days, months, or even years in Libya, with longer periods of settlement more common before the Libyan civil war, NATO airstrikes, and the eventual fall of Gaddafi in 2011. Many who arrive in Malta had no concrete plans to move to Europe at all, wishing initially only to find a safe place to live and work. However, aspirations shift during their stint in Libya, in part due to their experiences in the country and the presence of smuggling networks that readily provide information and facilitate travel to Europe by sea (Interviews: 2006–15). From Côte d'Ivoire, Marc made the journey and arrived in Malta in 2007. He commented on the impact of these networks:

> When I came to Tripoli, I made a lot of friends .... Someone [told] me to go to Europe. I say, eh? Europe? Me, in my life, I'm not planning to go to Europe before .... I spend my life [in Libya] doing small jobs.... One day, my friend comes and tells me, if you go [to Europe] you can manage in one year, you can get some money, you can come back, you can start a business.
>
> (Interview: April 2009)

---

[2] For more detail on its operations (HERA I, HERA II, HERA III, and INDALO 2007), see Frontex's Annual Reports (Frontex 2007: 12; 2008: 20–4).

Decision-making is a dynamic process, influenced not only by experiences in Libya, but expectations of life in Europe. Some people arrive in Libya with the explicit intention of moving on, often relying on networks of friends and family who supply them with money at intervals along their journey or working in order to save for the price of a place on a boat that they hope will transport them safely to the shores of Southern Europe. Aammiina, a twenty-one-year-old Somali woman, explained how she secured a place on a boat bound for Europe, saying, 'I paid $900 .... [I have] two sisters: one she stays in Norway, the other she stays in America. She sent me the money and I [paid] them for the boat' (Interview: April 2009). Well-established smuggling networks make this journey possible, with evidence that the Libyan authorities have been complicit in smuggling both before and after the civil war (Interviews: 2006–15; cf. European Commission 2015a; 2016c). For example, Yonas, a young Eritrean, related how the Libyan police caught him attempting to leave the country on a small boat. The police beat and threatened him but eventually transferred him back to a large boat with other migrants, which made its way to Malta (Interview: January 2009).

Political developments on the northern and southern shores of the Mediterranean have affected the composition and volume of migration over the last fifteen years. After the initial increase in 2002, migration flows across the central Mediterranean remained fairly consistent, peaking in 2008 at around 40,000 (Frontex 2017a). In 2009, arrivals dropped precipitously after the Italian–Libyan Treaty on Friendship (2008) ushered in 'pushbacks', interceptions and forced returns to Libya from the high seas, as well as joint operations to patrol Libya's coastline. The outbreak of the civil war and the collapse of the Gaddafi regime in 2011 put an end to this much-criticized pushback policy, which was condemned by the European Court of Human Rights in 2012 as contrary to the principle of non-refoulement.[3] By 2013, smuggling operations were back in business, unhindered in the absence of a functional government. The deteriorating security situation in Libya, as well as violence and poverty further afield, in Nigeria and Eritrea for example, caused the number of people travelling along the central Mediterranean route to increase over the next few years (see Graph 3.1).[4] In 2016, over 180,000 people arrived in Italy by sea (UNHCR 2017c; Frontex 2017a).

---

[3] The principle of non-refoulement is a cornerstone of international refugee law and forbids return to a country of origin or transit where a person has reason to fear persecution. It is considered customary international law and is thus binding on all states (UNHCR 2011b: 5).

[4] Initially, observers predicted that new barriers to migration across the Aegean that formed part of the 2016 EU–Turkey deal would lead migration flows to divert to the central Mediterranean (e.g. Dearden 2016b). Although the central Mediterranean route was indeed the main point of entry into

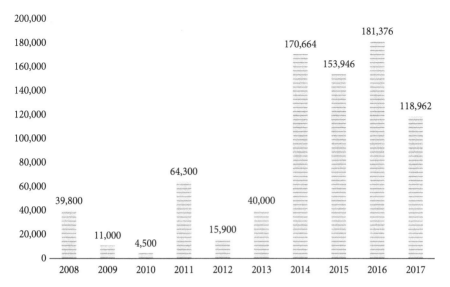

Graph 3.1. Central Mediterranean migration flows

Data collected by Frontex which they classify as 'Illegal border crossings on the Central Mediterranean route (including Apulia and Calabria)'. This does not include people who have died or are missing. The Frontex data is available at: https://frontex.europa.eu/along-eu-borders/migratory-routes/central-mediterranean-route/

Migrants arriving in Malta and Italy pay smugglers in Libya hundreds and sometimes thousands of dollars to facilitate passage across the sea. In contrast to the journey across the Sahara, crossing the Mediterranean Sea is a shorter voyage of a few days with very clear risks: it is a journey where 'you die or you live' (Interview: 2015; cf. Jones et al 2015). Smugglers gather migrants in safe houses along the Libyan coast in the days leading up to the voyage to facilitate quick departure. Vessels are generally overcrowded and inadequately supplied with food, water, life vests, and fuel.

Despite the European preoccupation with identifying smugglers on board, smugglers do not make the voyage across the Mediterranean. Rather, they provide rudimentary information on how to sail the boat, and occasionally also provide satellite phones. Migrants with some experience of piloting vessels at sea are sometimes selected by the smuggler or their fellow passengers to captain the ship and may be granted discounted or free passage. This more nuanced distinction between smuggler and migrant complicates the problematic and facile binary promoted by EU officials of migrants as victims and smugglers

Europe for refugees and migrants by 2016, Syrians, Afghans, and Iraqis did not make up a significant part of these flows which were dominated by sub-Saharan Africans. For instance, in 2016, the biggest groups were from Nigeria (37,600), Eritrea (20,700), Guinea (13,300), Côte d'Ivoire (12,400), and Gambia (11,900) (UNHCR 2017b; 2017c). See Footnote 27 in this chapter for more on the EU–Turkey Deal.

as villains. The distinction between migrant and smuggler is even less obvious along routes prior to and through the Sahara where smugglers are more often family members, friends, or co-nationals. Here, migrants who run out of money en route sometimes turn to being 'connection men', a point of contact between smugglers and co-nationals, in order to raise money for the next leg of their journey (Interviews: 2006–15; cf. European Commission 2016a: 35).

The vessels used to cross the Mediterranean have evolved in response to changing political landscapes. In the mid-2000s, fiberglass boats carrying twenty-five to thirty people were common, and there was some evidence that factories along the Libyan coast manufactured them for this sole purpose. In 2009, however, smugglers began using inflatable dinghies in order to evade security forces in Libya amidst a crackdown on migration that was part of the Italian–Libyan pushback operation (Lutterbeck 2013). In the immediate aftermath of the fall of Gaddafi, the absence of controls in Libya allowed smugglers to deploy relatively large wooden fishing boats, sometimes carrying several hundred people. Most recently, large, Chinese-manufactured rubber dinghies with flat hulls and forty horsepower outboard motors have been used and usually carry around one hundred people. These vessels also appear to be purchased in bulk for the purpose of transporting migrants, as, in some cases, intercepted dinghies bear manufacturer serial numbers in ascending order (Interviews: 2015). Moreover, a leaked report assessing the first six months of the EU's naval mission, Operation Sophia, reveals that the boats are bought from China and shipped through Malta and Turkey in order to get to Libya. The same report also notes that the move away from large wooden vessels to more perilous rubber boats is due to the EU's practice of destroying boats: 'smugglers can no longer recover [wooden] smuggling vessels on the High seas, effectively rendering them a less economic option for the smuggling business and thereby hampering it' (Wikileaks 2016: 7; cf. House of Lords 2017; Heller and Pezzani 2017). Fuelled by instability in Libya, the operational capacity of smuggling networks remains intact despite EU operations at sea.

During the initial increase in migration flows in 2002, the majority of migrants arriving in Malta (and Italy) were young men from areas afflicted by conflict and poverty in the Horn of Africa, primarily Somalia and Eritrea.[5]

---

[5] Between 2002 and 2012, there were 16,664 boat arrivals in Malta, of whom 36 per cent were Somali (5,997), 15 per cent Eritrean (2,528), 6 per cent Nigerian (999), 5 per cent Sudanese (793), and 4 per cent Ethiopian (626). In 2013, of the 2,008 arrivals, 50 per cent were Somali, 23 per cent Eritrean, and 8 per cent Syrian. In 2014, Syrians were the largest group (23 per cent), followed by Somalis (21 per cent), Sudanese (14 per cent), Gambians (7 per cent), and Eritreans (7 per cent) (Caruana 2016: 10).

The make-up of these flows shifted after the outbreak of the Libyan civil war in 2011. Although Somalis remained the largest group arriving in Malta by boat until 2013, more women and children made the journey as the violence in Libya intensified in the wake of the NATO-led intervention (House of Commons 2016). For instance, in 2011, 21 per cent of arrivals were women as compared to an average of 13 per cent between 2002 and 2010 (UNHCR 2011a; 2012a). The number of unaccompanied minors also increased after 2011 due in part to indefinite military conscription, including of young boys, in Eritrea and child abduction and recruitment by al-Shabaab in Somalia (Human Rights Watch 2015; UNICEF 2017). In 2014, Syrian refugees eclipsed Somalis as the largest group of arrivals in Malta as Syrians began using the central Mediterranean route in larger numbers in response to the escalation of the Syrian civil war and new barriers along the eastern route into Europe (UNHCR 2015). Similarly, in Italy, 25 per cent (42,323) of arrivals were Syrian in 2014 (IOM 2016). By 2016, things shifted again as Nigerians, Eritreans, and Guineans made up the largest groups crossing the Mediterranean (UNHCR 2017c).

Defining the Sea: Search and Rescue in the Mediterranean

Once at sea, geographic markers recede into an unfamiliar watery panorama. Mohammed, a medical student from Somalia, described his experience crossing the Mediterranean: '[At sea,] there is something: fear. When you see the sea from all sides, and you see the sky above—blue and blue—there's nothing. It's just silent' (Interview: July 2011). Many recount tales of family members, friends, or fellow passengers dying at sea, as they have done in the desert. In a small office building, the only permanent structure in Malta's notorious tent city for migrants, Bisi, a spirited Nigerian man, intent on asking me questions as well as answering mine, described his experience travelling across the Mediterranean, 'We were less than thirty in number in my boat. I lost one lady.... She had two kids' (Interview: April 2009).

Thus, for many, the sea offers both the hope of salvation from the horrors they have experienced in Libya and new, yet familiar dangers. Indeed, today, the Mediterranean Sea is the deadliest region in the world for migrants: in 2017, over 3,000 people died; in 2016, over 5,000 people lost their lives.[6] These

---

[6] These figures are collected by the International Organization for Migration in their Missing Migrants Project. See https://missingmigrants.iom.int/mediterranean

deaths are in part due to the lack of assistance provided by European states to those in distress, despite clear international laws that mandate rescue. This section examines the politics of neglect in the Mediterranean and argues that, along with the associated spectacles of enforcement and humanitarianism, the practice of non-assistance depends on the portrayal of the Mediterranean as an empty space, void of its historical and contemporary connections.

The Mediterranean is a connected space: it is a region that people—whether as slaves, migrants, conquerors, adventurers, sailors, or refugees—have always crossed. The sea's geography has shaped this way of life. The relative proximity yet clear separation of opposing shores allows diverse cultures to interact and trade, to cooperate, coexist and confront one another. Islands, like Malta, narrow the distance between shores, acting as bridges and meeting points. Over the sea's long history, this connectivity and constant interchange has had an enriching effect, culturally and economically (Abulafia 2003: 26; Braudel 1995a; 1995b; Horden and Purcell 2000). As Braudel (2001: 15–16) notes:

> It is in fact the major feature of the sea's destiny that it should be locked inside the largest group of landmasses on the globe, the 'gigantic linked continent' of Europe-Asia-Africa, a sort of planet in itself, where goods and people circulated from earliest times. Human beings found a theatre for their historical drama in these three conjoined continents. This was where the crucial exchanges took place.

The history of movement and connection in the region continues to echo in the present day: currents and weather patterns that shaped historic trade routes now influence migration flows renewing connections across the sea. To draw a dividing line through this connected Mediterranean space, as the EU and its migration regime have done, is to erase the region's history and necessarily involves the frequent (re)production of the sea as *mare nullius*, an empty space easily divided and separating different peoples, 'Europeans' from 'foreigners'.

The depiction of the sea as *mare nullius* also obscures a legal space of overlapping responsibilities. After World War II, states moved aggressively to claim further control of seas and oceans and to exploit resources above and below the seafloor. Until then, territorial waters stretched just 3 nautical miles offshore, beyond which lay 95 per cent of the world's oceans and seas, open to fishing and free movement. The principle of the sea as common space, outlined in Hugo Grotius's *Mare Liberum* (1609),[7] persisted long after the

---

[7] The Dutch East India Company commissioned Grotius to write the legal essay in their defence after they captured a Portuguese cargo ship in Asian waters and sailed it back to the Netherlands. Although he argued that the deep sea must remain open to all, Grotius suggests an active regulatory form of stewardship of the sea and leaves open the possibility that the stewards would be a few major powers (Steinberg 2001: 89–96).

enclosure of common land that began in the 1600s. However, by 1982, the Law of the Sea Convention had enclosed much more of the oceans and transformed them into administered zones that expanded sovereign control: today, territorial waters, contiguous zones, exclusive economic zones, and search and rescue regions encompass progressively more area in seas and oceans (Jones 2016: 113–18).

Whether of land or sea, maps are key to making space legible and thus controlling access and resources. By the late sixteenth century, maps were more widely available and affordable due to new techniques in surveying and cartography, including the introduction of scale, isometric drawing, and the printing press. These maps were central to the enclosure of common land in England. Available to the elite, maps allowed lords to make their lands legible in new ways and to draw lines that marked their exact boundaries (Jones 2016: 97–8). England was in this way transformed from a vast space that belonged to the king and that people knew through local experience into 'a disciplined commodity, captured on paper and administered from a distance' (Jones 2016: 97).[8]

By contrast, oceans and seas would not be 'enclosed' for some time. Nevertheless, the availability of maps also played a role in how they were imagined. Maps from the mid-sixteenth century show the sea as an uninviting space for navigation, more textured than land and full of fierce sea monsters. By the early seventeenth century, these images were replaced by grids over an essentially featureless ocean. Seas and oceans were no longer imagined as wild, unruly, and untamable, but as an empty space to be crossed, absent of nature and society, still unpossessible but also unremarkable (Steinberg 2001: 99–109).

The representations of oceans and seas as empty and antithetical to territorial land continued throughout the industrial capitalist era and the contemporary postmodern period. Steinberg (2001: 112) argues that in the industrial capitalist era, as the tenet of free trade took hold, the deep sea was characterized as

> a *great void* outside society and insulated from social forces. It was constructed as the wild antithesis of society (or place), the space of *anti-civilization*. As an unconquerable and uncivilizable space, the deep sea provided an ideal arena for Enlightenment society to test and affirm its own level of civilization, whether through annihilating the marine 'other' or through scientifically analyzing it.   (emphasis in the original)

---

[8] Europe and North America would undergo similar processes of enclosure in the nineteenth century.

In reality, the sea continued to provide societies critical resources—the resource of connection as well as fish, minerals, petroleum, and gas—that required active governance. By the 1990s, the international community had taken responsibility for the stewardship of the deep sea and designated coastal waters as territorial extensions of the nation state (Steinberg 2001: 110–13).[9] After World War II, disputes over resources in the deep sea, including fish and oil, eventually led to the establishment of exclusive economic zones (EEZs) by the UN Convention on the Law of the Sea signed in 1982 (Steinberg 2001: 159–88).[10]

Article 98 of the Law of the Sea Convention also enshrined the duty to render assistance to and rescue any person in distress at sea. The law is a long-established principle of customary international law dating back centuries, which was also codified in international treaties as early as the beginning of the twentieth century. The 1974 Convention on Safety of Life at Sea (SOLAS Convention) and the 1979 Search and Rescue Convention (SAR Convention) are more recent examples of such treaty law. Following the adoption of the SAR Convention, and as part of the effort to clarify rescue obligations at sea, the International Maritime Organization divided the world's oceans into thirteen search and rescue areas, in which countries were tasked with delimiting their SAR regions. It was not until 1998 that provisional SAR plans for all these areas were completed (Trevisanut 2010).

This enclosure of the seas has resulted in a 'complex web of joint, overlapping and clashing assertions of authority', where no single state exercises exclusive sovereignty (Aalberts and Gammeltoft-Hansen 2014: 445). The Commander of the Maltese Armed Forces summed up this state of affairs:

> When you have a land border, here is country A and therefore the subject of law is country A, and here is country B, there is no limbo in between. At sea it's different. Here you have country A, here you have the high seas and here begins the jurisdiction of country B. But in between, on the high seas, things are a little bit delicate.   (quoted in Klepp 2010: 1)

---

[9] The tension between the desire to maintain the ocean as a non-territory, an empty void ungoverned by any particular power, and the need to standardize practices at sea meant that it wasn't until 1897 that international shipping regulations were achieved in Brussels at the first meeting of the Comité Maritime International. It was not until the twentieth century that states signed agreements to self-regulate fishing practices in areas where deep-water fishing techniques endangered fish stocks, especially highly migratory, deep-water species such as halibut, salmon, tuna, and whales. Marine pollution remains inadequately and ineffectively regulated today (Steinberg 2001: 110–13).

[10] Here, freedom of movement prevails, but coastal states have exclusive rights to resources. Today, EEZs extend between the 12-mile limit that demarcates territorial waters and the 200-mile start of the high seas.

Indeed, in the Mediterranean, the EU has added its own legal regimes and policies, discussed further in Chapter 1, to the multitude of different zones drawn onto the sea over the last forty years, giving rise to characterizations of the Mediterranean as a Harlequin cloak (Trevisanut 2010: 538).[11]

As with land enclosures in previous centuries, the enclosure of the seas was largely motivated by an economic logic to extract resources.[12] Moreover, in both these cases, enclosure allowed states to not only control access to resources, but to also exclude people. Although exclusion is often most visible when states violently deny entry with border walls, deportation flights, and maritime 'pushbacks', states also exclude and kill through omission and neglect. The overlapping legal regimes, as well as the lack of a single sovereign authority at sea, enable a particularly explicit politics of neglect. In the central Mediterranean, this was the status quo until 2014 as Italy, Malta, and other EU states refused to deploy assets to facilitate rescue at sea and to allow disembarkation. This politics of neglect is a quieter, less visible form of exclusion in which states depend on the depiction of the sea as an empty space to eschew their responsibility for deaths at sea and shift blame onto smugglers, rough seas, and migrants for risking their own lives (cf. Heller et al 2012).

Daniel, an Ethiopian asylum seeker summed up the consequences of the politics of neglect as he described his journey across the Mediterranean in 2011:

> We saw NATO [ships] after sixteen hours... airplanes and plenty of NATO ships, warships. But nothing changed.... When we saw a boat, we go to that boat to get help. In one day, we saw about ten ships, also cruise ships. None helped us. When we came closer they went away. We saw mountains, I don't know which mountains. We don't know where it was. Maybe it was Lampedusa, but still nothing. Nobody helped.   (Interview: June 2011)[13]

For most of the twenty-first century, Italy and Malta quarrelled over responsibility for migrants in distress within Malta's SAR region. Although Malta's landmass totals only 316 square kilometres, its SAR region, a relic of British colonial rule, extends across the central Mediterranean for over 250,000 square kilometres. It encompasses the Italian island of Lampedusa and overlaps with parts of Italy's SAR area. As Figure 3.1 illustrates, any boat leaving

---

[11] For a visual representation of the multiple and overlapping maritime jurisdictions in the Mediterranean, see map published by Heller, Pezzani and Stierl (2017), available here: http://spheresjournal.org/files/2017/06/HellerPezzaniStierl_image1.jpg

[12] Economic interests also drove (and still drive) the contrary imperative to maintain free movement on the high seas (cf. Mann 2016: 14–15).

[13] Derek Lutterbeck conducted this interview for a project on which we collaborated (cf. EU Agency for Fundamental Rights 2013).

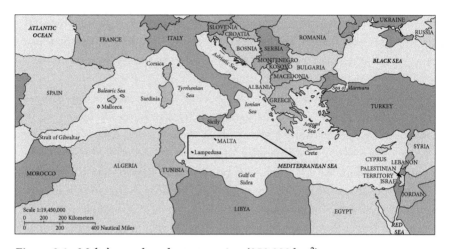

Figure 3.1. Malta's search and rescue region (250,000 km²)

Map reproduced from https://commons.wikimedia.org/wiki/File:Mediterranean_Relief.jpg SAR region approximated and inserted by author.

Libyan shores must pass through Malta's SAR region before it reaches Italy. Maltese politicians have often pointed to this large SAR area as another element of the disproportionate 'burden' the country bears as a migration gatekeeper on the EU's frontier. However, the Maltese government has roundly refused suggestions that it should relinquish some of the area as the region coincides with Malta's highly profitable Flight Information Area, which earns the country over €8 million in air traffic control fees every year (Grech and Sansone 2009; Trevisanut 2010: 524; Vella 2007).

Before Malta joined the EU in 2004, the coastguard's informal practice was to aid any boats in distress in the country's SAR region before allowing them to continue their journey to Italy, generally migrants' professed destination (Interview: Director of Policy Development and the Permanent Secretary, Ministry for Justice and Home Affairs, July 2006; Maltese Member of the European Parliament, July 2006). However, Malta's accession in 2004 came with new responsibilities towards people travelling through the region: the Dublin Regulation stipulates that asylum seekers must lodge applications in the first member state in which they arrive. Moreover, as the number of people travelling across this stretch of sea rose, disputes between Malta and Italy over disembarkation increased in parallel.

Formally, the Maltese Armed Forces (AFM) have an obligation to aid boats in the SAR area if they are in distress; other boats, even if carrying migrants, may pass through unhindered. Migrant vessels in distress may be identified in a number of ways: (1) AFM patrols, either by sea or air; (2) fishermen, other commercial vessels, or in more recent years, NGO operations at sea; or (3) telephone calls from someone on board either directly to the AFM or via an NGO (Interview: AFM Maritime Squadron Commander, July 2009). Once the AFM is aware of a boat in distress, they are obliged to coordinate the rescue of passengers under the United Nations' Law of the Sea (1982).[14]

However, in the great expanse of the Mediterranean, monitoring is limited, ambiguity remains, and politicking rules the day. Activists have argued, for instance, that states take a narrow definition of distress and leave migrants at sea until the last possible moment, greatly increasing the risk of death (e.g. Council of Europe 2012; Euro-Mediterranean Human Rights Network 2014). Migrants confirm this and recount how AFM officials encourage them to continue to Italy even when their engines are broken and their boats are taking on water (Interviews: 2006–15).

A loophole in international maritime law also exacerbates the situation. A country is responsible for the coordination of rescue within its SAR area. However, it was, until 2004, unclear where rescued persons should be disembarked. The SAR Convention (1979) only required states to 'ensure that assistance be provided to any person in distress at sea', to 'provide for their initial medical or other needs, and deliver them to a place of safety'. This ambiguity resulted in cases in which commercial ships rescued people and subsequently encountered great difficulty with disembarkation. In response, the International Maritime Organization amended the SOLAS and SAR Conventions in 2004. The amendment established that a state responsible for an SAR area is also responsible for finding a safe port for disembarkation. However, under no legal obligation, Malta did not ratify the amendment, which came into force in 2006 (Maritime Safety Committee 2004; cf. Klepp 2011).

Conflict over rescue and disembarkation has characterized Maltese–Italian relations at sea for much of the twenty-first century, especially when boats were found in distress within Malta's SAR region but in closer proximity to Lampedusa or Sicily than to the Maltese Islands, or when there was uncertainty about whether a boat was still in Libyan waters. With both states acting within their narrow legal commitments, heated negotiations ensued between Italy and Malta, often while migrants were left adrift for extended periods of time without proper attention or rescue.

For example, in May 2009, a four-day stand-off between Italy and Malta occurred when a Turkish cargo ship, the *Pinar E*, came across two boats carrying 154 people in need of rescue 45 nautical miles from Lampedusa. Having taken the migrants on board through coordination with Malta's

---

[14] See also the previously mentioned 1974 SOLAS and 1979 SAR Conventions.

Operations Centre, the question arose as to whether they should be taken to Lampedusa, which was closer, or to Malta, in whose SAR region they had been found and rescued. The Maltese government insists that in such cases, where boats are found outside Malta's territorial waters but inside its SAR region, the government's obligation lies only in coordination and migrants should be taken to the nearest safe port. In line with the 2004 amendment to the SAR Convention that it championed, Italy maintained that they should be disembarked in Malta.[15] In the *Pinar* case, Italian officials informed Malta's Operations Centre that since 'this event is developing in your SAR, and Lampedusa isn't a safety [*sic*] place, the MV PINAR E must head to Malta where the migrants will be recovered.' Although, ultimately, Italy capitulated and agreed to transfer the migrants to their patrol boats, the negotiations between the two countries lasted for four days while the migrants remained on board the Turkish cargo ship with minimal provisions for their health and safety (Ministry for Foreign Affairs 2009).[16]

With callous disregard for the human toll, Malta and Italy continued to dispute responsibility for rescue and disembarkation in the Mediterranean until 2013. Their positions created a vacuum in which state assets were often not deployed quickly enough. This politics of neglect came into sharp relief in October 2013, when 400 people, mostly from Somalia, Eritrea, and Syria, drowned less than half a mile from the Italian island of Lampedusa—an incident Pope Francis I declared a 'disgrace' (Yardley and Povoledo 2013). The politics of neglect also created an incentive for merchants and fishermen, often the first to spot boats in distress, to ignore their legal responsibilities as rescuing migrants, or even alerting officials to the presence of migrant boats, was likely to result in long delays and a loss of profit (Interviews: fishermen, 2011). The Maltese and Italian governments provide no compensation to fishermen or commercial vessels when they assist migrants in distress. In these instances, fishermen engaged in smaller business operations incur more significant losses relative to their income. Although some maintained that they provided food, water, and directions to migrants at sea, others noted that any engagement with migrant boats and their passengers was too risky (Interviews: migrants; fishermen, 2006–15).

[15] The two countries made similar arguments in EU negotiations over Frontex guidelines for operations at sea (see Chapter 1; cf. Mainwaring 2012a).

[16] Other such incidents include, for example: a Spanish trawler rescuing fifty-one people, who remained stranded on board for five days while Spain, Malta, and Libya negotiated responsibility for their disembarkation in 2006 (UNHCR 2006); in 2007, the tuna-pen incident detailed in the introductory chapter; and in 2011, an incident involving one hundred people rescued by a Spanish frigate under NATO control (Times of Malta 2011). In 2018, these types of disputes between Italy and Malta resurfaced (e.g. Borges 2018).

Fishermen also fear legal ramifications. In 2007, Italy arrested seven Tunisian fishermen, and charged them with smuggling, after they had rescued forty-four migrants and brought them to Italy (Council of Europe 2010; Statewatch 2007). Although a Sicilian court later acquitted the men and the Maltese government has not brought similar charges against fishermen, the fear of legal sanctions remains. Moreover, one fisherman involved in the tuna-pen incident in 2007 noted that the government threatened him with legal sanctions for rescuing the migrants and bringing them into Malta's SAR area (Interview: 2011).[17]

State conflict over rescue and disembarkation, and the associated disincentive for merchant ships to respond to distress signals, place those making the journey across the Mediterranean in more danger. For example, Eyob, an Eritrean care worker, described his experience at sea:

> It was rough weather...and we kept on asking for help. We were just two days on the sea. At the end, we managed to contact the...Malta AFM. There was a Russian vessel which was passing...and they came to help us, to rescue us. When we [spoke] to them, they didn't want to take us from the sea as they were waiting for a reply from Malta. And then in that situation, the weather was very rough and we sank down into the sea. And we were just scattered because it was rough weather and they didn't want to help us. So, three of us died in that moment and after two hours, we managed to be rescued by that Russian boat .... [T]hen at the end we came to Malta.
>
> (Interview: April 2009)

EU member states' responsibility for deaths at sea is obscured by a discursive strategy that imagines the sea as a void, a lawless space where migrant lives depend only on their vessel, the elements, and their own physical strength (Doty 2011; Squire 2014; Stierl 2016a; Walters 2008: 5). In early 2015, states reactivated this imaginary void when a large cargo vessel carrying 970 migrants but with no identifiable crew was observed heading towards the Italian coast. Media reports painted a picture of an unseaworthy cargo boat steaming toward the Italian coast with no one at the helm, condemned to crash if it was not for the Italian navy's quick response and interception. The boat was one of three quickly dubbed 'ghost ships' that made headlines around the world and became symbolic of smuggler cruelty and new threats emanating from the sea and the South. Although Frontex eventually admitted that evidence for the existence of 'ghost ships' was lacking (Stierl 2016a: 565),

---

[17] See Chapter 1 for more details on the tuna-pen incident in 2007.

the spectre of unmanned boats brimming over with dark masses of unknown, risky bodies took hold in political, public, and media circles and was exploited to reinforce fears of ruthless smugglers and an invasion of migrants untethered from any history or context (Interview: Malta Police Superintendent, 2015). In this narrative, migrants once again were cast as either passive beings, packed on boats silently awaiting their fate, or as cruel smugglers endowed with a dangerous sense of agency.

Within the visual political economy, the migrant boat becomes a powerful symbol of disorder alongside images of land border crossers crowded into containers or travelling by foot across deserts. In the North American context, Michael Andreas (2010: 59–60) argues that US Customs and Border Protection 'excessively documents acts of failed migration...[and] has a particular interest in exposing these migrant bodies, unbelievably concealed in speaker boxes, glove compartments or seats, and presents them as vulnerable individuals, hiding in trunks or under hoods, encapsulated by dashboards or even sewn into seats'. Similarly, in the Mediterranean, shipwrecks become the perfect visual conveyor of the migration 'crisis', further dehumanizing migrants by portraying them en masse taking unfathomable risks (cf. Bleiker et al 2013; Mainwaring and Brigden 2016).

The diplomatic tension between Malta and Italy was at least temporarily resolved by a volte-face in Italy's approach to rescue in the central Mediterranean. In the wake of the deaths of so many migrants in October 2013, the Italian government launched a 'military-humanitarian' SAR operation, Mare Nostrum. During the year-long operation, Italy dispatched patrol boats throughout Malta's SAR region, and near Libya's coast, at an expense of €9 million per month. The operation marked a significant shift not only in Italy's approach to search and rescue but also to disembarkation. The long-standing disputes between Malta and Italy disappeared overnight as Italy began to disembark the majority of migrants on Italian soil, even when they were found in Malta's SAR region or were rescued by the AFM.

Rumours still abound as to the nature of the agreement that Maltese Prime Minister Joseph Muscat made with then Italian Prime Minister Matteo Renzi to bring about this volte-face. The most prominent claim remains that Muscat traded rights to oil exploration in an offshore area disputed with Italy. Another partial explanation put forward by politicians is that Italy and other EU member states turned a blind eye to migrants moving north from Italy to other European countries (Anonymous Interviews; cf. Faiola 2014). It is also likely that the agreement between the two countries was only feasible because the number of people arriving in Malta was never very large, especially in comparison to those arriving in Italy. The deadly disputes over disembarkation between the two countries were always largely symbolic.

Although Mare Nostrum oversaw the rescue of more than 150,000 in 2014, 3,165 migrants still lost their lives in the central Mediterranean that year and the sea was described as 'the most lethal route in the world' by the United Nations (Day 2014).[18] Moreover, many politicians in Italy and in other EU countries opposed the operation, arguing it acted as a pull factor and encouraged more people to cross the Sea (Dinmore and Segreti 2014). For example, the UK Minister for Foreign and Commonwealth Affairs said, 'We do not support planned search and rescue operations in the Mediterranean' because they create 'an unintended "pull factor"', encouraging more migrants to attempt the dangerous sea crossing and thereby leading to more tragic and unnecessary deaths' (Travis 2014). There was widespread condemnation of this position, dubbed 'drown a migrant to save a migrant' (Hodges 2014), with critics pointing to a lack of evidence for the claim and the multitude of other factors contributing to the rise in migration that year, including the ongoing civil war in Syria and the deteriorating situation in Libya (Heller and Pezzani 2016a).

Nevertheless, due in part to these reservations, a much smaller Frontex mission, Operation Triton, replaced Mare Nostrum at the end of 2014. Triton's operating budget was a third of Mare Nostrum's (€2.9 million per month), it officially operated only 30 nautical miles from Italian and Maltese coastlines, and did not involve ongoing patrols, but rather responded to distress calls (European Commission 2014a; ECRE 2014a). Indeed, a leaked letter from Frontex Director of Operations to the Italian Immigration and Border Police encouraged Italy to proceed with a narrow interpretation of what constituted distress. Written in November 2014, just before the launch of Operation Triton, the letter states:

> Frontex is of the opinion that a satellite phone call is not per se a SAR [search and rescue] event and strongly recommends that actions should be taken to investigate and verify and only afterwards, and in case of distress, activate other maritime assets. Frontex doesn't consider the use of the [Operational Patrol Vessel] for such initial investigations outside the operational area as necessarily operational and cost effective activities .... General instructions to move to an area outside [European Patrol Network] Triton operational

---

[18] Heller and Pezzani (2016b) have also argued that as Italy expanded its practices at sea under Mare Nostrum, due to the public outcry over deaths at sea, it simultaneously withdrew protections for migrants and refugees on land.

area are not coherent with the operational plan and unfortunately will not
be considered for the future.   (quoted in Campbell 2017)

The deaths of 1,300 people in just one week in April 2015 bore out the
predictions of Members of the European Parliament and human rights
advocates who had opposed the scaling down of rescue operations in the
Mediterranean, arguing that it would result in more deaths at sea. It was only
after these fatal shipwrecks that Operation Triton's budget was tripled and its
SAR activities extended. Nevertheless, in the aftermath of these deaths,
Frontex Chief Fabrice Leggeri made the organization's priorities clear, stating
that saving migrants' lives 'shouldn't be [a] priority' (Kingsley and Traynor
2015; cf. Frontex 2014). Moreover, a wide-reaching investigation carried out
by Forensic Architecture revealed that Frontex and other EU actors were
aware of the increased risks to migrants and chose to prioritize deterrence
over their lives. In a document circulated internally before Operation Triton
commenced, Frontex stated plainly that 'the withdrawal of naval assets from
the area, if not properly planned and announced well in advance, would likely
result in a higher number of fatalities.' Squarely rebuffing the 'pull factor'
hypothesis, the Forensic Architecture investigation also demonstrates that the
deployment of a smaller operation in the Mediterranean in 2015 did not lead
to fewer crossings by migrants but instead to more deaths. The probability of
dying at sea increased thirty-fold during the first four months of 2015, as
compared to the same period in 2014 (Heller and Pezzani 2016a).

As Heller and Pezzani (2016b) have noted, the EU politics of non-assistance
in the Mediterranean Sea have ebbed and flowed since 2014. And yet, despite
the expansion of sovereign control over the sea, despite the unequivocal and
long-standing international legal obligation to rescue at sea, despite the over-
laying of EU laws and policies ostensibly aimed at reducing deaths at sea, and
despite the proliferation of rescue vessels and missions in the Mediterranean
in the twenty-first century, the Sea remains the deadliest space in the world
for migrants (e.g. IOM 2017b).

Migrant Agency and Negotiations at Sea

Despite the material and discursive efforts of states to dissuade migrants from
arriving on their territory, people continue to negotiate and overcome these
barriers. Examining the journey across the Mediterranean reveals instances
where, in spite and because of the difficulties they face, migrants demonstrate
agency in micro-level negotiations with smugglers, border guards, and other

migrants. Taking seriously the experiences of migrants en route also uncovers false narratives that states (re)produce about the migrant journey and the spaces they travel through. As Arundhati Roy reminds us, 'There's really no such thing as the 'voiceless'. There are the deliberately silenced, or the preferably unheard.'[19]

The focus here is primarily on negotiations that take place on the high seas, where little oversight is possible and where one expects that migrant agency is extremely limited and state power blunt. Drawing on the work of Agamben (1998; 2005), scholars have often characterized such spaces as states of exception where migrants are reduced to 'bare life', subject to the law but with no power to exercise any rights (e.g. Salter 2008; Vaughan-Williams 2008; cf. Dines et al 2015; Mountz 2011b). 'Pushback' policies and reports of boats 'left to die' would seem to corroborate this bleak picture.

Before setting sail across the Mediterranean, migrants negotiate with smugglers over the price of passage and the time of departure. Although these negotiations take place between two unequal actors, migrants leverage kinship, friendship, and their own knowledge in order to gain small advantages. Kamara, a Liberian man, recalled how a friend used his maritime skills in order to negotiate a lower price for their passage from Libya: 'I paid $300 .... [T]hey used to collect $1,200, but me I am lucky because my friend he knows how to drive' (Interview: April 2009). Others have less success and describe attempts to negotiate with smugglers as moments of powerlessness.

> Even when we start from Libya, it was broken the seating [in the boat]. And we told them, it was broken, we said to the Libyans. [They said,] Fuck, move, move, there is no time for me. If somebody saw me from the government, they will kill me .... Go, we don't care about you. And we did. We pray to God and we arrived here.   (Interview: April 2009)

Faced with challenging, dynamic situations, migrants draw on past experiences, skills, and networks in their negotiations in both these examples. This differentiated agency across time and space illustrates both the barriers to mobility, the violence and marginalization that people face en route, but also the room for manoeuvre they find.

People who arrive in Malta usually have not negotiated their destination with smugglers in Libya, but rather simply buy passage to Europe.[20] Nevertheless, as

---

[19] Quote from Roy's 2004 Sydney Peace Prize lecture, available here: http://sydney.edu.au/news/84.html?newsstoryid=279

[20] Scholars have documented this type of negotiation occurring elsewhere (e.g. Van Liempt and Doomernik 2006). In Malta, although many migrants report having wanted to go to Italy, others leave

is demonstrated below, migrants engage in negotiations over rescue and disembarkation with coastguards and other actors once at sea. If we consider journeys more broadly, migrant accounts reflect a dynamic process where they respond to new information, as well as structural opportunities and challenges along the route (cf. Havinga and Böcker 1999; Day and White 2002).

In the central Mediterranean, migrants negotiate their passage at sea amongst themselves and with other actors, such as fishermen and mariners on commercial vessels. Migrants negotiate amongst themselves in order to decide who will captain the boat, how to distribute very limited food and water, what rules should be followed at sea such as whether smoking is permitted, and where to disembark. Disembarkation must also be negotiated with border guards as states adopt policies that discourage rescue. During these negotiations, migrants demonstrate awareness of international rules, knowledge they can deploy in order to exert some degree of control over their rescue. For instance, Eyob described how his fellow travellers were aware they needed to reach Maltese or Italian waters in order to be rescued by a European country.

> We were twenty-four men and one woman. And when we start our journey from Libya, it was on the fifteenth of October. It was very rough weather. And from the minute we left Libya, we were calling for international help to Italy, to Malta, to everywhere. But they keep on telling us just that we were on the territory of Libya. So, we came forward, we came forward. At the end, we were at the international line. We were in Malta's territory and then we ask for help.   (Interview: April 2009)

Here, migrant manoeuvres can be understood as dynamic improvisation informed by and in dialogue with past experiences, future goals, and situational contingencies (cf. Emirbayer and Mische 1998: 979). Knowledge gained in the past shapes migrant expectations that they will be rescued in international waters. This informs their strategy of calling repeatedly for help while they move through Libyan waters.

Contrary to the Maltese state narrative that migrants who depart from Libya do not want to come to Malta,[21] migrant testimonies reveal a different

Libya without a specific destination. Moreover, even those who are trying to reach a particular country recall the overwhelming imperative to reach any safe place while at sea.

---

[21] Maltese politicians maintained this position in the interviews I conducted and in the media (Interviews: 2006–15; Gonzi 2011; Soares and Joy 2014). Similarly, members of the AFM Maritime Squadron and other officials emphasized that many migrants do not want to be rescued at sea and refuse help from Maltese officials (Interviews: Senior Policy Officer, Ministry for Foreign Affairs, April 2009; various interviews conducted at AFM Maritime Squadron base, July 2008). The issue of intended destination is discussed further in Chapter 4.

picture: most people who find themselves in distress at sea maintain their priority to be rescued over arriving at an intended or specific destination. For instance, Marc, from Côte D'Ivoire, said,

> After four days, six o'clock [at] night, we see Malta. We see the light. We say, yay, God is big, so we see another country. Even if we here in Malta, in Tunisia, anyplace, just so we keep ourselves and not die .... I give my life to Allah, to God. Any place is good for me. Italy, Malta all the same.
>
> (Interview: April 2009)

Migrants report that, in situations of distress, the Maltese Armed Forces (AFM) exerted pressure on them to continue to Italy by delaying rescue, with threats of the long detention period or other difficulties they will face in Malta, and with incentives of food and petrol to facilitate onward mobility (Interviews: 2011; 2015). For example, Aammiina, the young Somali woman, reported being advised to continue to Sicily by Maltese officials at sea. '[W]e stayed at sea [for] four days and three nights... [On the boat it was] very crowded, very hard. All the people they sitting like this', she said as she demonstrated a crouched position and continued:

> All the families, they are hungry and thirsty... nobody can speak. All the people [were] like that because [for] four days they did not eat, they did not drink water. The [Maltese AFM] boat they give me biscuits, water, a jacket... and they say to me go to Sicily, Italy because they say to me Malta is not good, it's small. Yes, the police they say Malta is small, it's not big. Go to Italy, Sicily. [But] the people because they're afraid, they said no, we want Malta.   (Interview: April 2009)

Thus, the most protracted and significant negotiations often take place between coastguards and migrants, where despite their limited power, migrants exploit their familiarity with international laws that require rescue at sea, and their knowledge of national flags and languages in order to identify vessels. Khalid, a twenty-eight-year-old Somali man, described such an encounter:

> the Maltese rescue team, they arrived. One day before that, there was a helicopter taking some photos and I think they called the AFM. They came and they talked to us, where do you go, you guys? Do you want to call Malta or do you want to call Italy? I spoke to them and I said no, we need just help from anybody. We don't need Italy, we don't need Malta, we just need help. And one of them came to our boat .... He said if you have a problem with the machine, I will fix it and then I will give you some petrol and then you

can go to Italy. I said we don't know where Italy is. And he said we'll help you, we'll help you. How you can help us is to put us on your boat [I said]. No, you can just go this way ....So, then one of them said we'll give you some time, two hours, then you have to decide if you go to Italy or not. And I asked him, what happens if we don't go to Italy, because we don't know Italy. We just need help. We cannot go with such a boat. Because inside the boat, we had holes, so the water was coming in. And we are worried about it capsizing....

After two hours, they [came] back and said, any decision? We say we want to stay here. And then, one of us, [a fellow passenger], told me, this guy is from Malta. I said how do you know, because I hadn't seen the flag before. But he said I know the flag. And when they came back, I told him [the AFM member], we're going to Malta. And he said, do you know where's Malta? I say yes. It's not far away from here. And he said, are you going to swim? Because he didn't like to take us. He was pressuring us to take help like food and petrol and repair the machine and go on to Italy. I said, no. And after when they see we are very serious, they came close and then they evacuate people.   (Interview: April 2011)

Present in this account are elements of agency: the contextualization of a social experience in light of past experiences and future projects, through deliberation with others and oneself, in order to negotiate possible trajectories. As Emirbayer and Mische (1998: 1006–7) argue '[a]ctors who face changing situations that demand (or facilitate) the reconstruction of temporal perspective can expand their capacity for imaginative and/or deliberative response.'

Moreover, Mark Salter (2006) reminds us that specific rules of entry are never exhaustive, and some discretion is left with the border guard within the state of exception. This discretion is evident in the interaction described and other migrant accounts of negotiations with border guards over whether boats will continue to Italy or remain in Malta. This discretion allows space for acts of migrant agency. Leveraging their knowledge of international law and state flags, migrants presented themselves to the sovereign as border crossers intending to enter Malta.

Within the central Mediterranean, the overlapping space between border guard discretion and room for migrant agency also indicates the potential for collaboration between these two actors. In some instances, the interest of border enforcement actors and migrants converge in a desire for migrants to continue to another country (in this case Italy).[22] Such overlapping interests

---

[22] This dynamic has also been evident more recently in the responses of some EU member states and their border guards to the high numbers of refugees arriving from Syria, Afghanistan, and elsewhere since 2015.

underscore the complexity of unauthorized border crossings and indicate that there is more room for manoeuvre for migrants than is usually assumed. More broadly, migrant experiences reveal the porous nature of these maritime borders, contrary to the national and regional discourse of 'Fortress Europe', and the agency of travellers in exploiting these crevices.

The agency described by people crossing the sea and other border zones could be characterized as 'individual acts of desperation' (Ellermann 2010: 409). However, I contend that these acts can reflect more robust expressions of agency that subvert state migration controls and belie the security spectacle at the border. They constitute the creation of what Reece Jones (2012: 685) calls 'spaces of refusal', where alternative ways of knowing, seeing, and being interact with sovereign state practices. For example, the acts described above force the hand of the AFM and result in migrants' disembarkation in Malta. Having arrived in Europe, people continue to resist policies and practices such as immigration detention through protest and escape, and to resist marginalization in the host community through the creation of support networks, acts of political organization, and demands for rights at the national and EU levels (Interviews: 2006–15).[23] Migrants also cooperate with lawyers and NGOs in order to legally contest state practices. Longer periods of settlement can allow for more organized forms of resistance to emerge. Such efforts are discussed further in Chapter 1 and, in some instances, result in legal condemnations of state practices, such as mandatory immigration detention and 'pushbacks' at sea, and thus a narrowing of the boundaries of the state of exception.

The Mediterranean Sea is scripted as a lawless space, a wilderness where migrant deaths may be attributed to the elements, the ruthlessness of smugglers, or even migrants' own folly in taking the risks involved with the journey. In this narrative, state and commercial personnel, assets, and activity at sea are made invisible. It is an imaginary that allows politicians to propose bombing migrant boats to tackle migrant deaths at sea (Mainwaring 2015; Chen 2015). It is a narrative that academics, activists, and artists have countered with accounts that reveal how people are left to die at sea despite the presence of other actors. For instance, Forensic Architecture reconstructed the fatal journey of the 'Left-to-Die Boat' to reveal how nobody responded to the distress signals sent by people on board despite the presence of many

---

[23] In speaking to reporters and researchers about their experiences and grievances, migrants also demonstrate an agency that challenges their subjectification and subverts state narratives about them and their journeys (cf. Appendix: Reflections on Methods and Ethics).

military vessels, aircrafts, and other actors in the central Mediterranean that formed part of the NATO-led intervention in Libya in 2011. Their report demonstrates how state and commercial actors neglected their legal responsibilities to rescue at sea and contributed to the deaths of sixty-three people (Heller et al 2012).

Engaging with migrant accounts of the journey and acknowledging their agency reveals the ways in which state bordering practices produce clandestine migration flows, encouraging these journeys across the Sea. Without access to legal channels into the Global North, migrants undertake transnational clandestine journeys both despite and because of state bordering practices. The excerpts above highlight the trauma that many suffer before arriving in Europe. Being unable to procure the travel documents and airplane tickets that are available to the wealthier classes, these people must travel longer, more dangerous and arduous routes.

Externalizing Migration Control, Shrinking Spaces of Mobility and Refuge

The migration 'crisis' is constructed by casting the Mediterranean as *mare nullius* and casting migrants alternately as victims and villains. The history of movement and connections across the Sea and the contemporary negotiations and challenges to sovereignty and borders described above are erased, replaced with simpler narratives of borders that demarcate sovereign territory and separate 'us' from 'them'. This sleight of hand locates the crisis outside of Europe and in doing so encourages the externalization of migration controls beyond European territory.

Indeed, as the politics of neglect and the practice of non-assistance at sea have fluctuated, especially after 2014, the EU's emphasis on externalizing migration controls beyond its borders has remained constant. Similarly, despite the diplomatic tension between Malta and Italy over rescue and disembarkation, the two states have long agreed that Libya is the real culprit due to its unwillingness to prevent departures from its shores. Both southern EU member states have pursued an agreement where Libya would patrol its coast to stop migrant departures and accept the readmission of third-country nationals who transit the country, an agreement similar to those signed by Spain with West African countries in the early 2000s. For many years, however, Libya's long-standing leader Gaddafi leveraged his strategic North African position and large oil reserves to resist such an agreement (Paoletti 2008).

Only after years of negotiation, and in the wake of the *Pinar* incident described above, did former Italian Prime Minister Silvio Berlusconi succeed in securing a Treaty on Friendship, Partnership, and Cooperation (2008) with Libya. The Treaty ushered in joint operations between the two countries to patrol Libya's maritime border. In return for Libya's cooperation in curtailing migration and providing access to the country's oil reserves, Italy pledged $5 billion in colonial reparations over twenty-five years. Although there was no formal readmission clause in the Treaty, the agreement resulted in Italy returning boatloads of migrants and refugees to Libya from the high seas, without granting them access to asylum procedures in Europe.[24]

The UNHCR reported that Italy refused entry to at least 900 people after the agreement came into force in May 2009. Along with NGOs and other international organizations, it voiced its dismay at these events and pointed to Italy's contravention of the principle of non-refoulement and other international norms (UNHCR 2009a; Fortress Europe 2007; Human Rights Watch 2009). These groups highlighted Libya's record of human rights' abuses and the lack of asylum legislation in a country that is still not a signatory to the UN Refugee Convention. In 2012, the European Court of Human Rights (2012) subsequently ruled that the pushback practice was contrary to the principle of non-refoulement. The grave consequences of denying access to asylum procedures in Europe came to light as reports emerged from those who were returned to Libya, only to suffer abuse at the hands of Libyan authorities or to be repatriated to countries where their lives were in danger (Fortress Europe 2007; Human Rights Watch 2009).

The Maltese government publicly supported Italy's Treaty on Friendship without reservation over human rights issues, having unsuccessfully pursued its own readmission agreement with Libya.[25] Malta thus supported the

---

[24] Italy had previously used this tactic of interception and pushback in relation to Albanian refugees arriving in the late 1990s. In March 1997, Italy signed a similar bilateral agreement with Albania that allowed for the return of Albanians in return for Italian financial, policy, and humanitarian assistance (Albahari 2006: 3–8).

[25] Malta's own relationship with Libya had changed quite significantly since it joined the EU. Despite persistent maritime disputes, Malta and Libya historically enjoyed good relations, as formalized in the 1984 Treaty of Friendship and Co-operation. Among other things, the Treaty allowed Maltese and Libyans to travel between the two countries without a visa, a practice that was upheld until 2004 when Malta joined the EU. Malta also acted as a mediator between the international community and the isolated Libyan state (MaltaToday 2009b; Boissevain 1991; Metz 2004: 230–2). Despite this history, as Malta's political framework shifted to an EU context and there was simultaneously a volte-face in Libyan–EU (and Libyan–US) relations as the international community began to accept Libya back into its fold, Malta's relationship with Libya paradoxically suffered. The influx of migrants from Libya to Malta increasingly strained relations between the two countries. Frustration grew among Maltese authorities and the wider public who believed that Gaddafi was turning a blind eye to migrants leaving Libyan ports (Interviews: Maltese MEPs, government officials, 2006–9). Nevertheless, Maltese officials maintained that they continued to play an important role as a mediator between the

externalization of migration controls beyond its shores, despite having wholly rejected similar proposals to externalize migration controls to Malta: Italy had previously suggested that Malta be responsible for all migrants and refugees travelling through its SAR region, and that the EU create large detention centres in Malta and Cyprus to house all of Europe's 'irregular' migrants (Grech 2010; Interviews: government officials, 2008–10, especially Maltese Ambassador to Libya, July 2008).

The Italian–Libyan agreement and the associated 'pushback' policy produced a 40 per cent drop in migrant arrivals in Malta between 2008 and 2009, and an almost complete cessation in 2010, with only twenty-eight people arriving by boat that year.[26] The Maltese government thus embraced Italy's Treaty on Friendship due to its effectiveness at shutting down the central Mediterranean migration route, albeit temporarily, but also in the hopes that the agreement would resuscitate negotiations for a multilateral EU readmission agreement with Libya (Interviews: government officials, 2008–9). The outbreak of hostilities in Libya in 2011 temporarily disrupted those plans. However, Maltese Prime Minister Joseph Muscat again proposed a multilateral, EU deal with Libya in 2017 as Malta took the helm of the EU's rotating presidency. Raising the spectre of crisis once again, Muscat claimed: 'There is no doubt that unless the essence of the Turkey deal is replicated in the central Mediterranean, Europe will face a major migration crisis.'[27] Médecins Sans Frontières (2017a) responded that EU leaders were 'delusional' about Libya, given the human rights abuses occurring there.

EU and Libya. For example, the Maltese government organized a meeting in July 2005 on the issue of saving migrant lives in the Sahara Desert and the Mediterranean Sea that Libya only attended because it took place in Malta, according to Maltese officials (Interviews: Permanent Secretary, Ministry for Justice and Home Affairs, July 2006; Maltese Ambassador to Libya, July 2008).

[26] There were 1,475 arrivals in 2009, compared to 2,775 in 2008. Arrivals resumed in 2011 due to the outbreak of the civil conflict in Libya: over 1,500 people arrived that year in Malta. See Graph 4.1, 'Migrant arrivals by boat, 1995–2017', in Chapter 1.

[27] In March 2016, the EU signed a deal with Turkey to stop migrants from travelling across the Aegean from Turkish shores towards the Greek islands. People who arrive in Greece can be returned to Turkey, which under the agreement is designated as a 'safe third country'. In exchange, Ankara received €6 billion in aid, visa-free travel to Europe for Turkish nationals, and the promise of a scheme to transfer Syrian refugees from Turkey to EU countries once 'irregular' arrivals dropped. The agreement includes a 'one in, one out' clause that stipulates that for every person returned to Turkey from Greece, an asylum seeker in Turkey will be resettled in the EU. However, after a year, fewer than 1,000 migrants were returned from Greece to Turkey and just over 3,500 refugees had been resettled from Turkey to the EU. Over 3 million Syrian refugees remain in Turkey. Moreover, although the deal (temporarily) reduced the number of people arriving in Greece, it has been widely criticized on a number of grounds. In practice, it remains extremely difficult for refugees, especially non-Syrians, to access protection in Turkey, a country that is not a full signatory to the UN Refugee Convention. The deal has also resulted in migrants being trapped in limbo on Greek islands in inhumane conditions. After the deaths of three men in Moria camp on the island of Lesvos in January 2017, one man described the camp: 'This is a grave for humans. It is hell' (Collett 2016; Gogou 2017).

Although the EU Commission and the EU's Foreign Minister rejected the proposal and a deal has not been reached, Frontex began training Libyan border guards in Malta (Rankin 2017). In July 2017, the EU also approved a €46 million programme under its Trust Fund for Africa 'to reinforce the integrated migration and border management capacities of the Libyan authorities' (European Commission 2017h). As before, Italy had already forged ahead with bilateral attempts to externalize migration controls to Libya, despite the violence and instability in the country. They too trained Libyan border guards, and in February 2017, Italian Prime Minister Paolo Gentiloni signed an agreement with the Libyan premier, Fayez Serraj, to curb migration from Libyan shores in return for money, patrol boats, technology, and medicine. The controversial deal involved Italian support to establish detention centres in Libya (Pianigiani and Walsh 2017). By August, the deal between the two countries had evolved and become even more contentious: Italy began operating in Libyan territorial waters to stop migrants from departing and return them to Libya. The Italian operations in Libyan waters took place despite opposition from other factions in Libya, including General Khalifa Haftar, who controls the eastern part of the country and called the move a 'violation of national sovereignty', threatening to bomb Italian vessels (Murphy 2017). Moreover, reports emerged that the fragile Serraj government was paying militias involved in smuggling to stop migrants from crossing the Mediterranean. EU funds were being funnelled to militias, increasing their power and access to arms and further destabilizing the country (Michael 2017).

These developments exemplify the trend towards externalizing migration controls and asylum procedures outside of European territory, and towards the co-option of member states on the periphery into this policy logic. In practice, such policies and politics make migrant journeys longer and more dangerous, and shrink spaces of asylum available to refugees, confining them to the Global South (cf. Hyndman and Mountz 2008). Even if one puts aside the moral arguments against externalizing migration controls and denying access to asylum within the European Union, evidence overwhelmingly suggests that these types of deterrent policies displace rather than deter migration flows (e.g. Andersson 2016). Indeed, the popularity of the central Mediterranean route increased in the early 2000s in reaction to the reinforcement of the Strait of Gibraltar with military and semi-military hardware to restrict migration flows from Morocco to Spain. In 2009 and 2010, Libya's cooperation in stemming flows across the central Mediterranean caused a diversion of migration routes towards the eastern Mediterranean (Frontex 2010a: 5–6; Lutterbeck 2006). Similarly, in 2017, there are early indications that the clampdown on migrant departures from Libya has been a contributing factor to the increase in journeys across the Strait of Gibraltar (McMahon 2017). The evolution of routes in response to new patrols and other barriers to mobility also indicate the importance of migrant agency.

The performance of humanitarian and enforcement scripts in the Mediterranean Sea locates the migration crisis and its solutions at and beyond Europe's edge. In this manner, Europe defines itself in opposition to the constructed disorder as a unified, stable force trying to 'save lives at sea', civilized in contrast to smuggler cruelty and the afflictions of the Global South. Chapter 4 works to further unravel this narrative by analysing both migrants' continued marginalization and their challenges to the state and its borders after they arrive in Europe.

4

At Europe's Edge

Arrival on the Maltese Islands

…it is easier for the world to express concern and outrage for the unknown refugee who drowns, or otherwise perishes, for he makes no demand on any nation. It is far more difficult to be reconciled to resolving the problems of those who live…

Poul Hartling, United Nations High Commissioner
for Refugees, 1979

On 6 September 2014, around 500 people left the Egyptian port of Damietta on a boat and made their way across the Mediterranean towards Europe. Most on board were Palestinian and Syrian refugees fleeing war and poverty. Four days after they departed, the boat sank 300 miles south-east of Malta. Almost all the passengers drowned. The eleven survivors endured days in the sea while their fellow passengers died around them. With limited life jackets, some clung to dead bodies to stay afloat.

Ibrahim was lucky. He and his brother were on the top deck when the boat sank and, in the chaos that ensued, they managed to find each other as the boat disappeared beneath the sea with many still on board. A bag of dates and some bottles of water drifted their way from the wreckage and would sustain them over the next five days as they trod water in the middle of the Mediterranean. They linked arms to form a circle with the other hundred or so initial survivors, but deaths and rough seas soon split them into smaller groups. By the fourth day, Ibrahim was removing his life jacket as his hallucinations become ever more real and he believed that he was back at his mother's house in Gaza. Ibrahim doesn't remember much after that, except being rescued by the crew of a French merchant ship, the *Antarctica*, on the fifth day. His skin was so damaged from the many days in the sea that it came off like dry paper where crew members grabbed hold of his body (Interview: December 2014).

European leaders and media outlets were quick to lament the deaths of so many at the edge of the European Union and label the incident a tragedy. However, the focus soon narrowed in on accounts that suggested that another vessel carrying smugglers had rammed the migrant boat causing it to sink. Though there were conflicting accounts and a great amount of uncertainty about what had happened to cause the shipwreck, this narrative cast the smugglers as villains who wilfully murdered helpless migrants. Media accounts reported that the smugglers laughed as they watched the boat sink. In contrast, there was limited emphasis on the EU's own border regime and immigration controls, which bar access to the Union for most people, especially those fleeing war, poverty, and persecution, and thus produce such journeys.

While such incidents are sometimes considered 'tragedies' and migrants and refugees are momentarily seen as vulnerable victims of villainous smugglers at sea, as they move onto EU territory, they transform into security threats. Ibrahim and his brother were shocked to be detained immediately upon arrival in Malta. Dehydrated and with severe skin problems, they saw a doctor only briefly and were offered paracetamol, a mild pain reliever (Interview: December 2014). Their swift detention reveals the sharp limits of Europe's humanitarianism. At sea and in death, migrants may be pitied as part of tragic shipwrecks. However, once ashore on EU territory, migrants become risky bodies, threats that must be contained and deported.

These two seemingly contradictory frames of understanding migrants as victims and as villains, through lenses of humanitarianism and enforcement, respectively, are in fact intertwined: framing migrants as victims at sea, defined by deficiencies and dependency, condemns them as 'other', as not fully human, and allows for exceptional policies that continue to marginalize them after arrival in Europe. As Douzinas (2007: 13) argues, '[w]e do not like these others, but we love pitying them. They, the savages/victims, make us civilised' (cf. Perkowski 2016: 332).

This chapter examines the tension inscribed in the epigraph above that Poul Hartling (1979) identified forty years ago: the ways that policymakers continue to lament deaths at sea and at their borders, while failing to resolve 'the problems of those who live'. Here, I first briefly trace Malta's migration history, analysing how we arrived at this moment of 'crisis' in the twenty-first century. Then, I turn to migrants' experiences once they arrive on EU territory, examining the sites and processes where they continue to be securitized: detention, economic and social marginalization, and deportation. The analysis reveals how these processes and related sites contribute to the constructed crisis. Even when rescued at sea and within EU territory, migrant journeys continue as their economic, social, and political marginalization discourages integration and encourages onward mobility. Finally, the chapter examines the resistance demonstrated by migrants despite their marginalized positions.

From Post-War Emigration to the Migration 'Crisis' of the Twenty-First Century

Malta's geographic location in the Mediterranean has shaped its migration history. Its strategic economic and military position attracted successive waves of conquerors, most recently the British who occupied the islands from 1814 until independence in 1964. This colonial legacy, coupled with high birth rates and the widespread bombing and destruction of much of the islands during World War II, encouraged levels of emigration after the War that have not been rivalled since. The period between 1946 and 1974 was dubbed the 'Great Exodus' as it saw the highest rates of emigration in the world at the time, with 3 per cent of the population leaving the country every year.[1]

Immigration has also been a feature of Maltese history, albeit on a smaller scale. Of those who emigrated from Malta between 1946 and 1996, over a quarter (115,973) returned to the island.[2] Besides those with Maltese heritage, British retirees continued to settle on the island, lured by the warm climate, the prevalent use of the English language, the cultural ties to Britain that lingered after colonialism, and the lower cost of living.[3] Towards the end of the twentieth century, a small number of asylum seekers arrived on the island every year, with even fewer people arriving by boat without authorization. Fewer than 200 people claimed asylum in Malta annually between 1995 and 2001, and only fifty-seven people arrived without authorization on the island in 2001.

Maltese asylum and refugee policies reflect this history of mobility. Before Malta's accession to the EU in 2004, the only relevant legislation promulgated in the latter half of the twentieth century was the Immigration Act of 1970, implemented to 'restrict, control and regulate immigration into Malta' (Malta 1970). Although Malta signed the UN Refugee Convention in 1968, it held a geographic limitation that restricted eligible asylum applicants to European nationals until 2001. Moreover, the United Nations High Commissioner for Refugees (UNHCR) was responsible for the majority of asylum and refugee matters in Malta. The UNHCR office in Rome oversaw the asylum adjudication process and the resettlement of refugees to other countries with the help of

---

[1] In total, 44 per cent of the population (138,000 people) emigrated during this period, mainly to Australia, the UK, the US, and Canada (Delia 1982; Jones 1973). Similar emigration patterns were present across Southern Europe, although they constituted a smaller percentage of the population (Venturini 2004: 9). Maltese citizens also did not emigrate to countries in Northern Europe, apart from the UK, as did many other labour migrants from Southern Europe at the time (Jones 1973: 108).

[2] Data from Emigrants' Commission Malta, see http://www.maltamigration.com/statistics/

[3] In the 1960s, these retirees were known as 'sixpenny settlers' because they profited from Malta's low tax rate of six pence to the pound (2.5 per cent) (King 2009).

the Emigrants' Commission, a non-governmental organization that formed in Malta in 1950 to assist Maltese citizens settling abroad.

Accordingly, there was no national refugee or asylum legislation before the implementation of the Refugees Act in 2001 (Malta 2001). The Act aligned Maltese policies with EU legislation, creating a national asylum system to be administered by a newly established Refugee Commissioner's Office. In 2002, this young asylum system faced the unexpected arrival of 1,686 migrants and a subsequent rise in asylum applications that peaked at 2,608 in 2008 (NSO 2011).

After 2002, 'boat people' continued to arrive in greater numbers than ever before, as Graph 4.1 demonstrates.[4] These arrivals peaked in 2008 at 2,775. Despite the long tradition of mobility that stretches back far beyond the twentieth-century snapshot given above, and despite the relatively small number of people arriving, this most recent migration development took centre stage. Successive governments have framed the arrivals as a crisis, establishing migration as a key political issue in the twenty-first century both domestically and at the EU level.

Since 2008, migrant arrivals have fluctuated. Initially, the Italian agreement with Libya and the consequent practice of returning people to Libya after interception at sea resulted in a decrease in arrivals, which fell to forty-seven in 2010. However, the outbreak of hostilities in Libya and the collapse of the Italian-Libyan agreement caused migrant arrivals to increase once again—to

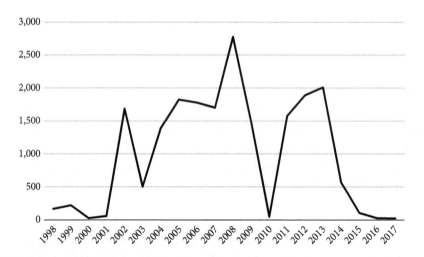

Graph 4.1. Migrant arrivals by boat, 1995–2017

Source: For 1998–2001, see Simon 2006: 39; for 2002–14, see NSO 2015; for 2015–17, see UNHCR-Malta 2018.

---

[4] The year 2003 was an exception to this general trend: only 502 migrants arrived in a clandestine manner. No official reason is given for this decrease (NSO 2011).

over 2,000 by 2013. As discussed in Chapter 3, Italy reversed its long-standing practice of resisting responsibility for rescue and disembarkation of people found in Malta's search and rescue region after two fatal shipwrecks near Lampedusa in October 2013. Italy's new practice of disembarking the vast majority of those rescued throughout the central Mediterranean caused arrivals in Malta to once again decrease. In 2017, only twenty-three people arrived in Malta.

The decrease in boat arrivals since 2014 has been accompanied by an increase in asylum applications from so-called 'non-boat arrivals', people who have not arrived via the maritime route from Libya. This includes people who arrive by plane, as well as those who apply for asylum after residing in Malta for some time. The number of asylum applications from 'non-boat arrivals' rose from 347 in 2008 to 1,584 in 2015 and 1,763 in 2016. The majority of these asylum seekers were from Libya and Syria, with a smaller number from Ukraine, Egypt, and Nigeria. In line with this trend, asylum applications increased from 1,280 in 2014 to 1,733 in 2016, despite the drop in arrivals by boat (Caruana 2016: 10; UNHCR-Malta 2018).

In the face of the fluctuating number of migrant arrivals on the island, the government's crisis rhetoric has remained relatively constant. For instance, in January 2017, Prime Minister Joseph Muscat discussed his government's agenda for the EU presidency at a European Parliament Plenary Session in Strasbourg:

> Now the issue is much more pressing and time is not on our side. We have been harping on for more than a decade that the migration situation in the Mediterranean is unsustainable…yet we were left almost alone for many years trying to overcome a crisis which was not our making.[5]

In the speech, Muscat's emphasis on crisis overshadowed his brief mention of the drop in arrivals to Malta since 2014. Although Malta experienced virtually no arrivals after 2015, an unrelenting emphasis on the migration 'crisis' remains politically convenient as it frames Malta as a key migration gatekeeper in the EU. Indeed, since it joined the EU in 2004, Malta has emphasized the 'invasion' of 'illegal migrants' in order to garner ever-increasing financial and logistical support from other EU member states (Interview: Officer, Ministry for Foreign Affairs, January 2009). Prior to 2014, the number of migrant arrivals, coupled with questions of security, was used to justify exceptional policies such as the practice of automatically detaining migrants and refugees for up to eighteen months. For example, the Minister for Home Affairs defended the policy of forced detention by noting that the number of arrivals in 2002

---

[5] Full transcript available at: https://www.eu2017.mt/en/news/Pages/Speech-Prime-Minister-Joseph-Muscat-EP-Presidency-Priorities.aspx

was equivalent to half the annual births in Malta (Council of Europe 2004: 4). When asked about the role of detention, another senior official in the Ministry for Foreign Affairs responded, 'We can't have a sudden influx of people roaming about on the streets of a small country' (Interview: May 2009).

The focus on clandestine migration presents a distorted picture. Malta has been a net immigration country since the 1970s. Today, EU and non-EU citizens migrate to Malta in substantial numbers: in 2016, over 9,000 non-EU nationals and 25,000 EU nationals were employed in Malta. The largest group of non-EU nationals are Filipinos (1,625), many of whom are employed as domestic labourers (Parliamentary Question 2017). Malta also accommodates over 1 million tourists every year.[6] Moreover, in 2014, Malta launched a lucrative and controversial Individual Investor Programme to sell citizenship to the super rich. An investment of over €650,000 secures access to Maltese and thus EU citizenship (Cooper 2016; Peel and Khan 2018). In Malta and elsewhere, migration is not solely about numbers. It is a deeply racialized and classed issue, influenced in Malta by the EU framework.[7] Asylum seekers and 'irregular' migrants are rendered a drain on the welfare state and economy. At the EU level, this portrayal allows the government to underline Malta's vulnerability to migration flows in order to acquire more support. Moreover, this narrative disregards the contribution that migrants and refugees make to the economy on the island, working primarily in construction, agriculture, and the service industries. One official stated it plainly: 'We want migrants to satisfy our economic [needs], our labour market mismatches, but at the end of the day I don't think we would want them to stay here permanently' (Interview: Ministry for Justice and Home Affairs, April 2009).

Migrant arrivals on the island are also portrayed as accidental, a narrative that reinforces the message that they do not belong. Most politicians maintain that migrants and refugees 'do not want to come to Malta' and that 'Malta is not a country where asylum seekers would choose to settle' (Interviews: Ministry for Foreign Affairs; Ministry for Justice and Home Affairs, April 2009). Yet, some migrants reported their intention to come to Malta while in Libya or in their countries of origin, either because they already had friends or family on the island or due to advice from acquaintances in Libya (Interviews: 2009). The majority of migrants did report wanting to reach Italian shores, from where they can more easily travel to other EU countries. However, the exceptions to

---

[6] In 2008, an estimated 1.3 million tourists visited the island; by 2017, this number had risen to over 2 million (NSO 2009; 2018).

[7] The relationship between Malta and the EU and how it shapes migration policies, practices, and discourse is discussed further in Chapter 5.

this trend are nevertheless significant and highlight a flawed, politicized logic in the government's rhetoric. Interviews also bring to light how most migrants' plans remain flexible and are affected by new opportunities and barriers, whether in their country of origin, in countries of transit, such as Libya, or at sea. On the high seas, people's initial ambitions are often eclipsed by a desire to find land and safety. Moreover, although migrants and refugees are frustrated by the limited opportunities in the country, they nevertheless report feeling 'safe' in Malta and some wish to remain. Hassane, a refugee from Niger, explained:

> I worked in Libya for a few months .... There is a lot of work in Libya, but the problem is that you don't feel safe in Libya .... Frankly speaking, there's a lot of work in Libya, but if you are not concerned about the money but peace, even if you have money, if the whole money in this world is given to you and you have no peace, there is no [point] .... So, there is a lot of money in Libya, there are a lot of jobs but no peace. That's why we leave Libya and come to Malta. Though Malta, there is a difficult situation in Malta, but we are very, very happy because we are in a peaceful place.
>
> (Interview: April 2009)

There is ample evidence that suggests Malta is, and will remain, an intended destination for migrants and refugees (Interviews: migrants, 2006–15). Since 2014, there are reports of migrants, who are rescued by and disembarked in Italy, subsequently travelling to Malta in order to find work (Interviews: 2015; Tory-Murphy 2018). It is important to make two observations here. First, it is politically expedient for Malta to maintain that most migrants do not want to remain, a logic which helps the government portray Malta as a victim of geography and EU legislation. This false narrative redoubles the sense of 'burden' and is consistent with attempts to shift responsibility for disembarkation to Italy, as well as Libya. Second, the narrow logic disregards global patterns of migration and inequality which point to the likelihood that Malta, a relatively wealthy state, will continue to receive migrants and refugees in the coming years. It also conveniently ignores how Maltese policies and practices, such as detention and the granting of temporary forms of protection, shape people's desires to remain on the island.

In the Name of Deterrence: Detention, Marginalization, and Deportation

The nascent asylum and migration systems in Malta were unprepared for the number of arrivals in 2002. The government responded with an 'ad hoc arrangement...made by the police immigration authorities' (Interview: Ministry for Justice and Home Affairs, April 2009). The makeshift response forcibly confined those who arrived in detention centres established in military barracks. Although one might excuse the initial failings of the reception and asylum systems due to the unexpectedly high levels of immigration, the continued depiction of migrant arrivals as a crisis more than a decade later is far less convincing. This section examines key moments, processes, and sites where migrants are securitized after they cross the border: through their detention, economic and social marginalization, and deportation. In doing so, it argues that the crisis is reinforced through expressions of disorder and alarm constructed in specific spaces and at specific times. The state benefits from the disorder because, as Jenna Loyd and Alison Mountz (2014: 28) argue, 'Nation-states...are inherently unstable forms whose legitimacy must constantly be renewed; this need perpetuates states and infrastructures of crisis and exceptionalism.'

Detention

We are not criminals.

Aman, April 2009

Ibrahim and his brother arrived in Malta dehydrated, ill, and disoriented after spending five days treading water in the middle of the Mediterranean. Upon their arrival, they met António Guterres, the UN High Commissioner for Refugees, as well as Angelina Jolie, a Special Envoy for the UNHCR. Although the media coverage of their high-profile rescue framed them as victims, worthy of meeting a celebrity activist, it did not prevent their securitization as risky bodies: after these meetings, they were quickly shuttled to detention having received only minimal medical care. Ibrahim was only taken to hospital three days later after repeated requests and after his condition worsened in detention (Interview: December 2014; cf. Divers 2014).

For most of the twenty-first century, Malta maintained the longest and arguably harshest detention policy in the European Union. Although Malta decriminalized unauthorized entry into its territory in 2002 as part of the pre-accession process, detention remained in place as an administrative fiat (Council of Europe 2004: 4). Moreover, until 2016, it was the only EU member state that automatically detained all migrants and asylum seekers who arrived without authorization for up to eighteen months.[8] In line with the EU's 2003

---

[8] After years of campaigning by migrants and NGOs, the Maltese government announced it would end the automatic and mandatory detention of asylum seekers in December 2015. This is discussed

directive on minimum reception standards, asylum seekers were released once their claim was successful or after twelve months' detention if their claim was still pending.[9] Rejected asylum seekers were held in detention for eighteen months. In 2013, the average time spent in detention in Malta was thus more than three times longer than in any other EU member state: migrants were held for an average of 180 days (European Commission 2014c: 5).[10] Suleyman, a Sudanese man from Darfur, explained the trauma of being detained upon arrival, with very little access to the outside world or information about his asylum case.

> When we arrived in Malta, they took us somewhere and took our fingerprints and gave us a number and put us in detention. I had never been in detention before. I was very confused and didn't have a phone to call my family. It made me crazy. It is like a jail. I applied for asylum but heard nothing for three or four months. I kept having nightmares and knew that I couldn't stay in detention.   (Interview: January 2009)

Although EU membership shaped Malta's immigration detention practices in the twenty-first century, the policy was legally sanctioned in 1970 by the country's Immigration Act. The Act gave the government the power to hold migrants in detention indefinitely, with detention ranging between twenty-two and twenty-four months on average (United Nations 2010: 9). However, the number of people in detention remained small. Indeed, the government only opened a detention centre in 2002, an ad hoc measure as part of the pre-EU accession process. The centre was established in the Hal Far military barracks and, based on the assumption that migrant arrivals would remain relatively low, had a capacity to hold eighty people (Interviews: government officials, NGOs, 2008–10; UNHCR Malta Representative; Maltese MEP, 2006).

The 1,686 people who arrived in 2002 far exceeded the capacity of the Hal Far detention centre and prompted the government to open new detention

---

further below. Prior to this, vulnerable migrants, including children, the elderly, and people with mental or physical disabilities were regularly detained upon arrival. Although government policies allowed for early release of vulnerable people, the process required either self-identification or identification by NGOs or government officials working in detention. As a result, not all vulnerable people were identified, especially when migrant arrivals were high and detention centres overcrowded. Even when identified, release was often not immediate. For example, unaccompanied minors were detained during the age determination process. Among children interviewed by Human Rights Watch (2012: 38) who were detained between 2008 and 2012, the average length of detention was 3.4 months and the most egregious case involved a child detained for seven months before release (Mainwaring 2016b: 119).

---

[9] Article 11 of the Directive stipulates that asylum seekers must have access to the labour market after one year.

[10] Estonia had the second longest detention period of fifty-eight days. The average across all member states was forty days, with the lowest averages seen in Sweden (five days) and Finland (twelve days) (European Commission 2014b: 5).

centres in Hal Safi and Lyster military barracks. Nevertheless, the policy of automatic detention coupled with lengthy asylum and expulsion processes quickly caused detention centres to become overcrowded (Council of Europe 2004). As the detainee population increased and conditions in detention centres deteriorated, NGOs launched campaigns to reform and abolish immigration detention. The Council of Europe (2004; 2005) sent delegations in 2003 and 2004, which lambasted the government for its unnecessarily punitive policy, and for subjecting detainees to violence and inhumane conditions. Although these challenges prompted Malta to establish an eighteen-month limit to detention, the government deflected responsibility for any legal transgression, locating the source of the problem 'beyond its shores'. In response to the Council of Europe, the government stated,

> It has to be reiterated that the smallest EU member state, possessing very limited resources, and, to complicate matters, having one of the highest population densities in the world, cannot be expected to adequately address this complex and multi-faceted problem having roots beyond its shores by itself....Malta simply cannot be left to struggle alone and, at the same time, expected to uphold international obligations to the letter, with its resources stretched to the limit and carrying more than a proportional share of this human tragedy....Malta will continue to insist that the European Union and its member states need to show solidarity with the border states that are bearing the brunt of this problem; at the same time, the countries of origin and the countries of transit must also shoulder their responsibilities.
>
> (Council of Europe 2007: 6)

Over the following decade, Malta detained 16,000 migrants and refugees, averaging 1,500 people per year (Human Rights Watch 2012). In parallel, the number of detention centres on the island increased (Interviews and fieldwork, 2008–10; cf. Global Detention Project 2014b). Advocacy organizations continued to regularly criticize the conditions in which people were detained for being overcrowded, unhygienic, and inhumane. For example, in February 2009, Médecins Sans Frontières (MSF) suspended their work at the centres after just six months due to the conditions they found. MSF (2009) subsequently published a scathing report detailing the unacceptable conditions, which concluded that:

> The undignified conditions in the Maltese detention centres and the risk they pose to the health of migrants and asylum seekers compound the suffering of people who have already fled danger and hardship in their countries of origin and who have survived long and risky journeys overseas.

MSF's (2009) report corroborates the grievances that migrants and refugees raised in my interviews. Deprived of their liberty, they objected to the material and psychological circumstances of their detention, including: (1) neglected and inadequate toilet and sleeping facilities, (2) a lack of physical security, (3) inadequate health provisions, (4) a lack of privacy, (5) a lack of education and, more broadly, mental and physical stimulation, (6) inadequate identification of vulnerable groups, (7) limited communication with families and the outside world, (8) the absence of visitation rights for friends on the island, (9) a lack of information about the reasons for their internment, and finally, (10) a lack of information about the asylum process (Interviews: 2006–15).

Migrants routinely referred to the detention centre as a 'prison' and maintained that they were 'not criminals' (Interviews: 2006–15). The majority were detained in the biggest centre in Safi, a military barracks that housed hundreds of men in a single open room.[11] Detainees hung tattered and dirty sheets between the rows of bunk beds, only a few feet apart, in an attempt to create some semblance of privacy. Those with a bed were lucky; others were merely allocated a mattress on the floor. The lack of windows at human height intensified the cramped atmosphere.[12]

Arriving in Malta in 2006, Nahom, an Eritrean man who was eventually granted subsidiary protection, spent fourteen months in detention and described the oppression of being prohibited from going outside for eight months. He said, 'Detention is amazing. You don't treat an animal like that. You don't get any newspapers, information. You lose so much in there. You lose your talent, everything. You need books to read, fresh air' (Interview: April 2009).

Although conditions in detention have improved over the last decade, they have improved most markedly when the number of arrivals decreases and thus remain susceptible to deterioration, especially when large numbers of people arrive on the island. These conditions, coupled with the well-documented psychological stress of long-term detainment, result in lasting psychological and physical damage to detainees (Steel et al. 2006). They also produce an unwieldy population for the government to control, prone to protests and escape attempts. For example, 1,614 detainees escaped from the Safi and Lyster Barracks detention centres between 2004 and 2012 (Parliamentary Question 2014; cf. Peregin 2011; Ameen 2009; UNHCR 2005).

---

[11] For example, 950 people were detained here in July 2008 (Interviews: migrants and refugees, 2009; Head of Detention Services, 2008).

[12] This description draws upon the author's first-hand experience of visiting detention centres during fieldwork between 2006 and 2010 (cf. MSF 2009). Although arrivals have dropped drastically since 2015, the government still operates a detention centre in the Safi Barracks and, in 2016, detained twenty people there (AIDA 2017).

Although detention is ostensibly mandatory for every 'prohibited immigrant' who either arrives or is found in Malta without leave to remain, in practice the policy is racialized and classed: the detainee population has comprised primarily Africans rescued at sea by the armed forces. In contrast, those asylum seekers arriving by plane have not generally been detained (Interview: 2006–15).[13] The policy is also an expensive one. In 2008, the Maltese Government spent over €8.2 million on immigration detention, approximately €23,000 per day and an increase from €6.8 million in 2005 (Parliamentary Question 2009).

Despite sustained criticism, successive governments have maintained and defended Malta's lengthy immigration detention policy. The justification has generally hinged on three points: security, deterrence, and Malta's gatekeeping role within the EU. References to the number of people arriving, and the related sense of crisis, framed justifications for the policy (Interviews: government officials, Ministry for Justice and Home Affairs and Ministry for Foreign Affairs, April 2009). For instance, a senior official in the Ministry for Foreign Affairs shrugged off the poor conditions in detention by attributing them to the high number of arrivals: 'I hope those conditions will be improved, but it all depends on the arrivals. The moment you have a sudden influx, it creates problems' (Interview: April 2009).

Security concerns have also been central to the government's defence of immigration detention, with discourse based on 'control' and 'order' juxtaposed against vulnerable borders. For example, the Home Affairs Minister defended Malta's immigration detention policy as the 'only way of safeguarding national security'. Despite a lack of evidence, the minister also claimed detention was necessary in order to ascertain that migrants and refugees were not terrorists (Times of Malta 2013). Such unfounded, sensationalist comments aside, government discourse and practices in Malta habitually reinforce the image of migrants and refugees as criminals. For example, a government policy document states:

Although by landing in Malta without the necessary documentation and authorisation irregular immigrants are not considered to have committed a criminal offence, in the interest of national security and public order they

---

[13] This trend appeared to change in 2016. Jesuit Refugee Services (JRS) reported that in the absence of boat arrivals, all asylum seekers arriving by plane in 2016 were immediately detained, rather than being taken to the Initial Reception Centre, as mandated under changes to the detention policy in late 2015 (see below for further discussion). Moreover, those using false documents to enter the country were brought before the Magistrate Court and most were sentenced to a prison term. JRS and other NGOs raised concerns about the criminalization of asylum seekers in this manner and reminded the government that the 1951 Refugee Convention prohibits states from penalizing refugees who enter their territory irregularly (AIDA 2017: 14–15).

are still kept in detention until their claim to their country of origin and other submissions are examined and verified.

(Ministry for Justice and Home Affairs 2005: 11)

The rationale assumes that people arriving on the island are in some way dangerous: they must not only be identified but also detained in order to protect the community (cf. Mainwaring 2014; 2012b). The practice of hand-cuffing detainees while transporting them only furthers their criminalization. In this context, calls to limit detention can be easily dismissed with vague references to 'national security'. Some officials have gone further and argue that detention is necessary 'in order to protect migrants' (Interview: Government official, 2009).

With some exceptions, the Maltese judiciary has echoed this political rhetoric that frames detention as a necessary policy in a country faced with exceptional circumstances. For instance, in a case brought against the Commissioner of Police in 2009, the Constitutional Court (2014: 13) ruled that:

> Detention can be considered, in the particular circumstances of our country, as a necessary measure required for the stability of the country so as to, as much as possible, avoid a deluge of 'irregular' people running around Malta, and this without having established the prima facie interest and disposition of the person.

Alongside such security concerns, policymakers and politicians have also long viewed immigration detention as a 'powerful deterrent' (Council of Europe 2005; Interviews: 2006–15). Outlining the reasons for immigration detention, the Minister for Foreign Affairs said, 'The message needs to…be received by everyone that entering Malta illegally will not go unpunished' (Interview: April 2009). Another official explained that the policy 'is good to persuade [illegal migrants] that they have to go back home….It's good that they contact their relatives and say, listen, don't come to Malta because it's terrible here' (Interview: Senior Policy Officer, Ministry for Foreign Affairs, April 2009).

Despite these claims, evidence suggests that detention fails to deter future migration flows (e.g. Edwards 2011: 13; IDC 2015). Migrants and refugees report not knowing about Malta's detention policy before arrival (Interviews: 2006–15). Moreover, the use of immigration detention as a deterrent is prohibited within international law, particularly in relation to asylum seekers (UNHCR 2012b; Council of Europe 2005). Detention nevertheless remains in place as a perceived deterrent in Malta. It has also been employed to coerce migrants into participating in assisted voluntary repatriation (AVR). Established in partnership with the International Organization for Migration in 2007, the

AVR scheme offered people up to €2,500 to return to their country of origin. AVR recruitment initially took place in open centres but was moved to detention centres as government officials believed the punitive nature of detention would increase participation. An official within the Ministry for Foreign Affairs (Interview: January 2009) explained:

> If they are in detention, they're not enjoying it for sure. In detention they can't dream, but once they are in open centres they can dream of escaping Malta....I think detention is tough on the individual and conditions could be improved, but for us it's a blessing that people get disgusted and want to leave.

Nevertheless, AVR had limited success: only thirty-nine people participated in 2012. In contrast, the government forcibly removed 266 people that year (EMN 2013: 48). The enduring belief in Malta and elsewhere that detention encourages participation in AVR and deters arrivals—despite an absence of evidence—creates a disincentive to improve detention conditions and to review detention policies and practices more generally.

The defence of immigration detention as a deterrent and security measure is intimately linked with Malta's membership and geopolitical position in the EU. The EU's emphasis on controlling migration along the external border in order to 'secure' the Union and compensate for relaxed internal controls encourages member states on the periphery to adopt securitized rhetoric and practices of control. Senior officials in the Ministry for Justice and Home Affairs[14] thus justify the lengthy detention policy by invoking 'the smallness of the country,' issues of influx in a short time' and highlighting that 'there isn't a convenient border which you can take them to and allow them to skip off to the other side as has been the case with several other countries .... It's our method of controlling and containing at the same time' (Interview: Ministry for Justice and Home Affairs, April 2009). Maltese officials are also quick to discredit EU criticism of the detention policy, pointing to the responsibility the EU simultaneously places on the country to control migration and secure the external border (Interviews: government officials, 2008–11).

After more than a decade of campaigns to reform and abolish immigration detention, the government announced in December 2015 that they would end the automatic and mandatory detention of asylum seekers. Asylum seekers may still be detained but only for up to nine months and only in particular circumstances, such as when a person's identity is not confirmed or when

---

[14] The Ministry was the Ministry for Justice and Home Affairs until 2013 when it was divided into the Ministry for Home Affairs and National Security and the Ministry for Justice, Culture and Local Government.

there is a risk of absconding. People who do not apply for asylum or whose asylum claim is rejected may still be detained for up to eighteen months. Alongside pressure from advocacy organizations, the change in policy was also prompted by amendments to the EU Reception Conditions Directive made in 2013 that required transposition into national legislation by 2015 (Interviews: 2015; Ministry for Home Affairs and National Security 2015; cf. AIDA 2017). Significantly, the reform occurred during a steep decline in arrivals, especially by sea, when migration was much less in the public eye. Time will tell whether the reforms will endure, especially in light of the unravelling of the informal Italian–Maltese agreement on disembarkation and an associated increase in arrivals in 2018 (Wintour et al. 2018).[15] Even after announcing the reform of Malta's detention policy, Prime Minister Muscat still maintained that 'detention plays a role as a deterrent' (Interview: 2015).

The Spectacle of Detention

Detention does not achieve its ostensible aims. It does little to deter future migrants. It does not lead to deportations (European Commission 2014b). Many of those who are released gain refugee protection and fill labour market shortages (OECD 2014). Despite these failures, immigration detention promotes a spectacle of chaos and control (Mainwaring and Silverman 2017; Mountz and Hiemstra 2014). It reinforces the migration crisis, constructing migrants as a securitized threat in need of imprisonment. In doing so, immigration detention bolsters Malta's position that it faces a 'disproportionate burden' within the European Union (Mainwaring 2012b). Paradoxically, immigration detention simultaneously reifies the power of the state to control its borders and deport 'undesirable' migrants.

The architecture of detention and the role of the armed forces contribute to the spectacle of state power and migrant threat. In Malta, detention centres are located within operational military barracks, surrounded by high walls and chain-linked fences topped with barbed wire. The architectural design promotes control, observation, and the denial of privacy and intimacy: for example, where detainees are housed in large rooms rather than a warehouse, they are not permitted doors. Barred windows and limited outdoor access create further layers of exclusion. The military barracks not only transmit a message that migrants are criminals requiring confinement in securitized spaces but also produce barriers to access for and to detainees. In response to

---

[15] Advocacy organizations in Malta have already noted instances where people arriving by boat have been taken directly to detention (AIDA 2017). For more on disputes over disembarkation between Italy and Malta, as well as the informal agreement struck between 2013 and 2017, see Chapters 3 and 5.

calls in 2011 by the Council of Europe (2013: 26) to allow visitation rights, the government responded that 'due to the layout of detention centres, which are located within active military barracks or police centres, regular visits cannot be allowed for security reasons.'

The detention centres' remote locations contribute to the spectacle of detention. Alison Mountz (2010: xvvii) observes how migration controls oscillate between obscurity and hypervisibility. Remote detention centres distance detainees from legal representatives, and advocacy and kinship networks, leaving them further physically and socially marginalized. The centres' far-flung locations also make invisible the material structures of detention, thereby obscuring the violence inherent within them. Yet, immigration detention centres are made visible in particular moments: for instance, when the state responds with military force to protests in detention, and in discourse that assures citizens that the state is 'tough on migration' and reminds non-citizens of their deportability. Indeed, even when the physical structures are absent from the landscape, for migrants, the threat of detention and deportation is omnipresent (De Genova 2002).

Immigration detention centres provide the crisis with an infrastructure (cf. Loyd and Mountz 2014: 31–2), whose architecture mirrors detainees' lack of global mobility (cf. Bauman 1998). Adding insult to injury, the largest detention centre in Malta abuts the international airport: airplanes literally take off and come in to land over the detention centre, providing a constant aural and visual reminder to its inhabitants of the mobility they are denied and the state's power to deport.

The role of the military in housing and running detention facilities contributes to the criminalization of migrants and refugees.[16] The increase in migration since 2002 expanded the role of the armed forces in Malta, which now includes responsibility for rescuing migrants at sea and managing immigration detention. Under the remit of the Ministry for Home Affairs and National Security, Detention Services oversees the management and day-to-day operations of detention centres. The majority of its staff members are current or former police officers and military officials. Lieutenant colonels in the armed forces have also filled the position at the head of Detention Services throughout the twenty-first century.

Placing detention centres under the remit of the military was initially part of the 'ad hoc arrangements' in the face of a large increase in the number of

---

[16] This occurs elsewhere as well. In Italy, for instance, border police operate particular detention facilities at ports of entry, such as Lampedusa. In Greece, former army camps and military barracks have been transformed into detention centres (ARCI 2012; Global Detention Project 2014c). In other contexts, the use of private security companies also contributes to the criminalizaton of migrants and the spectacle of detention (Mainwaring and Silverman 2017; Mainwaring and Cook 2018).

arrivals (Interview: Ministry for Justice and Home Affairs, April 2009). However, this practice remains in place, without consideration given to the negative impact of entrusting the welfare of often-vulnerable people to those trained in the use of force. Indeed, the militarization of immigration detention has exacerbated inhumane conditions and limited access to social services.

Detainees and advocacy organizations highlight the risks of bestowing the custody of vulnerable groups to military and police officials. Eyob, a young Eritrean man who arrived in Malta in 2006 and spent twelve months in Safi Detention Centre, describes his experiences:

> As I told you, I've been in prisons in a lot of places and…I can say that [the detention centre in Malta] was the worst prison I've seen. Because what makes it the worst for me is that [it] was not my expectation. And in other countries, I was in prison because I broke the rules, but in Malta I didn't break any rules. The only crime I committed is just that I asked for asylum….I can tell you that [in detention] I was cut off from everything. I had no communication with family; I had no communication with other people who live on the outside. I was doing nothing, just eating, waking up…for months, doing nothing….During my time, there [were] a lot of problems happening in detention, but…you cannot go and tell someone who is in charge….If you want to speak to the soldiers—soldiers, they are soldiers and they are trained to be soldiers, not trained to be a social worker or a care worker. They are trained to be soldiers…so I don't expect anything from them.
>
> (Interview: April 2009)

Migrants feel that detention reduces them to criminals, animals, or worse. In extreme, though not uncommon, cases, detention becomes a matter of life and death: two men died in Malta after being beaten by detention staff in 2011 and 2012 (aditus foundation et al. 2012). The 2012 death of Mamadou Kamara, a thirty-two-year-old Cameroonian asylum seeker, at the hands of detention staff prompted a public inquiry with a report released belatedly in 2014. The inquiry revealed how Kamara escaped from detention but was recaptured by detention officers, who handcuffed him, placed him inside a steel cage in the back of their detention van, and beat him to death. The forensic expert concluded that Kamara died from a heart attack due to blunt trauma (Valenzia 2014; cf. Diacono 2015). Three former soldiers are charged with Kamara's murder.[17]

The report also documents the conditions that allowed for systemic violence and abuse to take place with impunity. The former head of Detention Services noted that one sergeant would prey on women in detention, 'entering their

---

[17] At the time of writing, the case was ongoing (Schembri 2017).

rooms during the night and taking a woman back to his office with him.... Even condoms were found in the room.' Indeed, the report revealed that relationships were occurring between multiple members of staff and detained women, noting that consent was questionable under the circumstances. No disciplinary action was taken (Valenzia 2014; cf. Diacono 2015).

The release of the report added to the chorus of criticism against the government made by NGOs and international actors, including the European Court of Human Rights. Ruling against Malta in two cases brought by former detainees, the Court found violations of the right to liberty, the right to an effective remedy, and the prohibition of inhuman and degrading treatment (ECHR 2013a; 2013b). Aslya Aden Ahmed, a Somali national detained for a total of eighteen months, was one of the plaintiffs. In her case, the court noted,

> [the] exposure of detainees to cold conditions, the lack of female staff in the detention centre, a complete lack of access to open air and exercise for periods of up to three months, an inadequate diet, and the particular vulnerability of Ms Ahmed due to her fragile health and personal emotional circumstances.   (ECHR 2013c)

The Court concluded that Malta's immigration detention policy was a 'defective national system hindering human-rights protection' (ECHR 2013b).[18] Yet, the spectacle of detention—the order it purportedly establishes in the face of chaotic migration flows—has been politically useful for Malta as it reinforces the crisis and thus warrants calls for more 'burden sharing' within the European Union. Indeed, as the government responds to the migration 'crisis' with immigration detention as a 'solution', detention simultaneously creates and reinforces the crisis: it corroborates the populist impression of out-of-control flows of non-citizens amassing on the border while also signalling that the state is in control, working to identify and punish this population (Mainwaring and Silverman 2017).

At the Edge: Asylum, Employment, and Rights

People are... [not] 'housed' in the open centres. They are 'tented' or put into containers and therefore contained, far from being housed.

Interview: Director, Jesuit Refugee Services, 2010

---

[18] The judgement echoes conclusions of the Council of Europe (2011) that the policy is 'irreconcilable with the requirements of the European Convention of Human Rights (ECHR) and the case-law of the Strasbourg Court'.

Living in the tents is like living in the ghetto .... [I]magine under the tarpaulin, there are sixteen people, up and down, up and down [in bunk beds] .... It's very, very bad. Last time when there was heavy wind and the rain was falling, the heavy wind took off the tent. So, our property, everything, we lost it. It was destroyed. You can see why some [tents] are new, some are old because it takes some days, one week for them to replace the broken tents. So, you see, it's really bad because you feel cold when it is winter, it's bad. When it is summer, it's bad, it's too hot, very hot. In winter, it's very cold, so there's never a time it's comfortable. And problems, problems, problems: fighting [and] different things. You know in the night you cannot sleep because of the wind. You see maybe there's a hole... when I was sleeping the rain was falling and it was falling on my body because the tent is old. Even my clothes, my foodstuff, my flour, everything was wet and damp .... We don't have anywhere [else] to go.

Interview: Mahan from Somalia, 2009

All of us have problems, just different stories.

Interview: Hassana from Somalia, 2009

Once people are released from detention, they are moved to one of the open centres on the island. Without underestimating the significance of the freedom gained when released from detention, the physical conditions in open centres and detention centres have generally been similar: overcrowded, dilapidated, and not suitable for long-term residence. Intended as temporary accommodation for released detainees before they either integrate into Maltese society or are repatriated, the centres have often become permanent holding centres for those who have limited opportunities to create independent lives for themselves in Malta or to resettle in other countries.

The centres fall under the remit of the Ministry for Home Affairs and National Security. In 2008, the government consolidated migration policies and services under the auspices of the ministry, ostensibly to provide more cohesive migration policies. However, this move also signalled the establishment of separate bureaucratic channels and procedures, unequal to those provided to citizens. For example, the ministry established the Organisation for the Integration and Welfare of Asylum Seekers (OIWAS) in 2007, adopting responsibilities from the Ministry for Social Policy, which previously oversaw welfare and integration matters for asylum seekers and refugees along with its task of maintaining these provisions for Maltese nationals. In stark contrast to its titular focus, OIWAS emphasized resettlement and repatriation as long-term strategies for Malta and claimed that 'very few are interested in integration' (Interview: Head of OIWAS, January 2009). This emphasis was confirmed when in 2009 the organization modified its name to the Agency for the Welfare of Asylum Seekers, conspicuously abandoning any reference to integration.

The agency oversees the open centres in Malta and has run up to ten of them. The largest are those for single men, with smaller centres accommodating single women, families, and unaccompanied minors. Combined, the centres can officially accommodate 2,200 people. However, the number of residents fluctuates with arrivals: for instance, in January 2009, the centres accommodated 3,100 people, more than 40 per cent over official capacity (Interview: Head of OIWAS, January 2009). The number of residents decreased after 2014 and stood at 673 by the end of 2016. Since 2016, residents have included those refugees resettled in Malta from Italy and Greece under the EU's relocation scheme (AIDA 2017: 36, 44–5).[19] The centres vary widely in terms of their material conditions, ranging from small houses to industrial hangars and canvas tents erected in Malta's most infamous 'tent city' in Hal Far, which has the capacity to house around 700 people.[20] Although living conditions in all the centres are extremely challenging, the conditions in smaller centres and those run by NGOs and religious organizations, such as the Peace Lab in Hal Far, are markedly better.

Like the detention centres, the open centres are concentrated on the southern end of the island, historically poorer and dotted with far fewer holiday resorts than the north. Thus, the dilapidated centres and their residents remain hidden from the more than 1 million tourists who visit the island every year. This geographic isolation limits mobility around the island, making it more difficult for migrants to search for employment opportunities and to integrate into Maltese society (Interviews: migrants and NGO representatives, 2006–15).

Open centre residents are excluded from social welfare benefits and instead given a minimal per diem allowance from the government.[21] To receive this

---

[19] Before being transferred to an open centre, these refugees are initially held in an 'Initial Reception Centre' (IRC) for a few days where they are 'medically screened and processed by the pertinent authorities' (Ministry for Home Affairs and National Security 2015). The IRC was established in Malta in late 2015 in line with the changes to detention policy: asylum seekers who arrive without authorization are now not immediately detained but instead taken to the IRC. From here, the principle immigration officer assesses their cases against the (limited) grounds to detain asylum seekers. The applicant is then either transferred to an open centre or a detention centre (AIDA 2017: 14).

[20] In April 2012, these tents were replaced with pre-fabricated, metal containers (Times of Malta 2012). Nevertheless, living conditions in this and other open centres remain inadequate (AIDA 2017).

[21] Asylum seekers and those recognized with humanitarian or subsidiary protection receive a daily allowance of €4.66 (equivalent to €139.80 for a thirty-day month); rejected asylum seekers receive €3.49 (€104.70); and children are allocated €2.33 (€69.90). Asylum seekers returned from other EU countries under the Dublin Regulation are only provided a per diem of €2.91 (€87.30), effectively punishing attempts to leave the island (information provided to the author by OIWAS in January 2009; cf. AIDA 2017: 42; Caruana 2016: 15).

support, residents must register three times a week. If they fail to register on one day, they are no longer entitled to their allowance for that week and, in addition, must pay the centre eight euros per week for their accommodation. If this occurs over three consecutive weeks, they are expelled from the centre. The registration system is intended to prevent residents from collecting an allowance if they are working. However, those lucky enough to find work, mostly do so on a casual and part-time basis; many work seasonally during the peak tourist months and then have difficulty finding employment during the rest of the year. Although all migrants, even those whose asylum application has been rejected, have a legal right to work if they apply for a work permit, most do so without permits or contracts.

In this cycle of precarious employment, underemployment, and unemployment, many returned to the centre after a period away to find their bed taken and their belongings thrown out. They had been 'terminated' in the words of one centre coordinator. These short-sighted and punitive policies result in people being left destitute, with only the help and generosity of their friends to rely on. They also provide a disincentive for migrants to search for employment, encouraging them to remain dependent on the government's subsistence allowance, ultimately increasing government costs (Interviews: open centre coordinators and residents, 2006–15).

Despite the risk of losing the security of a steady, if minimal level of income and accommodation, the overwhelming majority of people interviewed were actively looking for work, accepting the risks involved with precarious labour in order to gain some semblance of independence and dignity (Interviews: open centre coordinators and residents, 2006–15). Mahan, a young asylum seeker from Somalia, explained,

> When I was working, I stopped signing because I was working. And I want to help the government, so I went to get a flat on my own. Unfortunately, I lost the job. So, after I finish my money, spending it on food, clothes and [my] house, then I came back here to the tent, to start signing again, [but] they could not allow me. So, for seven months now, I don't work, I don't receive money. Some of my friends who receive money, they help me....I don't have a place of my own, even a tent here. I don't have a place because when I stopped signing, I lost my bed, even a tent here....They take over my bed. So now I don't have a place to stay outside, I just move from camp to camp.
>
> (Interview: April 2009)

Although the open centres have become much less overcrowded as boat arrivals have dropped in Malta, migrants remain socio-economically marginalized.

A recent study carried out by the Jesuit Refugee Services in Malta and aditus, a local human rights' NGO, found that 80 per cent of asylum seekers[22] in Malta were at risk of poverty, more than five times the rate in the general population.[23] Perhaps most tellingly, those who have resided in Malta for longer are no less likely to be at risk of poverty than new arrivals. Moreover, poverty and material deprivation were consistently high in this population, regardless of protection status. For example, the households surveyed had an average disposable income of €4,800, well below the poverty threshold (€7,600). A staggering 45.8 per cent were unemployed, compared to the national unemployment rate of 5.2 per cent, with a further 20.8 per cent employed part-time. Of those who were employed, more than half did not have a formal work contract (Caruana 2016).

The accounts above illustrate how the presence and absence of migration policies create precarious labour and precarious lives. Neglected open centres in relatively remote areas and minimal financial support cause migrants to be vulnerable to exploitation and limit their ability to integrate into Maltese society. Services that would encourage further integration, such as English and Maltese language classes, are only provided by NGOs. Indeed, the complete absence of an integration policy, despite the arrival of migrants for over a decade, signals the government's lack of commitment to integration and its focus on deterrence and the construction of a crisis.[24] As a result, Malta ranked thirty-third out of thirty-eight countries surveyed by the Migration Integration Policy Index in 2015.[25]

Asylum

In line with the lack of emphasis on integration, the Maltese government favours granting temporary subsidiary protection to asylum seekers over

[22] The study interviewed people who had at some point applied for asylum regardless of outcome, including those granted status, rejected asylum seekers, and people still awaiting an asylum decision.

[23] Across the EU, the at-risk-of-poverty threshold is calculated at 60 per cent of the median national equivalized income. In Malta, the average household gross income and the mean disposable income stood at €29,948 and €24,730, respectively, in 2014. The at-risk-of-poverty threshold was thus €7,672 (up 5.7 per cent from 2013). In the general population, the at-risk-of-poverty rate was 15.9 per cent, whilst among persons below the age of eighteen, the rate was 24.1 per cent. Rates of material deprivation are also significantly higher amongst the asylum-seeking population surveyed: the severe material deprivation rate was 49.5 per cent, close to five times the national rate of 10.2 per cent, and the overall material deprivation rate was 85.3 per cent, while the rate in the general population was 20.2 per cent (Caruana 2016: 16, 29–30).

[24] The government announced it would launch an integration policy in 2017. However, betraying the lack of commitment to the issue within the government, the Minister for Civil Liberties noted that the issue was 'complex' and required 'changes to the policies being implemented by different parts of government' (Diacono 2017).

[25] The index focuses on eight policy areas and assesses migrants' access to the labour market, family reunification, education, health, political participation, permanent residence, and nationality, as well as their ability to be free from discrimination. See results at: http://www.mipex.eu/malta

permanent refugee status. Compared to other EU member states, Malta has relatively high rates of international protection: between 2004 and 2015, 63 per cent of all asylum application were given some form of international protection (see Graph 4.2). Across the EU, only 33 per cent of asylum applications resulted in positive decisions between 2008 and 2015 (European Parliament 2015a; Eurostat 2016a). Indeed, Malta often maintained the highest rates of international protection within the EU, pointing to this as evidence of the 'disproportionate burden' it faces. Despite this, only 4.3 per cent of applicants were granted full refugee protection between 2004 and 2015, with 54.5 per cent granted subsidiary protection (UNHCR-Malta 2018; Ministry for Justice and Home Affairs 2005: 5). Over this decade, Malta often maintained a refugee protection rate that was among the lowest in Europe, especially between 2007 and 2010 when less than 1 per cent of applicants were granted refugee status.[26] This runs contrary to overall EU patterns, where a smaller percentage of people are granted some form of protection, but a much larger percentage of those given a positive decision obtain refugee status. For instance, in 2015,

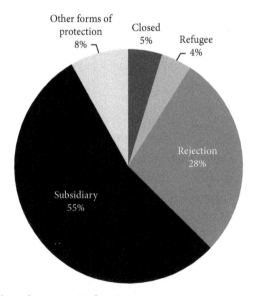

Graph 4.2. Asylum decisions, Malta, 2004–15

Source: For more on data used see UNHCR-Malta 2018; Ministry for Justice and Home Affairs 2005: 5.

[26] Calculations are based on the number of people who had their asylum claim processed during one year, either receiving some form of protection, being rejected, or withdrawing their application. The number is not necessarily equal to the number of applicants who lodge claims during one year as the Refugee Commissioner's Office has experienced delays in processing claims since its creation in January 2002 (Eurostat 2010; Interview: Refugee Commissioner, July 2006; statistics provided by the Refugee Commissioner's Office, August 2011).

74 per cent of positive decisions across the EU were people granted refugee status, 18 per cent were granted subsidiary protection, and 8 per cent were authorized to stay on humanitarian grounds (Eurostat 2016a: 3).[27]

Temporary forms of protection leave recipients in a legal limbo where the government may at any time decide that it is safe for them to return to their country of origin. They also bar access to family reunification provisions, a particularly cruel facet of European migration policies. For instance, Fatumo, a young mother from Somalia, has lived in Malta for six years. She made the dangerous journey to Europe without her three children who live with her sister in a Kenyan refugee camp. Having only been granted temporary protection by the Maltese government, she has no hope of being reunited with her children on the island (JRS et al. 2016). Such policies hinder integration and encourage onward mobility. In Malta, many attempt to leave. They travel on tourist visas or false documents to other member states and reapply for asylum in the hope of finding a more secure and less transient existence. For example, Somalis and Eritreans, who are usually granted temporary protection in Malta, are aware that other European countries are more likely to grant them refugee status (Interviews: 2006–15).

Subsidiary and temporary forms of protection have changed over the years, reflecting the dynamic and politicized process of creating migrant categories. Humanitarian protection was awarded as a form of temporary protection in Malta until 2008, when subsidiary protection was introduced as an additional category, a category harmonized at the EU level. Since then, the majority of asylum applicants have been awarded this status. In 2010, a policy decision made by the Minister for Home Affairs introduced another category, 'Temporary Humanitarian Protection New' (THPN), as a form of ex-gratia national protection. THPN was given to people whose asylum application was rejected but who after many years could not be deported and had 'showed effort and some measure of success at integration'. Although the government vehemently denied it, the status was effectively a form of regularization, albeit with limited rights and benefits. In 2012, the government stopped granting THPN in new cases, but continued to annually renew the status of those already holding it (aditus foundation et al. 2016; European Migration Network 2010; Sansone 2017a).

In late 2016, the Minister for Home Affairs announced that he would permanently suspend THPN: no renewals would take place after October

---

[27] Similarly, in 2008, 53 per cent of positive decisions in the EU were those granted refugee status (Juchno 2011). Others have discussed the origins of temporary protection and its prevalence across Europe (e.g. Koser, Walsh, and Black 1998).

2017. Those in possession of temporary protection were told to procure documentation from their country of origin (Ministry for Home Affairs and National Security 2016). The announcement came during the high-profile detention and deportation attempt of thirty-three Malians, discussed further in the next section. Deportation fears quickly spread in the community, especially as the majority of the 1,300 people who held the status were also from West Africa. The group, which included children born in Malta, had all resided on the island for at least nine years, some for as many as eighteen (Sansone 2017a).

Individual and group protests erupted after the announcement. In an unprecedented step, the three biggest media outlets in Malta joined forces to condemn the move as 'guided by opportunistic politics rather than reasoned policy' (Times of Malta et al. 2017). In the midst of the uncertainty, a thirty-three-year-old Ghanaian, Frederick Ofosu, who had been in Malta for eight years, took his own life. He left behind an audio recording detailing how he was being made to feel like a criminal when he had done no wrong (Grech, Herman 2017). The following day, the government retracted their plan to suspend temporary protection status (Sansone 2017a).

The mercurial policies that structure the lives of migrants and refugees once they leave detention entrench their position at the edge of society. With no dedicated integration policies, migrants remain economically and socially marginalized with few opportunities to find long-term housing and secure employment, regardless of their status. Temporary forms of protection deny them the right to reunite with their families. Suspended in a space where integration is hindered and where return to countries of origin is inconceivable, many see moving further into Europe as their only option (Interviews: 2006–15). These policies not only encourage illegalized onward mobility but also signal that migrants and refugees do not belong in Malta, that they are only tolerated temporarily. Detention centres, 'tent cities', and temporary forms of protection reinforce the political message that Malta is 'full', overburdened at Europe's edge, and, as a result, long-term settlement is foreclosed as an opportunity even for refugees. In short, the temporal and material features of migration controls within the border reproduce the crisis.

Deportation

In Malta, policymakers point to the eighteen-month mandatory detention policy as a means of facilitating deportation of rejected asylum seekers and other people with no right to remain on the island. Despite this, a lack of diplomatic relations with many countries of origin hampers the government's ability to deport people. Even when diplomatic relations exist, countries of origin may resist accepting forcibly returned migrants. Across the EU, the spectacle of detention obscures the fact that most detainees are not deported (cf. Mainwaring and Silverman 2017). According to the European Commission (2014b; 2018), there is a significant gap between those issued a return order and those removed from EU territory: for example, in 2012, 484,000 people were given a return order and only 178,000, or 37 per cent, were removed. This trend was similar in 2016 (45.8 per cent) and 2017 (36.6 per cent).

Despite these low figures, deportations are still the costliest element of the EU's migration regime: the bloc spends €1 billion a year on deportations, according to the Migration Files. Even in Malta, where on average the state only deported 400 people per year between 2008 and 2014, the country spent €22 million on deportations over these seven years (Eurostat 2017; Journalism++ SAS et al. 2015). Charter flights and the necessity of police 'escorts' contribute to these high costs. For example, in 2014, the EU's border agency, Frontex, chartered forty-six planes for forced removals.[28] The flights not only forcibly returned 2,281 people but also required the presence of 4,081 staff escorts. Indeed, in most cases, planes are filled with more staff than deportees (Stahnke et al. 2015).

The violent and contested nature of removals has prompted governments across the EU to employ private security firms and to charter flights in order to avoid public scrutiny. For example, the 'unlawful killing' of Jimmy Mubenga on a commercial British Airways flight in 2010 revealed the violent nature of forced removals. Mubenga was being deported from the UK to Angola and died while being restrained by three Detainee Custody Officers, employed by the private security firm G4S. Testimonies from other passengers on the plane thwarted an initial attempt at a cover up by G4S and the Home Office (Sambrook 2013; cf. Walters 2016).

The confined, regulated space of commercial airplanes may expose state violence, as well as facilitate resistance. Fellow passengers need only to stand and refuse to fasten their seatbelts to disrupt a deportation (e.g. Crouch 2018; Indymedia UK 2011). When charter flights are used, more radical tactics are needed: in March 2017, fifteen activists grounded a mass deportation flight from the UK to Nigeria and Ghana by chaining themselves to the airplane on the Stansted Airport runway for eight hours (Graham 2017).[29]

---

[28] This does not include flights chartered by individual member states, which are more numerous. For example, the UK removed over 2,000 people on at least sixty charter flight in 2012 (Corporate Watch 2013: 18).
[29] Such resistance is not without risk: the UK government charged the fifteen activists with a terrorist offence under the 1990 Aviation and Maritime Security Act. The activists were convicted but received suspended sentences (Gayle 2019).

Deportations, like detention, are alternately obscured and made hypervisible by states (cf. Mountz 2010: xvii; Walters 2016). Occasional high-profile deportations remind citizens, non-citizens, and other countries that the state is 'tough' on migration and in control of its borders. On the other hand, states attempt to obscure the inherent violence of forced removals and the resistance they engender. Similarly, states present deportations as finite, one-way journeys that deter other migrants, while research demonstrates the likelihood that deportees reattempt migration after being returned and that deportation does not act as a deterrent (Hiemstra 2012; Schuster and Majidi 2013).

Nevertheless, the threat of deportation looms large for migrants in Malta and elsewhere (De Genova and Peutz 2010). Precarious legal status alongside high-profile deportations contribute to this fear. For instance, in 2002, prior to EU accession, the Maltese government forcibly deported 220 Eritreans. Upon arrival in Eritrea, all the deportees were detained in the Adi Abeto military detention centre. Three women, deported in advanced stages of pregnancy, gave birth in the prison with very little medical attention. Men of conscription age were kept incommunicado and tortured (Amnesty International 2004: 30–1). One deportee described the experience:

> I was on the last of the four planes [leaving Malta], among 57 Eritreans who were flown back to Eritrea. That night at 3am we were woken up, handcuffed, and taken to the airport—some even without their shoes. There were two Maltese Special Force soldiers to each prisoner, holding our arms. Some of us were crying but the soldiers were laughing and joking in their language. We couldn't resist. In the plane, we all had one soldier on each side of us, and there were others with their guns in the centre aisle.
>
> When we landed at Asmara, the airport was quiet. The Maltese handed us over. There were no relatives meeting us. When the Maltese plane left, the soldiers took us in a military bus to Adi Abeto prison. The women, girls and children were separated. There were interrogation rooms and we were called one at a time, with two guards, one asking the questions, the other doing the beating.   (Amnesty International 2004: 30)

Although this deportation received significant attention and criticism, Malta generally has limited success with forced returns. Over the past decade, the government deported 400 people per year, on average. The government points to its limited diplomatic representation in Africa and related difficulties in procuring identity documents as the main reason for its inability to increase the number of forced removals (Interviews: 2006–15; Eurostat 2017). Nevertheless, the government has exploited the threat of deportation. In July 2013, 102

Somalis, including forty-one women and two babies, arrived by boat in Malta, having departed from Libyan shores. They were immediately detained, denied any opportunity to apply for international protection, and threatened with deportation to Libya. The government booked the forty-five adult men on an Air Malta plane to Tripoli that very night. Eleven advocacy organizations on the island responded swiftly, issuing a joint statement that condemned the government's deportation attempt. They argued that, if returned to Libya, the Somalis would face gross human rights violations.

> [T]hose we met detailed the abuses they faced [in Libya], especially in detention, among them brutal beatings and shootings, which left some permanently disabled. Those who return to Libya after attempting to reach Europe are singled out for especially harsh punishment .... The action contemplated by the government is precisely what the Prime Minister says it is not: it is a pushback, sending people who have come to our shores to seek well-deserved refuge, back to a country where they may well be killed.
>
> (aditus foundation et al. 2013)

The organizations also appealed to the European Court of Human Rights, which quickly intervened with an emergency interim order that blocked the deportation (ECRE 2013). In response to the widespread criticism, Prime Minister Joseph Muscat admitted that the move was a symbolic one, a tactic carried out to send a message to Brussels just four months after he came to office. Yet, he defended his actions, claiming, 'This is not pushback, it is a signal that we are not pushovers.' Muscat maintained that Malta would not continue to receive migrants and refugees without more support from the EU (ECRE 2013; Interview: 2014). He also noted that a beneficial effect of the threat was that 'immigrants are more afraid to come to Malta now' (Interview: 2014). Lambasting this position in their statements, the NGOs said, '[I]t is unacceptable to use innocent people to score points and to bargain, in a bid to put Malta in a stronger position at the European burden-sharing table' (aditus foundation et al. 2013).

Malta again used migrants' deportability to demonstrate to Brussels and its fellow member states that it was tough on migration in the months leading up to its adoption of the rotating EU presidency. In November 2016, the government detained thirty-three Malians who had lived in Malta for many years, claiming that they were 'failed asylum seekers'. The men were detained when they arrived at routine appointments in police stations to renew their documents, a requirement they had to fulfil every three months. A Malian government delegation accompanied by Frontex officials arrived on 5 December and identified nine detainees as Malian nationals.[30] The other twenty-four were released. After three months in detention, the remaining nine were released hours before a protest organized by NGOs, one of many that had taken place. The Minister for Home Affairs stated that they would be released but deported once documentation from Mali was forthcoming (Sansone 2017b). The climate of fear intensified as the police carried out a surprise raid and rounded up eighty-four Africans near the Marsa Open Centre one early Wednesday morning in April 2017. The migrants were taken to a police station to 'verify their documents and ensure they [were] in Malta legally' but were all eventually released. The raid is the first of its kind in Malta (Times of Malta 2017; Balzan 2017).

Symbolic raids and deportation attempts spread fear and fan the flames of crisis. They turn migrants and refugees into distrustful, dangerous bodies, made suspicious by their skin colour. Notably, these actions come on the heels of three years of low boat arrivals. In their absence, other measures are needed to sustain the crisis. The raid and deportation attempt also occurred during Malta's EU presidency and in anticipation of a national election.[31] They act as a symbolic demonstration of state power and encourage migrants to move on to other EU member states.

Malta's show of force is informed by a regional context where the EU has also prioritized deportations. In 2016, the EU launched a drive to sign 'partnership agreements' to facilitate deportations, including with Afghanistan, Ethiopia, Mali, Niger, Nigeria, and Senegal (Baczynska and Körkemeir 2016; European Commission 2017g). In these agreements, the EU's implicit and sometimes explicit threat is the withdrawal of aid. For example, a leaked 2016 memo from the European Commission revealed that the EU threatened to withdraw aid if Afghanistan refused to accept deportees. The mass deportations to Afghanistan have been particularly controversial given the ongoing conflict in the country, a conflict in which EU member states have played

---

[30] The move came as the EU was attempting to sign a €145 million deal with Mali to 'fight against irregular immigration', the first agreement with an African country to include a specific mechanism for deportation. The agreement was controversial and illustrated the difficulty in securing cooperation from countries to facilitate deportation. Even the Malian Foreign Minister maintained that he would not send officials to Europe to identify people for deportation (Baczynska and Körkemeir 2016; Euractiv 2016).

[31] At this time, the election was expected in 2018. The fallout from the publication of the Panama Papers resulted in a snap election called by the ruling Labour government and held in June 2017. The Panama Papers revealed that Konrad Mizzi, the Minister of Energy and Deputy Prime Minister, and Keith Schembri, the Prime Minister's Chief of Staff, held offshore accounts in Panama. Neither had resigned at the time of writing (Garside 2017). Despite these revelations and allegations of corruption, the Labour Party won the election with a large majority (55 per cent of votes) (Scicluna 2017).

a significant role (Rasmussen 2016). The same leaked memo outlined a 'deteriorating security situation' in Afghanistan while still encouraging more returns to the country.

> The main push factors are: a deteriorating security situation with record levels of terrorist attacks and civilian casualties (over 11,000 civilian casualties recorded in 2015), compounded by a deteriorating economic situation. Both are likely to grow stronger.   (European Council 2016: 3)

> The positive trend in the asylum application acceptance rate from 2014–2015 is an indicator that Member States are aware of the worsening security situation and threats to which people are exposed. Despite this, more than 80,000 persons could potentially need to be returned in the near future.
> (European Council 2016: 2)

The EU thus continues to encourage member states to increase deportations. For instance, although the EU Returns Directive came into force in 2010, the EU Commission subsequently drafted multiple 'Action Plan[s] on Return' in 2015 and 2017 to support member states to carry out more deportations (European Commission 2015d; 2017a). In May 2015, deportations were included on the European Agenda on Migration at the Valletta Summit. In March 2017, the European Commission (2017c) presented new measures to 'ensure swift return procedures and substantially increase the rate of return' that included: shorter appeal periods against return decisions, an increased use of detention, and the increased involvement of Frontex.[32]

The 'refugee crisis' has also been leveraged in order to argue that the EU must return more 'illegal migrants' before they can accept additional refugees (DeBono 2016).[33] Moreover, the rhetoric of 'exceptionally' high arrivals is used to justify undermining human rights protections. For example, Article 18 of the 2010 EU Returns Directive states that in 'emergency situations' where there are 'an exceptionally large number' of arrivals, derogations from limits on judicial review and maintaining conditions in detention may be justified (European Parliament and Council 2008: 106). What constitutes 'large

---

[32] After the expansion of Frontex's mandate and its rebranding as the European Border and Coast Guard Agency in 2016, the agency can now initiate return flights. As a result, it had returned more people in the first four months of 2017 (4,704 people on one hundred forced return flights) than it did throughout all of 2015 (3,565 people on sixty-six flights). Moreover, between 2015 and 2016, Frontex's budget for joint returns almost tripled from €11.4 million. By 2017, its operation budget for returns was €66.5 million (Civillini and Bagnoli 2017).

[33] In September 2015, the EU Commission proposed seven measures in response to the 'refugee crisis' in Europe. Four of the seven focused on external aspects of migration control, on either deterring people from migrating to the EU or deporting them once they arrived. They include: a common European list of Safe Countries of Origin; making return policy more effective; addressing the external dimension of the refugee crisis; and establishing a Trust Fund for Africa (European Commission 2015c).

numbers' is never defined. The Commission also encourages the use of long-term detention to facilitate deportation, noting that 'The maximum duration period of detention currently used by several Member States is significantly shorter than the one allowed by [the Returns] Directive 2008/115/EC and which is needed to complete the return procedure success-fully. These short periods of detention are precluding effective removals' (European Council 2017a).

The employment of an exceptionalist logic in order to undermine human rights continues. In 2017, Malta, with support from the EU Council, commis-sioned an EU report to 'examine how to interpret and apply' laws to deport people fleeing persecution by suspending the principle of non-refoulement during times of 'crisis' (Vella 2017; Maltese Council Presidency 2017). German officials also proposed relaxing human rights safeguards in order to be able to deport asylum seekers while their cases are still pending (Euractiv 2017).

False Rescue

Everybody wants my story; nothing changes.

Ibrahim, December 2014

Those rescued at sea face detention, deportation, legal disenfranchisement, and further socio-economic marginalization within the European Union. Journalists, activists, researchers, and celebrities sought Ibrahim's story after he survived days of treading water, while hundreds of his fellow travellers drowned in the Mediterranean. Yet, 'nothing changed' for him: he was never-theless scripted as a risky subject and faced detention and marginalization.

Kitty Calavita (2005: 154) argues persuasively about the relationship between the racialization of migrants and their economic position in Spain and Italy. She maintains that 'institutionalized economic marginality is integral to the racialization of immigrants (indeed, their very nomenclature as such)', and that their marginal economic position 'inevitably reproduces the visible markers of poverty, and further generates…material and social exclusion'. Following Calavita, I argue that this 'othering' occurs before migrants even arrive on EU territory and is fundamentally related to discourse, policies, and practices at sea. The language of rescue strips migrants at sea of agency, reduces them to victims, and in turn allows for their continued marginalization once they arrive on EU territory. Migrants are already constructed as inferior, racialized beings at sea, associated in political and media rhetoric with chaos, illegality, and need. This initial characterization allows for their continued criminalization, as well as their socio-economic and legal marginalization within the EU (cf. Maher 2002).

In Malta, the government's interpretation of migration patterns as temporary and accidental ignores the long-term presence of migrants and refugees and gives grounds for their continued marginalization. Integration remains elusive, especially due to the government's rhetorical and financial focus on deterrence, detention, and deportation. For example, the Third Country Nationals Unit within the Ministry for Home Affairs described their top priorities as (1) readmission agreements, (2) implementation of burden-sharing commitments in the EU, and (3) increased and better cooperation with African countries in order to facilitate migrant returns (Interview: January 2009). These echo Malta's priorities at the EU level. The lack of integration policy is justified with reference to the country's small size and to the perceived apathy felt by migrants and refugees towards Malta. A senior official in the Ministry for Home Affairs commented,

> They're not interested in being integrated in the local context. They would like to integrate but in an environment which is fertile in terms of their returns, their perceived returns. They see Malta as being small, constrained and the first thing they want is out .... [T]he fact is that [integration] is not a consideration for practically all of them.   (Interview: April 2009)

The absence of an integration policy results in ambiguity around the rights of migrants and refugees, especially in terms of their access to social services after they are released from detention, including healthcare, housing, employment, education, and social support. Information given to migrants about their rights is still limited and a common complaint is that regulations and rights are unclear to them as well as to Maltese providers (Luhmann et al. 2007; cf. Caruana 2016). Migrant and refugee experiences are therefore dependent on the individuals they encounter. Some report great kindness and generosity, while others encounter racism, especially when attempting to access services, such as in hospitals, at the Employment Training Centre, and with the police (Interviews: 2006–15; cf. Caruana 2016).[34]

An EU report found that sub-Saharan Africans in Malta experienced the second highest rates of discrimination in the EU: 66 per cent of those interviewed had experienced discrimination in the previous twelve months

---

[34] Calavita (2005: 152) defines racism as 'the systematic subordination, exclusion, or domination of one group by another, that is justified by prejudice against that group as inferior, and that is accompanied by perceived physical inscriptions. It thus has a structural/material dimension (subordination), an attitudinal one (prejudice), and a physical one (perceived bodily inscriptions).'

(EU Agency for Fundamental Rights 2010: 88). Warsame, a Somali man who arrived in Malta in 2004 and has been a leader in the migrant community, described his experience: 'You feel closed in. You can't leave, you can't go back, and the Maltese people don't want you here and don't want to know you. So you try to be invisible and worry about a future that may never come' (quoted in Bilefsky 2006b).

The Maltese government's continued assessment of migration as a crisis and a security concern hinders integration further. Government discourse and practices that (re)produce the crisis also discourage the Maltese population from accepting immigration realities on the island. For example, when surveyed in 2013 about migrant boat arrivals, the largest number of respondents (20.6 per cent) said that their greatest concern was migrants 'invading Malta'. A further 14.9 per cent responded that migrants 'come in uncontrolled numbers' (Debono 2013). Similarly, a survey conducted in 2009 reported that 84 per cent of respondents viewed immigration to Malta as a 'national crisis' (MaltaToday 2009a). Fuelled by the government's portrayal of the situation as a crisis, the Maltese peoples' initial sympathetic response to the plight of people arriving on the island has turned hostile, increasingly xenophobic, and racist.[35]

However troubling, the racism and xenophobia in Malta are hardly surprising. Government discourse largely paints Malta as a victim of migration flows and ignores the ways in which people who arrive contribute to Maltese society. Local NGOs as well as international organizations have criticized the government for not doing enough to curb the growth of racism. These organizations point to the distorted picture presented to the Maltese population through an emphasis on migration numbers and costs. Officials have also been accused of making racist remarks themselves, linking migrants and asylum seekers to crime, terrorism, and the spread of illness. The assistant director of Jesuit Refugee Services Malta, said,

> A lot of statements have been made, even by those in authority, associating immigrants with illness and with a security threat. Obviously, anyone can be sick…it has nothing to do with nationality. But, irregular immigrants have

---

[35] A poll conducted by the *Times of Malta* in 2005 revealed that 90 per cent of respondents perceived an African or Arab neighbour to be undesirable (Grech 2005). In 2006, seven cars at the Jesuit Refugee Services office were doused in gasoline and set alight over a three-month period. The assistant director's house was also set on fire. Stacks of fliers signed 'KKK' were left at the entrance of the Marsa Open Centre with the warning 'get out or we will start killing you' (Bilefsky 2006b). Carmen Sammut's (2007) report on the issue includes an interesting discussion of the ethics of newspaper reporting on migration, while Mark-Anthony Falzon and Mark Micallef (2008) provide a detailed account of the rise of the far right.

been publicly associated with illness or with the threat that they might be terrorists. Of course, so could anyone else and we're more likely to be than they are. No terrorist is going to come and spend eighteen months in Safi [Detention Centre] .... But, the fact that in the public mind we have made these associations is very dangerous.   (Interview: June 2006)

Ignorance and misinformation encourage the perception of being invaded by migrants, leading to xenophobia and racism. Two interrelated factors based largely on fear appear to fuel this racism: the fear of losing economic security and the related perception of material scarcity, an image propagated by the governments' rhetoric within the EU regarding Malta's small size and inability to cope with the migration 'burden'; and the fear of losing one's national identity, a fear exacerbated by stereotypes and myths relating to both the national culture and migrant cultures.[36] A 'historical amnesia' allows for the construction of a mythical, homogenous 'pre-migrant' society in Malta and elsewhere (Behdad 2005). Along with state practices of deterrence and exclusion, these national myths reinforce and justify racism (Schuster 2003a; cf. Hayter 2000: 21–36). The migrant is constructed as the inferior and threatening 'other', who challenges traditional divisions between nationals and non-nationals through the act of migration, as well as a group's sense of identity within a specific culture, territory, or ethnicity (Triandafyllidou 2001; Anthias and Lazaridis 1999: 1–11). Migrants' marginal position in the economy reinforces their otherness. As Tahar Ben Jelloun (1997: xiv–xv) poignantly states,

> Poverty has never been well-received.... At most, difference is accepted under condition that the person be rich, under condition that he has the means to disguise it and pass unobserved. Be different, but be rich! Whoever has no other riches than their ethnic and cultural difference are consigned to humiliation and every form of racism.[37]

Migrants' marginalization is not just physical, nor socio-economic. It silences them, erasing their bodies and voices from the community, except when they are exploited to further the crisis. bell hooks (1990: 209) reminds us that it is also oppressors who insist of those on the margins: 'tell me your story. Only do not speak in a voice of resistance. Only speak from that space in the margin that is a sign of deprivation, a wound, an unfulfilled longing. Only speak your pain.' More complex representations of migrants and their experiences rarely reach the public. Migrant accounts are routinely dismissed as biased or

---

[36] These claims are drawn from the extensive interviews done by the author. There is limited literature on the issue of racism in Malta (Borg and Mayo 2007; Calleja 2000).
[37] Quoted in Calavita (2005: 154).

false amongst policy makers. Many citizens have never had a conversation with them.[38] As Eyob, the young Eritrean quoted above, said, 'We have nowhere to speak. There is no mediator between the migrants and the government or between the migrants and the NGOs' (Interview: April 2009). Amongst government officials and the broader population, there is thus a limited understanding of migration realities in Malta.

Migrant journeys continue after they have reached Europe. Socio-economic marginalization, subsidiary forms of protection, and fear of deportation encourage people to leave Malta. Yet, onward mobility is prohibited and criminalized by the EU's Dublin Regulation. Those that travel to another EU country risk being returned. When Aslya won her case at the European Court in 2013, she had already suffered at the hands of a migration system that criminalizes movement, divides families, and increases suffering. A Somali national, she arrived in Malta in 2009 at the age of twenty-two and was immediately detained. Her asylum application was rejected, but she escaped from detention and travelled to the Netherlands. She applied for asylum there and hoped she could continue to Sweden to reunite with her father, siblings, and young son, who she had not seen since 2008. They had been granted refugee status in Eritrea and were awaiting resettlement to Sweden, which took place in 2011. However, the Netherlands returned Aslya to Malta in 2011 under the Dublin Regulation where she was immediately detained at Safi Barracks despite being two months pregnant. Soon after, the government initiated criminal proceedings against her and charged her with escape from a place of public custody, as well as using forged documents and making false statements to leave Malta. She was given a six-month prison sentence, during which she had a miscarriage. After release, she was once again held in immigration detention and only released after being detained for eighteen months (ECHR 2013a).

Negotiating Rights inside the EU

Faced with marginalization and significant challenges, migrants continue to make demands, negotiate their rights and interests, and demonstrate agency after arrival within EU member states. Aslya took her case to the European Court of Human Rights to protest her treatment by the Maltese government.

---

[38] In a 2013 survey, over 70 per cent of respondents in Malta said they had never had a five-minute conversation with 'a migrant from sub-Saharan Africa' (Debono 2013).

Ibrahim, the young Palestinian man mentioned at the beginning of this chapter, never intended to come to Malta. The boat he travelled on from Egypt sank en route to Italy, and he and his brother spent five days in the sea watching most of their fellow travellers perish before a French captain rescued them. Dehydrated to the point of delirium, they nevertheless were registered and sent immediately to one of Malta's detention facilities when they arrived on the island. Despite these traumatic experiences, Ibrahim and his brother both refused to be fingerprinted during the police registration process, aware that these fingerprints would follow them around Europe and would inhibit their settlement in Sweden where they had family they intended to join (Interview: December 2014).

Although often discounted in academic and policy circles, migrant agency and forms of migrant resistance to state practices influence state and regional policies, as well as state relationships. For example, the plight of refugees in Greece prompted the European Court of Human Rights (2011) to rule against returning an Afghan asylum seeker to the country under the Dublin Regulation in 2011. In these instances, NGOs often act as intermediaries, championing migrant causes at the regional and international level. The lobbying successes of NGOs in Brussels are based on their first-hand knowledge of the situation 'on the ground', with migrant testimonies forming an indispensable part of their expertise and campaigns (Hoffmann 2013).

In Malta, protests in immigration detention have led the EU to exert pressure on the country to improve conditions and to reconsider its mandatory eighteen-month detention policy. After their visit to Malta in 2005, the European Committee for the Prevention of Torture also compiled a report that specifically references protests held by detainees, as well as allegations of mistreatment (Council of Europe 2005). Legal action taken by migrants subsequently resulted in the European Court of Human Rights (2013a; 2013b) condemning Malta's detention policy.[39] Building on years of campaigning, these legal challenges, alongside the long-awaited release of a national enquiry into the death of Mamadou Kamara, prompted the government to announce that they would end the mandatory detention of asylum seekers in 2016 (Interview: senior government official, 2014; Ministry for Home Affairs and National Security 2015).

Lawyers involved in cases at the national and regional levels note the centrality of migrant participation and testimony. Indeed, the difficulty in

---

[39] Similarly, the Court used migrant testimony and data collected by advocacy organizations to condemn Italy's practice of returning people to Libya from the high sea (ECHR 2012).

identifying migrants who have been returned to another country or detained, and in ensuring their participation and testimony, often over a long period of time, can thwart attempts to launch such cases (Interviews: 2006–15). Nevertheless, lawyers, NGOs, and politicians have cooperated with migrants to overcome these challenges. In 2016, Italy signed a memorandum of understanding with Sudan to facilitate repatriation, and promptly deported forty Sudanese citizens. In response, a delegation made up of Italian lawyers and MEPs from the European United Left–Nordic Green Left coalition travelled to Sudan in late 2016 and met with the deported migrants. As a result, five of the Sudanese citizens filed a case at the European Court of Human Rights in February 2017 claiming that their deportation violated the principle of non-refoulement to a country where fundamental rights are not safeguarded and people risk being subjected to inhuman treatment (Civillini and Bagnoli 2017; GUE/NGL 2017).

In Malta, Tefarra, another young Eritrean refugee, was shocked when he was imprisoned in detention for twelve months upon arrival. After his release, in May 2007, he filed a case at the national court with the aid of a lawyer from Jesuit Refugee Services. The case was still pending six years later in 2013 and was cited in the European Court of Human Rights (2013a) judgment that year as evidence of the lack of an effective remedy. In 2017, the court eventually ruled on the case and found a breach of the protection from arbitrary detention, ten years after the initial application was filed and after forty-one court sittings were deferred and a further nineteen were adjourned (Camilleri 2018: 43–4; Civil Court—Malta 2007). The length of such proceedings diminishes the ability of migrants and NGOs to pursue these cases.

Nevertheless, migrant and NGO actions are influential in Malta. Malta's visibility within the EU with regard to migration across the Mediterranean amplifies this effectiveness. Having emphasized its vulnerability in the face of the migration 'crisis' (Mainwaring 2014), Malta attracts more attention from regional actors and simultaneously constructs a larger, more visible platform for migrants and NGOs. Migrant and refugee action can therefore affect a state's image, power, and relationships to varying degrees, depending on the levels of monitoring and oversight by non-governmental and supranational actors. NGOs play a crucial role in this process, as their advocacy work is sometimes the most powerful tool available to marginalized migrants and refugees, especially at the regional and international levels.

Although the discussion above demonstrates migrants' room for manoeuvre and ability to effect change, migrant agency and the contestation of the politics of mobility may be co-opted by the state. For example, Malta has exploited people's circumvention of their border policies in order to argue that the island faces a disproportionate responsibility for migration and asylum within the EU. Within this discourse, the inability of the state to secure borders and its vulnerability in the face of large, unregulated flows is emphasized and exploited for political gain. An ambivalent relationship between the state and unauthorized migration thus arises: although the focus is on deterring migrant arrivals, it is these very arrivals that have put Malta on the political map during the last decade. In this manner, the agency demonstrated by migrants and refugees in order to arrive on the island constitutes in part the power that Malta wields within the EU (Mainwaring 2016a).

5

Lilliputian Power? Malta's 'Crisis'

Twenty-three migrants arrived in Malta by boat in 2017. In 2016, twenty-five did. Yet, in July 2017, a spokesperson for the Prime Minister's Office said, 'All the efforts of Malta, Italy and others suffering from the immigration crisis should remain focused on persuading other EU countries not to shrug responsibility in the face of this humanitarian crisis' (Martin 2017). The significant decrease in arrivals since 2014 did not hamper the government's appetite for constructing a migration crisis, nor for positioning Malta as the EU's migration gatekeeper.

This construction and position date back to Malta's accession to the EU in 2004, when Maltese politicians began to express frustration, feeling caught between migrant arrivals and an EU that was slow to respond to demands for help from the Mediterranean island (Interviews: 2006–15). For example, reacting to criticism of Malta's inaction over the rescue of twenty-seven men stranded on the tuna pen in 2007, the Maltese Foreign Minister maintained, 'If the European Commission is sincere in its indignation, then it should push other EU countries to share the burden. Malta cannot become a holding area for all of Europe' (quoted in Bilefsky 2007b).

The government responded to this new geopolitical reality by framing the migration situation as a crisis. Regionally, it has lobbied for more 'burden-sharing' measures within the EU. In order to attract more EU funds, Malta has highlighted its vulnerability to migration flows, emphasizing its smallness, limited resources, and gatekeeping role. Nationally, the government has limited the rights and opportunities of migrants and asylum seekers in order to reinforce the interpretation of migration as a crisis and to deter further arrivals. Containment and control have been prioritized over integration and human rights. Both nationally and regionally, government officials have insisted that the answer to the 'crisis' lies beyond Malta's shores—in Brussels, in Italy, and in Libya.

This chapter explores the strategies that Malta has used in order to make its voice heard at the EU level. In this way, it continues to explore the theme of power at the margins but moves away from the migrant experience to that of a small state at the edge of Europe. As migrants assert their agency, constitute the border, and shape the Maltese landscape, Malta itself has worked strategically to influence EU policies to its own benefit, often by exploiting migrant arrivals to the island. Here, I demonstrate how Malta has exerted an unexpected level of influence on EU migration governance, despite its small size and limited resources, by emphasizing its gatekeeper role and adopting a discourse of crisis. Indeed, the island's geopolitical position within the EU defines and limits its strategies at the EU level. The institutional framework that Malta now finds itself in as an EU member state shapes its interests. Moreover, Malta's power to radically change the system is limited. The EU framework ultimately encourages a negative portrayal of the arrival of migrants on the island and provides a perverse incentive for Malta to continue to treat the situation as a crisis.

In the crisis narrative, migrants are reduced to symbols. Their agency is co-opted by the state as it transforms them into a threat to national stability and a burden that needs to be shared. Even while migrants demonstrate agency and make decisions that require action from nation states, they are discursively reduced to these symbols in government rhetoric. Although the migrant disappears as a complex actor, as a symbol he is a powerful tool and resource with which Malta can create the ideal threat and wield influence.

The chapter proceeds by first examining Malta's position within the EU with regard to migration. The second section looks more closely at the particular strategies Malta has adopted as a small state in its campaign for influence within the EU and for increased support from member states. Amongst its strategies, Malta has built key alliances, kept migration in the Mediterranean on the EU's agenda, and framed the migration situation it faces as exceptional. The third section traces Malta's efforts to influence key EU migration policy initiatives between 2008 and 2016: (1) the European Pact on Immigration and Asylum, (2) the Schengen Borders Code, (3) the Dublin Regulation, and (4) the Long-Term Residents Directive. These four interrelated initiatives are fundamental to EU migration governance as well as to the experiences of migrants on the edges of Europe. The final section examines the shortcomings of Malta's Lilliputian strategies and its construction of a migration crisis: it analyses the contradictions involved in Malta's position as well as the consequences of these policy positions for migrants and refugees.

Guarding the Gates of Europe

There has been a steady expansion of EU migration and asylum activities since the adoption of the Treaty of Amsterdam in 1999, which brought immigration under the first, community 'pillar'.[1] Soon after, the Tampere Council called for a common European approach to asylum and immigration. Although the EU has committed more money and attention to migration in recent years (Geddes and Scholten 2016: 146),[2] progress towards harmonization has been slow, and solidarity has appeared in rhetoric more often than in action. Member states remain reluctant to commit themselves to higher protection standards, which are perceived as costly and an infringement on sovereignty (e.g. Interviews: German and Cypriot Officials, EU Permanent Representation; Commission Officials, June–July 2010). Thus, harmonization has occurred most frequently in creating minimum standards, necessarily lower than those in many member states, and in standardizing restrictive legislation on border control and mobility (Trauner and Kruse 2008).

As discussed further in Chapter 2, a central feature of EU migration governance is the responsibility placed on its peripheries which exacerbates the lingering mistrust between northern and southern member states. The Schengen Agreement, which established freedom of movement within the EU alongside measures to fortify the external border, and the Dublin Regulation, which places responsibility for asylum applications on the first country of arrival, have arguably produced more asylum and immigration pressures on countries along the external border. Indeed, the implementation of the Dublin Regulation in 1997 decreased the number of asylum applications made in Northern Europe, especially in Germany and France (see Graph 2.1, p. XX).

Malta became a member state on the southern periphery in 2004 during the 'big bang' enlargement that saw ten countries accede to the European Union, eight along the eastern periphery, together with Malta and Cyprus in the Mediterranean.[3] Unlike Italy, Greece, Spain and Portugal, Malta adopted the Schengen Agreement and Dublin Regulation without participating in

---

[1] The EU has three pillars, which each strike a different balance between supranationalism and intergovernmentalism. The first pillar is the most supranational.

[2] For example, in response to the perceived migration crisis in Europe, Frontex was relaunched in 2016 as the European Border and Coast Guard (EBCG) with expanded powers and a budget that is set to double by 2020 (European Parliament and Council 2016). While, like Frontex, the EBCG is still a coordinating body very much dependent on member states' goodwill, participation, and resources, the rebranding increases the agency's powers: by 2020, it is projected that it will have 1,000 employees and a budget of €320 million. It will be able to purchase its own equipment and will have a rapid reserve pool of 1,500 border guards ready to be mobilized within five days. Its deportation powers have also been expanded: it can now propose and organize joint return operations, provide escorts, and charter flights (Carrera et al. 2017: 43–9; Eder 2016).

[3] Before the 2004 accession of Malta and Cyprus, the member states making up the southern rim of the EU included Italy (who entered the Union in 1952), Greece (1981), Spain (1986), and Portugal (1986). Spain and Portugal joined the Schengen area in 1995, followed by Italy in 1997 and Greece in 2000.

their development.[4] It also did not benefit from the flexibility afforded to the United Kingdom and Ireland in being able to opt out of such agreements. As the country acceded to the European Union, its borders were redefined as external borders of the EU in need of fortification.[5]

Malta is a considerably smaller country than Spain, Italy, Greece, or even Portugal in terms of its population, economy, and land mass. One might expect that this would circumscribe its power, and that it would have little impact on the development of regional migration and asylum policies. Surprisingly, however, its vociferous campaign for the redistribution of the migration 'burden' has earned Maltese policymakers and politicians a reputation as effective lobbyists (Interviews: European Council and Commission, July 2010).[6] For example, one Commission official working on asylum said,

> In Malta, my opinion is that they are the kings of lobbying.... For a country so small, they have been very, very strong, lobbying everybody at the EU level: the Commission, Parliament, all the member states.... I think the Maltese authorities should be congratulated, in the sense that even though it is a small administration with limited resources and so on, they have worked hard to lobby for their interests, much more than Greece, much more than Cyprus.
>
> (Interview: Official, Asylum Unit, Directorate General for Justice, Freedom and Security, henceforth DG JFS, July 2010)

Maltese officials have been successful at maintaining Malta's role as the EU's migration gatekeeper and as champion of Mediterranean states facing a high 'burden', despite other states sometimes facing larger numbers of migrant

---

[4] Historically, EU member states on the southern periphery have responded ambivalently to the new responsibility of migration control. In the 1980s and 1990s, the four states making up the EU's southern periphery—Greece, Italy, Portugal, and Spain—were transitioning from countries of emigration to countries of immigration. Moreover, informality was a prominent structural feature in all four economies, as were high levels of 'irregular' immigration. It was thus politically expedient for these states to adopt EU policies, like Dublin and Schengen, in order to comply with accession requirements, despite geographic, economic, and bureaucratic barriers to implementation (Baldwin-Edwards 1997). The countries used large-scale regularization schemes in order to address 'illegal migration', a practice the EU criticized as being a 'pull factor' (Maas 2010; Brick 2011; European Council 2008). Notwithstanding the limits to implementation, EU policies shaped migration controls in the four countries, encouraging for instance new readmission agreements with countries outside the EU and the introduction of increased border controls and new border technologies (Geddes 2003: 149–72). For a more detailed discussion on the migration histories of these four countries, see the special issue on 'Comparing the New Hosts of Southern Europe' (González-Enríquez and Triandafyllidou 2009). On Spain and Italy, see Wayne Cornelius and colleagues (Cornelius, Martin, and Hollifield 1994: 303–69).

[5] Of course, membership also brought with it concrete financial benefit: €1.18 billion in EU funds was earmarked for Malta between 2007 and 2013 (Interview: Ministry for Foreign Affairs, April 2009), constituting 20 per cent of Malta's annual GDP of €5.86 billion (in 2007).

[6] For more information on interviews conducted at the EU level, see Appendix: Reflections on Methods and Ethics.

arrivals. For instance, comparing Cyprus's role with Malta's, the same EU official said,

> Cyprus hasn't lobbied so strongly; they are not really very vocal. I mean, okay, they were in this Quadro Group and everything, but they are completely overshadowed by Malta in that aspect,... even though for many years, they have had more asylum seekers.
>
> (Interview: Official, Asylum Unit, DG JFS, July 2010)

Malta has led the call for more 'burden sharing' in the EU, and for an expansion of the notion of solidarity beyond financial transfers. In practice, the government demanded a relocation scheme whereby asylum seekers given protection in Malta would be resettled to other EU member states. The relocation of asylum seekers whose claims have not yet been decided and who may not ultimately qualify for protection was a longer-term goal of the Maltese government. However, this was even less popular with other EU member states (Interviews: government officials, 2008–9; European Council 2009a). More broadly, Maltese officials lobbied for a renegotiation of the Dublin Regulation in order to add a proviso that would exempt countries facing 'particular pressures' from being bound by the obligations to process asylum claims and accept those people returned from other EU countries, so-called 'Dublin returns'.

Malta renewed their calls for more 'burden sharing' in 2007 after twenty-seven men clung to a tuna pen in the Mediterranean Sea for three days, while Malta, Italy, and Libya argued over responsibility for their rescue (e.g. Bilefsky 2007a).[7] The country succeeded in garnering a limited amount of support for these demands at this time. For example, shortly after the tuna-pen incident, the EU's Justice and Home Affairs Council noted Malta's 'difficult situation' and 'reaffirmed the principle of solidarity and the need for taking into account the particular pressure which specific situations may put on individual Member States regarding assistance to persons in distress at sea' (European Council 2007). Overall, however, there remains little political will amongst member states to implement permanent intra-EU relocation schemes, as the more recent arrivals of refugees from Syria and elsewhere demonstrated.

Successive Maltese governments have centred their lobbying campaigns at the EU around the number of migrants arriving in Malta relative to its population and the limited space and resources to cope with these arrivals. Because of the small number of arrivals in absolute terms, the government has frequently

---

[7] For more on this incident, see Chapter 1.

made comparisons based on population, arguing, for example, that one person arriving in Malta is equivalent to 1,749 arriving in France. By this count, the 1,780 people who arrived in Malta in 2006 would be equivalent to over 3 million arrivals in France (Gonzi 2007: 42; Interviews: government officials, 2006–10). The government used this politicized counting to contend that Malta carries a disproportionate amount of the migration 'burden' in Europe. Arguing vociferously at EU fora, Maltese politicians have called for 'solidarity amongst member states' to resolve the crisis (Interviews: government officials, 2006–15).

The emphasis on the disproportionate number of migrant arrivals has been used to garner political attention and support yet is misleading. Out of fifty-one industrialized countries surveyed by the United Nations, Malta did record the highest number of asylum applications per capita in 2008, and the second highest (after Cyprus) for the period of 2004 to 2009. However, calculating the number of asylum applications based on gross domestic product per capita results in a different picture. Using this measure, Malta ranked 24th for the period between 2004 and 2009, amongst the forty-four industrialized states surveyed (UNHCR 2010b; 2009b).[8] As with arrivals, migrant deaths at sea also become symbolic of the exceptional crisis. The Coordinator of the Maltese Permanent Representation at the EU Council explained, '[I]mmigration in the Mediterranean is different to immigration from other routes, because you have the tragic aspect to it that you have so many drownings.... There may even have been incidents which we aren't even aware of and that automatically elevates it to a different level' (Interview: July 2010).

As noted in the beginning of this chapter, even when arrivals decrease significantly, as they did in 2010 and again after 2014, Maltese government discourse has continued to focus on its 'exceptional' situation, portraying migration as a crisis demanding more solidarity. For example, in January 2017, the EU presidency gave Prime Minister Joseph Muscat the opportunity to reinforce the sense of emergency around migration in the central Mediterranean. At a plenary session of the European Parliament, Muscat raised the spectre of crisis: 'Come next spring Europe will face a new heavy influx of migrants, this time through the central Mediterranean.' Muscat predicted that the EU would face 'a major migration crisis' within months unless it replicated the EU–Turkey deal in the central Mediterranean.[9]

---

[8] GDP per capita is calculated taking purchasing power parity into account, which equalizes purchasing power by using long-term equilibrium exchange rates.

[9] The full transcript of Muscat's speech is available at: https://www.eu2017.mt/en/news/Pages/Speech-Prime-Minister-Joseph-Muscat-EP-Presidency-Priorities.aspx

Lilliputian Strategies: Agenda Setting, Exceptionalism, and Alliances

Malta is a small state with limited power. Nevertheless, due to its EU accession and its geographic position on a major migration route, the small state emerged on the political map with a voice in EU fora. The government's persistent exploitation of clandestine migration to the island has further amplified this voice. As the Minister for Foreign Affairs (Interview: 2009) stated, 'We are punching above our weight.' Although other states on Europe's periphery act as gatekeepers to the EU, Malta has been particularly successful at wielding its Lilliputian power by exploiting its small state status and focusing primarily on migration in its lobbying efforts at the EU level.[10]

Malta adopted a number of interrelated strategies in order to achieve their migration goals at the EU level, including agenda setting, the propagation of an exceptional narrative, and the formation of alliances. In the absence of material power, many of Malta's strategies rely on non-material power, such as networks, moral authority, and symbolic capital, and are discursive in nature (Holzscheiter 2005).[11] Malta has deployed moral authority by arguing that it receives a 'disproportionate' level of migration in the EU. In particular, politicians have highlighted that the country carries a 'disproportion burden' in terms of asylum applicants. In its lobbying and rhetoric, Malta has turned its small size and migrant arrivals into symbolic capital. These strategies have led to a portrayal of Malta's migration situation as exceptional and to the interpretation of the migrant arrivals on the island as a crisis.

The former Minister for Foreign Affairs explained that it is his ministry's responsibility to ensure that migration 'is always on the agenda of the EU, [and] of other international fora in the Mediterranean, for instance in the United Nations or in the Council of Europe' (Interview: April 2009). Maltese politicians generally expressed their satisfaction in attaining this goal. A senior policy advisor in the Ministry for Foreign Affairs noted, 'With twenty-seven countries, you need to continually remind people of Malta's situation . . . . It's

[10] In contrast, Greece for instance has faced multiple 'crises', including its debt crisis. Like Italy and Spain, Greece's arguments about the migration 'burden' are also less compelling due to its size. In Cyprus, another small state in the Mediterranean, politics are dominated by the division of the island, which overshadows migration as a political issue (cf. Mainwaring 2014).

[11] My distinction between material and non-material power may be compared to Joseph Nye's discussion of soft power, the ability to obtain what one wants through co-option and attraction as opposed to coercion or payment, considered hard power (Nye 1990; 2004). Here, I instead draw the distinction between material and non-material power in order to highlight the material limitations faced by small states but more importantly as a critique of the notion of soft power as purely non-coercive (Mattern 2005).

good to keep up awareness' (Interview: April 2009). The goal of keeping Malta on the EU's agenda, along with the island's relatively weak position in the Union, creates an incentive to portray the situation as a crisis and Malta as indispensable to EU migration controls.

Maltese elites strategically adopt a discourse of exceptionalism that hinges on the portrayal of Malta as vulnerable in the face of migration flows. The state is presented as overwhelmed due to demographic and geographic factors but still playing a vital role as an EU gatekeeper. This allows responsibility to shift towards both the EU and countries outside the EU, such as Libya. The Director General of Operations in the Ministry for Justice and Home Affairs said,

> It is clear that [Malta] is a country so small and so limited at the frontier, unless we can get the cooperation of both Europe on one side and the countries of origin on the other side, both on a bilateral level but perhaps more effectively if it's taken in the European context, where you can have more potential development of agreements.   (Interview: April 2009)

The exceptionalist narrative is not a new strategy. In the 2004 EU enlargement round, Malta exploited its 'exceptional' smallness in order to negotiate the highest number of transitional arrangements and derogations. Many of these concessions were won and justified with reference to Malta's small size, revealing how a negotiation handicap can be creatively transformed into a successful exceptional logic (Pace 2006; 2002). Moreover, the government won some of the concessions on the very same grounds that now underlie migration rhetoric: population as a securitized issue. For instance, Maltese officials negotiated a permanent derogation on the acquisition of secondary residences and real estate by citizens of other EU member states on the basis of the size of the country, the population density, and the 'social effects' of a substantial increase in the demand for properties (Busuttil 2002). Similarly, in 2005, the government argued successfully that the formula used to distribute EU funds amongst member states should be adjusted to account for its high population density and small size (Camilleri 2005). More recently, the government employed the same logic of exceptionalism, based on the number of migrant arrivals, to successfully lobby for the seat of the European Asylum Support Office. Their bid began with a quote from then Prime Minister Lawrence Gonzi:

> I believe that Malta, situated as it is on the EU's southern border and standing right at the centre of one of the most important crossings of illegal migrants making their way from Africa to mainland Europe, is the ideal candidate to host the seat of the European Asylum Support Office.
>
> (Malta 2009)

The Office was established in Malta in 2010 with a budget of over €45 million for the first three years (Times of Malta 2009).[12]

Another strategy to increase bargaining power has been to create alliances with actors who will raise Malta's profile and draw attention to the issue of migration in the Mediterranean. In 2008, Malta spearheaded an alliance with Italy, Greece, and Cyprus, known as the 'Quadro Group'. The aim of the group was to raise awareness within the EU of the 'challenges posed by illegal immigration and asylum' in the Mediterranean, with a specific interest in the promotion of intra-EU relocation programmes, a revision of the Dublin Regulation, the strengthening of Frontex, and the continued negotiation of multilateral and bilateral readmission agreements (European Council 2009a). In its paper, presented to the Justice and Home Affairs Council in February 2009, the Group emphasized the disproportionate and specific pressures of asylum and 'illegal' immigration on front-line member states, 'with a view to put into practice the Union's principle of solidarity and fair burden sharing'. The relocation of refugees was fundamental to the Quadro Group's conceptualization of solidarity (European Council 2009a; 2009b; Interviews: Official, Asylum Unit, DG JFS; Anonymous Council Official, July 2010).

The Group's aim was thus to relocate responsibility for asylum and migration to other member states and to transit countries. It inverted long-standing rhetoric that depicted the Mediterranean as Europe's 'soft, vulnerable underbelly' (Haynes 1999: 19; Katrougalos and Lazaridis 2003: 169) and shifted blame northward to larger member states for their perceived lack of interest in controlling southern EU borders. For example, the Maltese Minister for Foreign Affairs (Interview: April 2009) said,

> What is an interesting development now is that Italy,...Cyprus and Greece have joined forces within the EU, mostly because they feel they are in the periphery and have been relatively abandoned on this issue and therefore they are offering a common front to see to it that more aid comes in their direction and as well not to increase [our obligations].

Although it would be another six years before the EU considered a large-scale relocation project, the Quadro Group's lobbying gained some traction, at least discursively. For example, the Council's presidency conclusions in June 2009 echoed their concerns and called for the 'internal reallocation of beneficiaries of international protection present in the member states exposed to specific

---

[12] Human rights organizations raised concerns over the success of Malta's bid, pointing to the country's lacklustre record of receiving refugees and its priority of preventing 'illegal' migration both nationally and at the EU level (Phillips 2009).

and disproportionate pressures and highly vulnerable persons' (European Council 2009c). The conclusions also noted the pilot relocation project that the Council initiated in Malta in 2009, a success for the island discussed in the section below, 'Moving through Europe'.[13]

The Quadro Group was largely inactive after 2009, with Malta championing many of its causes independently. However, in 2013, Cyprus revived the alliance with an informal meeting between the original four states (Cyprus, Greece, Italy, and Malta), as well as France, Portugal, and Spain (Republic of Cyprus 2014). In 2016, in the midst of increased arrivals of Syrian and other refugees on the EU's southern periphery and with many countries facing financial strain, the group formalized as the EU Med Group (also known as Club Med) and held its first summit in Athens (Kambas and Maltezou 2016). The demands and rhetoric of the Med Group remain similar to the Quadro Group. For instance, in a statement made after the third summit in 2017, the countries insisted that 'EU migration policy must be based on shared responsibility and solidarity with those countries affected by migratory pressure due to their geographical location at the external borders of the Union' (Torres 2017). A month earlier, Maltese Prime Minister Muscat reminded member states that '[s]olidarity is not à la carte. We need to be consistent and accept it even when it does not benefit the individual member state' (Bonnici 2017).

'Kings of lobbying?' Influencing a Region

In this section, I examine four different but interrelated migration policy initiatives that are fundamental to EU migration governance and to the experiences of migrants on the edges of Europe: (1) the European Pact on Immigration and Asylum, (2) the Schengen Borders Code, (3) the Dublin Regulation, and (4) the Long-Term Residents Directive. Malta has lobbied for particular outcomes in all these policy areas, with varying levels of success. The most significant success was the expansion of the concept of solidarity to not only include financial transfers but to also comprise the relocation of people, albeit still on a voluntary basis. Given its size, Malta has been surprisingly successful in its lobbying at the EU level. Yet, this success has come at a price: its construction and exploitation of a migration crisis reinforces the very emphasis on migration control at Europe's edge that it has resisted.

---

[13] A more ambiguous proposal for 'mechanisms for the voluntary and coordinated sharing of responsibility between the Member States' was also inserted into Article 6.2.2 of the Stockholm Programme, the EU's five-year plan for justice and home affairs between 2010 and 2014 (European Union 2010: 32).

The European Pact on Immigration and Asylum

A year after the tuna-pen incident, Nicholas Sarkozy proposed the European Pact on Immigration and Asylum when France assumed responsibility for the EU Presidency in July 2008. The Council subsequently adopted the proposal in October. Not legally binding, the Pact is a political document that proposes five commitments: '(1) to organise legal immigration...(2) to control illegal immigration...(3) to make border controls more effective; (4) to construct a Europe of asylum; [and] (5) to create a comprehensive partnership with the countries of origin and of transit' (European Council 2008). In negotiations over the Pact, Malta successfully campaigned for the inclusion of a reference to member states facing 'particular pressures', the first to appear in an EU document.

Over a hot summer that saw the number of boat arrivals soar in Malta, Maltese politicians and policymakers lobbied relentlessly to see their interests enshrined in the Pact. The 2,775 people who landed on Maltese shores in 2008 embodied the zenith of Malta's 'crisis', with asylum applications reaching similar levels that year. The country was ultimately successful in securing a reference in the Pact to 'Member States which are faced with specific and disproportionate pressures on their national asylum systems, due in particular to their geographical or demographic situation' (European Council 2008; Interviews: 2010).

Although calls for more burden sharing were common as early as 1992 after the onset of the Bosnian War and the resulting refugee flows into Europe (Thielemann 2003: 266), the Pact is the first EU document to encode the notion of disproportionate migration pressures. Evoking the 'spirit of solidarity', the Pact also notes that the EU should promote, on a voluntary basis, the relocation of refugees from member states facing such 'pressures' (European Council 2008). Maltese policymakers further credit their lobbying for the commitment to hold an annual debate on immigration and asylum in the Council (European Council 2008: 15). In 2010, the Coordinator of the Maltese Permanent Representation in Brussels (Interview: July 2010; cf. European Council 2008) explained how Malta leveraged the principle of EU solidarity to further its interests:

> One of the most important things in the Pact is that...the European Council will have an annual debate on the immigration and asylum scenario in the EU....[T]hat at least helps keep the subject on the agenda, and hopefully one day...my Prime Minister will stop having to come to the European Council, and every time he says, 'Listen, I need a proper commitment.

I cannot have my experts going to working groups after you have promised them certain things and your experts are telling them, "no way".' So, this is something... which is a success on our part of having introduced the subject of solidarity... of having ensured that prime ministers will discuss this on a regular basis ....And this principle of solidarity, we have been arguing [for it] since we entered the EU. We worked very hard to introduce it in the Pact.

Beyond these specific lobbying successes, Elizabeth Collett (2008) identifies the reference to the 'reception capacity' of member states within the Pact as a new concept. The idea that states have a (limited) 'capacity' to receive migrants is one that has been central to Malta's message to the EU. More generally, the Pact points to the EU's limited ability to receive migrants and creates an explicit trade-off between rights and numbers. The Pact states for instance that '[t]he EU does not have the resources to decently receive all migrants hoping to find a better life here.' Guaranteeing rights for migrants and refugees who are allowed in is explicitly linked to stricter migration controls within the document.[14]

Despite Malta's successes, the Pact is guided by nationalism and intergovernmentalism that undermine the elusive goal of common European migration and asylum policies, as well as Malta's demands for more 'solidarity' (Carrera and Guild 2008). The redistributive measures envisioned in the Pact, such as the relocation of people from member states on the periphery, remain voluntary and small in scale. A decade later, Malta and other southern states continue to demand more 'solidarity' from northern member states.

Although the Pact is not legally binding, it has shaped the direction of EU immigration and asylum policies. The principles within it were foundational to other EU immigration measures taken over the next decade. The initial reference to '[m]ember States which are faced with specific and disproportionate pressures... due in particular to their geographical or demographic situation' reflected a significant political gain for Malta: it would reappear in a multitude of subsequent policy documents (e.g. European Parliament and Council 2011; 2013b; European Council 2012a), and lead to a pilot relocation programme in Malta, as well as the large-scale relocation of refugees from Italy and Greece initiated in 2015.

---

[14] This trade-off was again at the heart of many EU policy proposals in the wake of the increase in refugee arrivals after 2015 (e.g. European Commission 2017b). It is notable that this ostensible 'trade-off' is generally only raised in the case of refugees and low-skilled temporary labourers (cf. Dauvergne and Marsden 2014; Ruhs and Martin 2008), and that the social and financial costs associated with deterrent measures used to reduce 'numbers' are rarely taken into account.

Rescue at Sea and the Schengen Borders Code

The Pact did not refer to the rescue of migrants in distress at sea nor to their disembarkation in a 'place of safety', points of contention that continue to shape migration in the Mediterranean as previously discussed in Chapter 3. The lack of legal consensus on definitions of 'distress' or a 'place of safety' creates a high degree of discretion with regard to rescue at sea, which member states have exploited in order to shirk their responsibilities. As a result, migrant deaths have soared in the twenty-first century, making the Mediterranean Sea the deadliest region in the world for migrants.

By examining the negotiations over the Schengen Borders Code amendment between 2010 and 2014, this section illustrates how Malta exerted power and shaped EU regulations over rescue at sea. Although it was ultimately unable to establish disembarkation at 'the nearest safe port' as the principal modus operandi for EU Frontex missions, it did secure disembarkation at the nearest safe port as an exception in the Schengen Borders Code. It also was a key player in the legal challenge that tabled the amendment until 2014.

All ships and coastal state authorities have an unambiguous and unconditional responsibility to rescue those in distress at sea, a responsibility embedded in customary international law and the 1982 United Nations Convention on the Law of the Sea. Although 'distress' is not defined in international law,[15] a number of cases have set a low bar and determined that 'there need not be immediate physical necessity' and vessels do not need to be 'dashed against the rocks' in order to constitute distress (Papastavridis 2011). The International Maritime Organization also 'maintains that even if a ship's passengers show no signs of distress, the suspicion of trafficking and transport in unsafe conditions only entitles states to take action in accord with humanitarian principles' (Pugh 2004: 59).

Nevertheless, as has been demonstrated throughout the previous chapters, rescue at sea is a politicized and dynamic issue where states continue to take a narrow interpretation of distress despite their clear legal responsibilities. Harrowing audio tapes from 2013 leaked to the Italian newspaper, *L'Espresso*, reveal how the delays, inaction, and disputes of EU member states cause deaths at sea. On the tapes, Mohanned Jammo, a Syrian doctor, informs Italian officials that the boat he and hundreds of other people are on is sinking. He begs the Italian authorities to rescue them. In his third phone call in an hour,

---

[15] As discussed below, the 2014 amendment to the EU's Schengen Borders Code defined 'distress' in more detail.

Jammo could not be clearer, 'We are dying, please.' Despite having a military vessel, the *Libra*, 20 nautical miles away, Italy refused to rescue these people and insisted they were Malta's responsibility. Malta also did not send a rescue vessel. Four and a half hours after Jammo's initial phone call, the boat capsized 60 miles south of Lampedusa. Two hundred and sixty-eight Syrians, including sixty children, drowned (Gatti 2017; Momigliano 2017b).

Similar delays and disputes over disembarkation put migrants in further danger as they deter commercial vessels from rescuing those in distress (Pugh 2004: 63). In 2006, a Spanish trawler encountered fifty-one people in distress 180 kilometres north of the Libyan coast. The Spanish captain, Giuseppe Dura, radioed Spain for help and was shocked to receive no reply. Dura and his crew decided that they must nevertheless provide assistance and transferred the migrants to their boat. The decision proved costly: he and the crew were stranded on the open sea for six days, while a diplomatic stand-off unfolded between Spain, Malta, Libya, and the European Union over responsibility for disembarkation (Bilefsky 2006a). Indeed, as previously discussed, private shipmasters must not only consider the potential commercial losses they may incur by rescuing people at sea but also face the possibility of being investigated for migrant smuggling (e.g. Council of Europe 2010; Statewatch 2007).

The disembarkation of migrants and refugees after rescue in the Mediterranean is a long-standing point of contention between Malta and Italy, and is discussed in more detail in Chapter 3. Malta's search and rescue (SAR) region overlaps with Italy's and encompasses the Italian island of Lampedusa; migrants have often been rescued within Malta's SAR region but in closer proximity to Lampedusa or Sicily. In these cases, Malta has insisted that disembarkation should occur in Lampedusa, the nearest 'place of safety'. Italy, on the other hand, insisted that Malta is responsible for disembarkation as the state coordinating search and rescue. By maintaining these divergent positions, both states complied with their international legal obligations as Malta has not signed the 2004 amendments to the SAR Convention and the Safety of Life at Sea Convention, which clarify that responsibility for disembarkation lies with the coordinating state (Klepp 2011).

In April 2010, faced with these intransigent positions on disembarkation, the EU Council passed an amendment to the Schengen Borders Code, which governs any rescue at sea carried out by Frontex, in order to clarify responsibilities (European Council 2010). The amendment confirmed that the Schengen Borders Code provides the legal framework for Frontex operations, even if conducted on the high seas. It also clarified rules for disembarkation. Both Italy and Malta lobbied zealously to see their preference reflected in the changes to the Code as the regulations would in large part determine how many people landed on their shores. It was Italy that was initially more successful. Article 2 in the amended Code notes that:

> [w]ithout prejudice to the responsibility of the Rescue Coordination Centre, and unless otherwise specified in the operational plan, priority should be given to disembarkation in the third country from where the ship carrying the persons departed or through the territorial waters or search and rescue region of which that ship transited and if this is not possible, priority should be given to disembarkation in the host Member State unless it is necessary to act otherwise to ensure the safety of these persons.
>
> (European Council 2010)

Malta's preference for disembarkation at the nearest safe port was thus made an exception rather than the rule, due to lobbying by Italian authorities who wanted to avoid disembarkation in Lampedusa or Sicily. Nevertheless, the insertion of the clause demonstrates Malta's power, as the Italians were opposed to its inclusion, even as an exception. Moreover, the rules on disembarkation were included in a non-binding Annex to the Code, in line with Malta's lobbying efforts (Interviews: Commission Official, DG JFS, June 2010; Coordinator of the Maltese Permanent Representation, July 2010). The new rules also placed more responsibility for disembarkation on the member state hosting the Frontex mission in question. In response, Malta refused to continue to host or participate in the Frontex mission in the central Mediterranean in 2010 (Camilleri 2010; Xuereb 2010).

The amendment to the Schengen Borders Code was also short-lived. In a move spearheaded by Simon Busuttil, a Maltese Member of the European Parliament (MEP), the Parliament challenged the amendment and referred it to the EU's Court of Justice. An MEP between 2004 and 2013, Busuttil was active in migration debates and cast himself as Malta's champion in the struggle for influence over EU migration and asylum policies.[16] He was a vocal advocate for Malta's 'burden-sharing' agenda at the EU Parliament, especially within the Civil Liberties, Justice and Home Affairs (LIBE) Committee on which he was the European People's Party coordinator. Busuttil advanced the legal case against the amendment on the basis that it exceeded the scope of the Schengen Borders Code through the introduction of rules on interception, search and rescue, and disembarkation, which went beyond surveillance as defined by Article 12 of the Code (European Union 2010: 34–5). The case

---

[16] In 2013, Simon Busuttil was elected leader of the Nationalist Party in Malta after their defeat in a national election that ended the party's almost twenty-year rule. The party remains in opposition. Busuttil resigned as leader after defeat in a snap election in June 2017.

also claimed that the Commission had exceeded its powers in passing the amendment through comitology, rather than the normal legislative process that would have given the Parliament a larger role.[17]

In 2012, the European Parliament won its case at the Court of Justice, which nullified the amendment (ECRE 2012). Despite this temporary victory, a new amendment adopted in 2014 reintroduced much of the same language. The Schengen Borders Code now prioritizes disembarkation in the third country outside the EU from where a vessel is assumed to have departed (ECRE 2014b; European Parliament and Council 2014). When this is not possible, disembarkation occurs in the member state hosting the Frontex mission.[18] In response, Malta refused to host any Frontex operations after 2010, although it participated in subsequent missions, such as Operation Triton, hosted in Italy between 2014 and 2018. More significantly for Malta, search and rescue in the Mediterranean had changed dramatically by 2014. Italy had reversed its policy of refusing to disembark people intercepted in Malta's SAR region after hundreds of migrants drowned near the island of Lampedusa in October 2013. It launched Mare Nostrum, a year-long 'military-humanitarian' SAR operation, and then continued to play the principal role in the subsequent Frontex operations in the central Mediterranean. As a result, migrant arrivals in Malta had already fallen in 2014, and would continue to do so over the next few years: in 2016, only twenty-five people arrived by boat. That same year, Italy disembarked over 180,000 people on its shores (IOM 2017b; UNHCR-Malta 2018).

Despite and in response to the new amendment to the Schengen Borders Code, member states and commercial vessels continue to use strategies to

---

[17] Comitology refers to the process by which the Commission executes its powers given to it by the legislative branch of the EU (i.e. the Parliament and the Council) with the assistance of particular committees consisting of representatives from member states.

[18] The new regulation also includes more explicit instructions as to how member states should respond to distress situations, binding rules which Malta and five other Mediterranean states—Cyprus, France, Greece, Italy, and Spain—vigorously opposed. The states argued that the new provisions were 'unacceptable for practical and legal reasons' and that international maritime law already dealt 'amply' with search and rescue situations (ANSAmed 2013). Although the new rules establish a scale with three different phases of urgency—uncertainty, alert, and distress—they nevertheless remain ambiguous on state responsibilities with no differentiation between types of state action necessary in each phase. Importantly, the regulation fails to specify when rescue operations must be initiated (den Heijer 2016). The amendment to the Schengen Borders Code has also been criticized for establishing a parallel legal framework for interception on the high seas that does not guarantee the rights afforded to asylum seekers and other migrants within EU territory or territorial waters, where the Asylum and Return Directives apply. The new amendment further undermines the right to asylum in the EU by allowing member states to return vessels intercepted on the high seas to a third country, and to alter the course of vessels intercepted in territorial waters to a destination outside those territorial waters. The amendment did not address the question of rescue in the territorial waters of a third country, a practice that became commonplace in the central Mediterranean where many migrants were rescued in Libyan waters after 2014 (den Heijer 2016; AIDA 2014; Thompson and Singhvi 2017).

avoid rescue, thus contributing to deaths at sea. For instance, in August 2014, the Rescue Centre in Rome alerted seventy-six ships to a vessel in distress in their vicinity. Seconds later, only six ships appeared on the radar screen. All the other ships had turned off their radar (BBC 2014). Moreover, although the Italian practice of disembarking people in Italy temporarily stayed the conflict between Malta and Italy over rescue at sea, the deal was a fragile one and accusations of Maltese inaction re-emerged. In 2017, the Italian Coast Guard operations chief lambasted Malta for severely limiting its search and rescue operations and for denying requests to disembark migrants.

> [Malta] tend[s] to underestimate the conditions of real danger that the boats are in in order to avoid the obligation of declaring a search and rescue operation and interven[ing]. They simply monitor the boats until they leave their territorial waters [to] avoid intervening in the flow of migrants, who then proceed to Italy. (ANSA 2017)

By 2018, the informal agreement between Italy and Malta on disembarkation had unravelled (Wintour et al. 2018). The politics and practices of rescue in the Mediterranean Sea therefore remain dynamic and contested, both by the people sailing across on boats and the states involved in delimiting responsibilities at sea.

Moving through Europe: Dublin and Relocation

At the heart of Malta's campaign in Brussels is the call to recast the Dublin Regulation due to the disproportionate responsibility it places on member states at the periphery. Debates over the Dublin Regulation strike at the core of the European project: how do twenty-seven sovereign states share responsibility for refugees and control of an external border? What constitutes solidarity amongst these states? Malta has lobbied tirelessly over the last decade to promote the idea of states facing 'particular pressures' and to expand the notion of 'solidarity' to not only include financial transfers to countries on the periphery but to also involve the relocation of migrants and refugees from the periphery to other member states within Europe. In this section, I demonstrate how this small state has been successful in many ways. Malta won the bid to host the European Asylum Support Office in 2010. In 2009, it secured the first intra-EU relocation project, EUREMA, which relocated refugees from Malta to other member states. Most fundamentally, Malta successfully expanded the concept of solidarity, even if it fell short of establishing a permanent relocation mechanism. The voluntary relocation of people within Europe is now a reality, an idea that member states dismissed almost entirely before 2015.

Questions of solidarity and the disproportionate responsibility placed on peripheral member states re-emerged in 2015 when over one million migrants and refugees arrived in Greece and Italy. The response by member states underlined the fragility of EU solidarity. Many fortified their borders: they erected walls and dispatched border guards, unconcerned about the implications for free movement and refugee protection within Europe. Very few states championed the idea of relocation. Only Germany briefly opened its borders to Syrian refugees. Despite these recent developments, the EU has grappled with the issue of 'burden sharing' and how to show 'solidarity' with member states on the periphery before the increase in arrivals in 2015. For example, in 2010, the European Parliament's LIBE Committee (2010) published a study on 'burden sharing' that outlined how some member states face disproportionate asylum pressures in terms of numbers and costs. The report identified Malta, Cyprus, Sweden, and Greece as states facing particular pressures and proposed an increase in financial compensation for such states, as well as suggesting the *voluntary* relocation of asylum seekers.[19]

After lobbying for more 'burden-sharing' since its accession in 2004, Malta's efforts came to fruition in 2009 in the first intra-EU relocation project, EUREMA, piloted on the island. However, without the force of legal obligation, only six member states participated, and only 227 people were resettled in the first twenty-four-month period. Moreover, France and Germany resettled the vast majority of people (197). Although member states explained their decision to participate in relocation activities as a political act of 'solidarity towards Malta, in line with the EU spirit of solidarity' (EASO 2012: 8), the minimal numbers resettled from the island—Luxembourg and Portugal resettled six people each, Slovenia resettled eight, and the UK resettled ten— belies the lack of robust solidarity within the EU (EASO 2012: 4).[20] In contrast and during the same period, the United States resettled more people from Malta in a bilateral relocation scheme.[21]

---

[19] The study acknowledges the difficulties in assessing asylum pressure due to the different results obtained when using various capacity indicators (e.g. GDP, population, or population density).

[20] The second phase, from 2012 to mid-2013, also experienced low resettlement numbers: seven member states pledged to resettle ninety-one people. Moreover, many countries chose to resettle refugees bilaterally rather than through the EUREMA structure (EASO 2012).

[21] The resettlement programme with the US operated between 2008 and 2017 when it was discontinued in the wake of President Trump's executive order on immigration, 'Protecting the Nation from Foreign Terrorist Entry into the United States'. By its end, the initiative had resettled over 3,000 people (Malta Independent 2017; IOM Malta 2017; UNHCR-Malta 2018).

The location of the European Asylum Support Office (EASO) is also a tacit admission of the unequal pressure on peripheral states. Malta won the bid, with minimal competition from Cyprus and Bulgaria, in part by emphasizing the migration pressures it faced. Established in 2010, the Office has a mandate to 'promote, facilitate and coordinate exchanges of information and other activities related to relocation within the Union' (European Parliament and Council 2010: 15, Article 5). Its mandate reflects developments in the negotiations over defining 'particular pressures':

> The Support Office shall coordinate and support common action assisting asylum and reception systems of Member States subject to particular pressure which places exceptionally heavy and urgent demands on their reception facilities and asylum systems. Such pressure may be characterised by the sudden arrival of a large number of third-country nationals who may be in need of international protection and may arise from the geographical or demographical situation of the Member State.
>
> (European Parliament and Council 2010: 16, Article 8)

Although the definition of 'particular pressures' remains vague, the references to demography, geography, and sudden influxes indicate the influence and interests of southern member states. The language echoes arguments made by the Maltese government in its advocacy for relocation and other forms of 'burden sharing', as well as its campaign for the EASO headquarters. The decision to establish the EASO in Malta reveals the success of these arguments at the EU level and the power of maintaining an image of a state overwhelmed by migration, regardless of the number of arrivals. As one Commission official presciently noted, '[I]t made sense to put [the EASO] in Malta, as long as there is an asylum problem in Malta, because if nobody arrives in Malta in the next three years, it'll be a bit strange!' (Interview: Official, Asylum Unit, DG JFS, July 2010).

Despite these successes, Malta's wider campaign for a more permanent relocation mechanism has been afflicted by setbacks. For example, Malta's attempt to invoke the Directive on Temporary Protection in the Case of Mass Influx in 2011 was unsuccessful. The directive would automatically grant temporary protection to displaced people arriving in the EU as part of a 'mass influx' for up to two years. It also promotes a 'balance of efforts between EU countries', although it does not explicitly call for the relocation of people (European Council 2001). Adopted in 2001, the Directive has yet to be used. Malta formally requested its activation in 2011, after the arrival of over 800 people fleeing political unrest and violence in Libya, in the hopes that it would allow these asylum seekers access to fast-track procedures in any EU member state. The EU ultimately rejected Malta's request (Beirens et al. 2016).

Italy experienced an even larger increase in arrivals over this period but claimed there was no 'mass influx' and did not support Malta's request to trigger the Temporary Protection Directive, which it viewed as a slow and ineffective mechanism. Instead, when faced with the arrival of 20,000 Tunisians in 2011, Prime Minister Silvio Berlusconi granted them temporary residence visas that allowed free travel throughout the Schengen area.[22] France's colonial legacy in Tunisia, alongside the overcrowded conditions in Italian reception camps, encouraged many of these migrants to journey towards the French–Italian border, attracted to the country by kinship networks and a common language (PA 2011).

In response, French President Sarkozy sparked a diplomatic crisis within Europe when he closed the border between France and Italy in order to obstruct a train carrying Tunisian migrants and activists at the end of April 2011. Sarkozy accused Italy of shirking its migration responsibilities and offloading the problem onto other Schengen countries. In both countries, Sarkozy and Berlusconi exploited the situation in order to placate their far-right constituencies (BBC 2011a; BBC 2011b). The dispute brought the lack of trust between northern and southern member states to the fore once again. The EU supported France's closure of the border in order to avoid disturbances to 'public order' (BBC 2011a).[23] The Commission concluded that both states were in 'formal compliance with EU law', but that 'the spirit of the Schengen rules [had] not been fully respected' (European Commission 2011d). In a thinly veiled reference to the Italian–French dispute, the Commission noted that visa waivers could lead to large-scale 'irregular immigration' and endanger security. The Commission thus proposed an amendment that would allow the reintroduction of visa requirements for third-country nationals under certain conditions. It also proposed a mechanism to temporarily reintroduce border controls within the Schengen area in situations where 'a Member State is not fulfilling its obligations to control its section of the external border, or where a particular portion

---

[22] Simultaneously, an agreement was reached with Tunisia to stop migrants departing from Tunisian shores. In return for Tunisian cooperation, Italy pledged to provide assistance and technical support to Tunisia's security forces.

[23] Border controls are still present along many internal borders within the EU, an exception allowed for in the Schengen Agreement 'where public policy or national security so require' (European Union 2000: Article 2.2). For instance, France reintroduced border controls with Belgium and Luxembourg in 1996, viewing them as transit countries for drugs coming from the Netherlands. More recently, Germany reintroduced border controls during the G20 Summit in 2017. Other countries have replaced border checks with police units that control migration directly inside the border, or have introduced obligations to carry national identity cards (Apap and Carrera 2003; Brouwer 2008: 45).

of the external border comes under unexpected and heavy pressure due to external events' (European Commission 2011b).

Throughout this period, both Malta and Italy continued to fan the flames of crisis, reducing migrants to symbols of disorder. For example, Robert Maroni, the Italian Interior Minister, warned of a 'biblical exodus', and Berlusconi referred to a 'human tsunami' in Lampedusa (Pop 2011; Grant 2011). This alarmist rhetoric benefited Malta as the EU agreed to extend the voluntary relocation project and member states committed to the relocation of 320 people from Malta (European Commission 2011c; 2011e).

The Schengen area of free movement has continued to fracture in recent years. In 2013, the EU amended the Schengen Borders Code in order to introduce the mechanism proposed by the Commission in 2011 to temporarily reintroduce border controls (European Parliament and Council 2013a). In May 2016, the Council invoked the article with reference to 'deficiencies in external border control in Greece and the subsequent secondary movements of irregular migrants entering via Greece and who move to other Schengen States'. Border controls were reintroduced for six months in five Schengen states: Austria, Germany, Denmark, Sweden, and Norway. The Council prolonged these 'temporary' controls multiple times; they are still in place and due to be reassessed in 2019 (European Council 2017b; 2018). Alongside these five countries, others, including France, Hungary, and Slovenia, also reintroduced border controls in 2015 and 2016.[24] On behalf of southern EU member states, the Cypriot Foreign Minister responded, 'The EU Med Group are the front-line states and we all share the view that unilateral actions cannot be a solution to this crisis' (Hadjicostis and Gatopoulos 2016).

During this time, the EU also launched its largest intra-EU relocation effort to date. Although the EUREMA project was much more limited in its scope, it was arguably the predecessor to the scheme agreed in 2015. The Commission indicated that they would propose 'a permanent relocation scheme, based on voluntary commitments by Member States and consent of beneficiaries' after the second phase of EUREMA (European Union 2011). However, the 2015 relocation effort remained voluntary even if more institutional pressure was applied on member states to resettle 160,000 refugees from Greece and Italy, countries that had seen the largest number of arrivals (European Commission 2015b).[25] Moreover, the divergent interests of EU countries crippled the

---

[24] For a list of all countries reintroducing borders control between 2006 and 2018, see European Council 2018.

[25] The European Commission (2015e) has proposed a permanent 'crisis relocation mechanism'. However, it currently remains obstructed by the EU Council.

scheme: even after member states committed to the relocation of 98,000 people, rather than the original 160,000, only 27,695 people (8,451 from Italy and 19,244 from Greece) were relocated by September 2017, the end of the project's two-year period. Member state intransigence condemned refugees to squalid camps in countries struggling to cope with arrivals, where high rates of suicide, rape, sexual abuse, destitution, and prostitution were well documented (European Commission 2017b; Nielsen 2017).[26]

Member states are generally reluctant to participate in such relocation schemes, preferring to resettle people directly from third countries outside the EU. Some argue that relocation from member states on the EU's periphery acts as a pull factor for migrants (European Commission 2010: 38-9). The EU has also offered greater financial incentive to resettle people from third countries than from other EU member states: the European Refugee Fund provided €4,000 for each person resettled from a third country, an amount that was increased to €6,000 in 2012 for countries accessing the Fund for the first time.[27] For many years there was no financial incentive in place for intra-EU relocation. Only in 2015 was a mechanism established to provide €6,000 for those relocated from Italy and Greece (European Commission 2010: 38-9; European Parliament 2010; Interview: Official, Asylum Unit, DG JFS, July 2010; European Council 2015).[28]

Negotiations over relocation raise the spectre of a lack of trust and solidarity amongst member states. Northern member states remain sceptical of southern member states' asylum processes both when too many and too few people are granted international protection. This lack of confidence in other states' decision-making processes is, moreover, embedded in EU law: the legal status of a refugee in one EU member state is not transferable to another member state. The principle of mutual recognition has not been applied to positive asylum decisions, although it is applied to negative asylum decisions, as well as decisions on refusal of entry and expulsion of third-country nationals (O'Dowd 2011; European Parliament 2015b). An official within the Commission explained:

[26] Malta was one of only two states, alongside Finland, to almost reach their target relocation figures from Italy and Greece. In July 2017, the Commission launched legal proceedings against Poland, Hungary, and the Czech Republic for refusing to relocate refugees (European Commission 2017b).

[27] Under the Asylum, Integration and Migration Fund (2014-20), all states receive €6,000 per resettled person and €10,000 per refugee belonging to priority categories and vulnerable groups (European Parliament 2017a).

[28] More recently, proposals have been put forward to penalize states not participating in the relocation scheme with fines of up to €250,000 per person not relocated (BBC 2016). In 2017, Malta proposed a more modest €60,000 fine per person, alongside a financial incentive of €60,000 per person relocated above each country's quota (Baczynska 2017).

There is not full trust [between member states]. So, member states do not trust the Maltese decision making, even though we in the Commission believe it's perfectly fine, and UNHCR also told us we are fine.... Because, it's true that in Malta, I think 60 or 70 per cent of the asylum seekers receive some kind of protection, which is very high. But why? Because they are Somali.   (Interview: Official, Asylum Unit, DG JFS, July 2010)

The limited trust between member states in recognizing each other's asylum processes as robust and legitimate undermines attempts at relocation as well as the broader project to create a common European asylum policy.

Malta has effectively widened the concept of solidarity within the EU beyond financial transfers. Nevertheless, states continue to favour unilateral and bilateral measures. The thin veneer of solidarity in the EU cracks easily under specific pressure, especially in the politicized realm of migration. Malta has ultimately been unsuccessful in recasting the Dublin Regulation in order to pool asylum applications in one central EU system to be shared 'equitably' across the Union or to suspend Dublin returns to a member state when it experiences a 'disproportionate burden' (Interview: Official Asylum Unit, DG JFS; Coordinator of the Maltese Permanent Representation, July 2010). Indeed, even more powerful states have been unsuccessful in pursuing similar measures. For example, Germany unsuccessfully proposed 'burden-sharing' measures at a European summit in Luxembourg in 1991 after receiving the highest share of asylum seekers in Europe that year (Bosswick 2000: 53–5; Schuster 2003b: 229–35). Germany's recent pursuit of solidarity on migration has also been hampered by a lack of political consensus amongst member states. Malta's ability to initiate and sustain debate around solidarity and 'burden sharing' is thus, in its own right, a success for the small state. Moreover, the issue of a permanent relocation mechanism, a political pipe dream when Malta joined the EU in 2004, is now very much on the table despite sustained opposition. In 2016, the Commission proposed recasting the Dublin Regulation yet again to include a permanent relocation mechanism (European Commission 2016a).

The Long-Term Residents Directive

As detailed in Chapter 4, migrants and refugees who survive the sea and reach Europe's shores continue to face economic, political, and social marginalization years after arrival. They confront barriers to rights traditionally associated with long-term residency despite being recognized as refugees or attaining other legal statuses. Temporary forms of protection preclude people from accessing family reunification. Access to citizenship continues to be racialized and classed. Contributing to this atmosphere of exclusion, Malta vetoed an EU proposal to extend long-term residency rights to refugees in 2008. This section analyses how, despite this expression of power, changes to the voting structure of the EU circumscribed the island's influence.

The Long-Term Residents Directive (2003) establishes the rights of third-country nationals who reside legally and continuously in a member state for five years. These rights include access to healthcare and other social services, as well as freedom of movement within the EU. In 2008, the Commission proposed an amendment to the Directive to extend its scope to the beneficiaries of international protection (i.e. refugees and those with subsidiary protection). Malta opposed the amendment and vetoed the proposal under the unanimity rules in place at the time. In 2009, the EU limited the power of small states significantly when it altered its decision-making procedures on migration from a system necessitating unanimity, which effectively gave every state veto power, to qualified majority voting. Under the current rules, a blocking minority must consist of at least four member states, comprising more than 35 per cent of the Union's total population. The change came into effect as part of the Lisbon Treaty and soon impacted the negotiations over long-term residency: despite Malta's protestations, the amendment passed in May 2011 and the country was obliged to adopt it in 2014 (European Council 2011).

In 2008 and 2011, Malta demanded the inclusion of an exception where, after one year, beneficiaries of international protection on the island would have the right to move to other EU member states. Malta argued that the five years needed to qualify for residency under the Directive could be calculated across different member states. Detailing Malta's political fears with regard to the Directive, the coordinator of Malta's permanent representation in Brussels explained,

> [T]his Long-Term Residents Directive, which is going to be extended to all beneficiaries of international protection, will grant a free movement right to persons after five years. But what that means in effect is that after five years when you would have given them so many more rights, then they will not leave.   (Interview: July 2010)

Another official in the Ministry for Justice and Home Affairs concurred,

> [F]or someone to qualify for long-term residence, so having been in Malta for five years, having health insurance, having employment, the necessary resources....If someone qualifies, if someone fulfils all of those criteria, then it means that they are perfectly well integrated. They're not the ones who really need to move.   (Interview: July 2010)

These political negotiations reflect Malta's focus on short-term deterrence. In the long term, the extension of residency rights to refugees would allow for their movement to other member states and therefore indirectly achieve Malta's relocation goal. A Commission official thus interpreted Malta's veto of the Directive in 2008 as 'shooting itself in the foot' (Interview: Asylum Unit, DG JFS, July 2010).

Despite the inconsistencies in Malta's position and its ultimate failure to block the Long-Term Residents amendment, it was successful in reducing its obligations. Compared to the Commission's original proposal, the 2011 amendment curtailed the rights of refugees in three important ways. First, it excluded people given protection under national law, rather than international law, from the scope of the Directive.[29] In Malta, those falling under this category are not an insignificant number: between 2004 and 2015, 1,700 people were granted 'other forms of protection', and by the end of 2016, 1,300 people on the island held a national form of protection (Sansone 2017a). Second, only half the time spent waiting for an asylum decision counts towards the five-year period necessary to obtain long-term residency. The original amendment envisaged that the entire period would be taken into account. Finally, the adopted amendment allows states to refuse long-term residence in cases where grounds for revocation of international protection exist (Peers 2010: 5–6).

A Crisis? Contradictions, Limits, and Consequences

Notwithstanding Malta's successes in lobbying at the EU level, the interpretation of migration as a crisis is not unproblematic. Even when exceptionalist discourse is effective, it has negative consequences for citizens and non-citizens, as explored in Chapters 3 and 4. Migrants face marginalization and violence as the island prioritizes deterrent and restrictive policies over those aimed at integration and access to rights. The criminalization of these populations has caused an increase in racism and xenophobia in Malta over the last decade (Council of Europe 2013).

The construction of a migration crisis in Malta involves the propagation of contradictions similar to those seen in the simultaneous deployment of humanitarian and security discourses and practices in response to shipwrecks

---

[29] While asylum seekers may acquire refugee status or subsidiary protection derived from international legal instruments such as the Refugee Convention (1951) or the EU Qualification Directive (2004), in cases where applicants do not meet the standards for international protection, states may also confer protection on a discretionary basis on compassionate or humanitarian grounds. These forms of subsidiary protection derive from national laws and policies.

in the Mediterranean. For instance, in constructing a crisis at the edge of Europe, Maltese policymakers simultaneously portray the island as weak and overwhelmed but also as an indispensable gatekeeper, essential to EU border controls. Migration is presented as a security issue in order to justify deterrent and restrictive measures, while also framed as a humanitarian concern in order to acquire support for relocation schemes and other solidarity measures within the EU. In these narratives, migrants' agency is distorted, either stripped away or exaggerated, as they are reduced to symbols of suffering and disorder.

This tension is resolved in part through granting temporary forms of protection, which allows the government to appear enlightened to Europe—as a state with high rates of refugee protection carrying Europe's moral burden—and defensive to their local electorate. In this way, the government addresses multiple audiences at the national and regional levels by exploiting different aspects of the migration phenomenon. Temporary forms of protection also align with a charitable, humanitarian framework, which resonates with the country's long Catholic tradition while also denying access to citizenship, family reunification, and long-term settlement (Zammit 2016).

Nevertheless, such inconsistencies weaken the argument made by Malta at the EU level, as well as having negative effects domestically. The contradiction is not lost on those who it affects most. Frustration is evident among migrants who recount experiences of being continuously told that Malta has limited capacity to provide for them but are nevertheless returned from other EU countries when they are apprehended. Some, having been sent back multiple times from as far away as Norway or the UK, despair that they will never manage to leave Malta and start their lives afresh. As was demonstrated in Chapter 4, many of Malta's policies and practices marginalize the migrant community and so encourage onward movement to other EU member states. Yet, in this cycle of state-enforced mobility and immobility, when people attempt to move to other EU countries, they are returned if their fingerprints are found in the Eurodac database. They despair that they will never be able to establish their lives fully as long as 'Malta has [their] finger'.[30]

One frustrated young Eritrean woman who had been returned under the Dublin Regulation to Malta after living in Norway for ten months said,

> I know Malta is small. If Malta's small, why are we sent back [here]? Because there are a lot of people in detention. Why do they send the paper and send

---

[30] This statement was repeated by many people in Malta who held subsidiary protection (Interviews: April 2009).

us back?…We understand that Malta is small. But when we come back to Malta, they say again: Malta is small, we cannot keep you.

(Interview: April 2009)

Another young Somali woman who had been granted subsidiary protection echoed these sentiments asking, 'If Malta cannot help, why does she say come back?' (Interview: April 2009).

The perpetuation of the Dublin system continues to restrict the mobility and opportunities of migrants within Europe. In desperate acts of resistance, people burn their fingers in order to conceal their identities and move to countries where they have better chances of being recognized as a refugee, securing employment, and joining friends and family (Grant and Domokos 2011). As Liza Schuster (2011) argues, EU policies effectively turn refugees into 'illegal immigrants'. In peripheral member states, like Malta and Greece, many are left in limbo without status or with temporary forms of protection that foreclose the possibility of family reunification. Others face everyday forms of marginalization and violence. There is therefore an enormous incentive to travel to other member states. When they do, the Dublin Regulation and the Eurodac database recasts these refugees as 'illegal migrants'.

As it shapes the identities of people on the margins, the EU has also shaped the identity and strategies of states on its periphery. Indeed, Malta's tactics at the EU level and the associated contradictions are fundamentally intertwined with its geopolitical position within the EU. On the one hand, the state argues that its geographic location on the periphery of Europe in the path of migration flows makes it vulnerable and exceptional. However, it is precisely because it is a gatekeeper that migration is so salient both nationally and within EU forums. Within the EU, a small country such as landlocked Luxembourg lacks this strategic power vis-à-vis migration because of its geographic location (and thus limited unauthorized migrant arrivals), and because it therefore cannot make the argument that it is 'exceptional'.[31]

At the EU level, Malta also treads a fine line of advocating solidarity measures, while resisting harmonization measures that would increase its obligations towards migrants and refugees (Interview: Official, Asylum Unit, DG JFS, July 2010). The island demands that other states increase their share of the migration 'burden', while trying to limit its own. Such a position reflects the primacy of national interests and the enduring intergovernmental nature of the European Union. For example, a Maltese official said,

---

[31] Migrants do, nevertheless, make up a large part of Luxembourg's population: in 2016, 40 per cent of the population was foreign (Eurostat 2016b).

[W]e have been trying to resist at the EU level...certain negotiations that would not be beneficial to us. It's that you cannot have a harmoniser, one shoe fits all, or one size fits all approach in the sense that you get the Commission that comes up with theoretically very nice proposals, always pro-harmonisation....And we have always tried to argue, and to a certain extent we have been successful, although now we look in the future for the Qualifications Directive and for the extension of the Long-Term Residents Directive, we are going to face, let's say, an uphill struggle.

(Interview: Coordinator of Malta's Permanent Representation, July 2010)

Similarly, when in 2010 the European Parliament appointed Simon Busuttil as the rapporteur for a legal review of the Frontex regulation, he championed the notion of 'compulsory solidarity' within the context of making member states' financial pledges to Frontex legally binding (European People's Party 2011). That same year, he simultaneously argued against expanding Malta's responsibility for disembarkation under the Schengen Borders Code amendment.

Beyond the contradictions involved in Malta's position, the persistence of crisis discourse for over a decade, regardless of fluctuations in migrant arrivals, raises questions. At what point does such an entrenched 'crisis' stop being an emergency and become the normal order of things? Does such crisis rhetoric become less effective and therefore less powerful with time? Amongst EU officials interviewed for this research, a palpable level of crisis fatigue was already evident even in 2010. For example, when asked if there was an incentive for Malta to portray arrivals on the island as a 'disproportionate burden', one Commission official responded,

If they say I don't have a big problem, then they will have to cope with the problem by themselves. So, there is an interest to call this [a disproportionate burden], even if it's not. I think it is, but even if it wasn't, they would like to call it a disproportionate burden. It is today, I don't have any doubt about it, but if the situation improves in the coming year, I think they will still [say] this is too much for us. But I think...Malta and Cyprus haven't come to terms with the idea that they are now in this rich club of twenty-seven member states ....They are immigration countries, they are not emigration countries anymore and sometimes we feel the Maltese authorities see their country as, well, we don't have any place here, nobody should come, only tourists or rich European tourists. And I think Malta has to accept that it has to take part of the burden, maybe not everything which falls on the island, but at least part of it.   (Interview: Official, DG JFS, July 2010)

These sentiments, and the discussion above, challenge the effectiveness of the crisis imagery perpetuated by Malta. Certainly, such inconsistencies are more apparent now that Malta has acquired a larger degree of political power within the EU with regard to migration and asylum. Its accession to the Union brought with it not only the opportunity to participate in and influence regional negotiations over migration but also more monitoring of domestic practices and policies. There are costs to political power, which can expose an actor in new ways and make them vulnerable. Nevertheless, the continuing attention and money that the island receives from the EU are a powerful incentive to stay the course.

What becomes apparent in discussions with Maltese policymakers is that the new incentive structure has shaped their interests and they are now wedded to the EU as an institutional framework. Although EU membership has provided new opportunities to exert power and promote interests at the regional level, this new structure also establishes new parameters to those interests. Indicative of this is the change in policymakers' attitude in the years after EU accession. In 2006, politicians joked about the idea of giving all 'illegal' migrants Maltese citizenship in order to facilitate their onward movement to Europe. Now, however, policymakers' rhetoric is one of solidarity with Europe and the need to carry one's 'fair share of the burden' (Interviews: government officials, 2006–15). In some instances, migrants and their advocates are able to exploit this new EU framework to expand the protection given to people making their way across the Mediterranean, through for instance the European Court of Human Rights (ECHR 2010). Overall, however, it has produced an incentive to emphasize illegality and exclusion.

Malta's geopolitical position within the European Union encourages the construction of a crisis around migration. The constructed crisis has reinforced the narrative that the country is overwhelmed and that solutions lie outside national borders. When asked about long-term solutions for the migration issue in Malta, one policymaker responded, 'Resettlement basically' (Interview: Official, Ministry for Justice and Home Affairs, April 2009). Some officials regard even resettlement schemes as too soft a touch, maintaining that they act as a pull factor. Echoing these sentiments, the Head of Detention Services in Malta averred that '[r]epatriation is the answer' and '[r]epatriation is best done from detention' (Interview: July 2008). In most cases, the message from Maltese politicians is clear: 'the solutions are not in Malta' (Interview: Official, Ministry for Justice and Home Affairs and Ministry for Foreign Affairs, April 2009).

EU membership conditions Malta's power to a large degree, shaping its interests and, in turn, its strategies. Within this context, Malta has constructed an ambivalent relationship with immigration. The emphasis over the last fifteen years has been squarely on deterrent policies to halt maritime migration flows. However, it is these very migration flows that have put the island on the European political map. At the very least, the 'threat' of migration is necessary, politically useful, and powerful.

6

The Future of Europe

— 2007 —

Appeals by Malta and Sweden for help in *sharing the burden* of thousands of African and Iraqi refugees streaming into the European Union were rebuffed Tuesday as the bloc's interior ministers clashed over how to solve the *spiraling crisis*.

To avert further *humanitarian crises*, Malta proposed that the EU states devise a new system under which migrants whose boats founder in non-EU waters would be distributed evenly among EU countries.

But Malta's call for aid was greeted with skepticism by EU migration officials, who argued *it could encourage rather than deter illegal migration*.

> Dan Bilefsky, 'EU divided as refugee crisis grows Malta's
> call for aid meets skepticism', *New York Times*, 13 June 2007
> (emphasis added)

— 2015 —

The *migration crisis* has turned into a major row within the European Union, which at the beginning of the year began an attempt to *discourage Mediterranean crossings by reducing rescues*.

Italy and Greece complained they were having to bear an unfair amount of migrants....

Now the EU is split over proposals to install a quota system...with Theresa May, the Home Secretary, saying it would create *an additional 'pull' factor*.

> Richard Spencer, '3,000 desperate souls crammed into
> just five open boats', *Sunday Telegraph*, 7 June 2015
> (emphasis added)

— 2017 —

EU officials, however, have been pursuing an explicit policy of staying away from the coast to *avoid encouraging more migrants to undertake the perilous passage*. So many aid agencies are now sailing so close to Libya, the EU argues, that they may be acting as *a pull factor* for migrants and a boon for smugglers sending out rubber boats....

The EU sought to *make the crossing more difficult* so people would stop attempting it, bringing down deaths overall, according to an EU report on the patrols. It warned, however, that the void could risk higher fatalities, at least at first, it said.

> Drew Hinshaw & Pietro Lombardi, 'Migrant Toll Rises as
> Quarrels Slow Rescues', *Wall Street Journal*, 20 April 2017
> (emphasis added)

As people continue to die at Europe's edge, the newspaper excerpts above confirm a depressing inertia over the last decade. Despite the efforts of migrants, activists, and academics, the false narrative of search and rescue in the Mediterranean as the most powerful migrant 'pull factor' persists. The propagation of this myth depends on a radical erasure of the colonial history and neocolonial present that connect Europe with Africa and other parts of the world, influence many push factors, and shape migration flows. Migration scholars have long noted that 'push' and 'pull' factors are simplistic concepts with which to understand dynamic migration flows, ignoring how they might interact with broader social processes and contexts, as well as migrant agency (Castles 2010; Castles et al. 2014: 28–31). The accounts of people in the pages of this book reveal a more dynamic and fragmented journey, shaped by experiences, barriers, and opportunities en route. Even if one narrows the analysis, the focus on search and rescue as the most significant pull factor is still unfounded, discounting the relative wealth, peace, and stability in Europe that surely act as bigger 'pull factors'. The focus on 'pull factors' also contributes to a narrative that casts migration flows as an infinite supply of Third World bodies ready to flood Europe. In reality, sharp increases in migration flows, like the recent one out of Syria, are limited in duration, caused by specific pressures. Even in these instances, the Global North is relatively sheltered from the effects, receiving a fraction of the refugees hosted in the Global South (UNHCR 2017d). More significantly, the pull factor myth casts migration flows as inevitable shifts from poverty to wealth, as if the entire Third World would head to Europe if they could. In this narrative, migration flows become inevitable, discounting the complex beings and dynamics involved.

Wedded to the pull factor myth, governments dismiss efforts to make the sea safer through, for instance, the establishment of legal channels into Europe. Rather, the creation of crisis around the long-standing migration phenomenon continues. Moreover, people still travel across the Mediterranean despite EU efforts to 'make the crossing more difficult', and thousands die as a result. The Mediterranean thus remains a fault line 'in the smooth space of globalization where...the worlds designated by the terms Global North and Global South confront one another in a very concrete, abrasive way, and where gradients of wealth and poverty, citizenship and non-citizenship appear especially sharply' (Walters 2011: 146).

By casting the Mediterranean as a space of migration crisis, the EU sets the stage for its 'humanitarian' intervention: migrants are reduced to helpless victims or to malevolent smugglers. The victims must be saved from the sea, from the smugglers, and from themselves. Borders must be fortified. The EU and its border guards become heroes in this script, defending sovereign territory and saving lives at sea. The ways in which Europe's border regime is deeply implicated in deaths at sea is made invisible.

Creating Fortress Europe

This book started with three questions. Why has the EU prioritized the fortification of external borders when many more unauthorized migrants arrive through legal channels? Why do people continue to attempt the Mediterranean crossing, and continue to die at sea, despite the emphasis on controlling this border? How have small member states on the southern periphery responded to the sudden spotlight and new responsibility for border control?

In part, the emphasis on control at the external border is what the EU calls a 'compensatory measure', an ostensibly necessary response to lifting border controls within the area of free movement. The Dublin and Schengen agreements place responsibility for asylum and migration control at the external borders. Yet, these border measures also work symbolically to highlight the power and control that the EU and its member states retain over their territory. Notions of management, control, and orderly migration loom large in debates over migration within the EU. The emphasis also squarely locates the migration 'problem' outside or at the edge of Europe, rather than a phenomenon created within the bureaucratic halls of the European Union.

Malta and other member states along the EU's periphery have also reproduced the emphasis on migration control at the external border. In its attempts to garner more 'solidarity' from the EU and bring about a burden-sharing agreement, Malta has emphasized the number of people coming across the Mediterranean and the need for further EU intervention. Despite Malta's protestations over increased responsibility for migration and asylum, its construction of a migration crisis has paradoxically reinforced the need to control the external border.

EU policies and hierarchies create an incentive for member states on the periphery to treat migration as a crisis. Migration in the Mediterranean, alongside the emphasis on control at the external border, has put Malta on the political map in Europe. The country's exploitation of its new gatekeeping role and its small state status has arguably increased its relative power within the Union. Regardless of the fluctuating number of arrivals, Malta has continued to use emergency rhetoric based on migrant arrivals and its small state status to construct and perpetuate a crisis that promotes xenophobia and barriers to inclusion and integration. Nevertheless, its power is circumscribed as the island's geopolitical position as a migration gatekeeper shapes its strategies at the EU level.

The analysis of the Maltese case study in this book traces how that crisis is constructed in practice, policy, and rhetoric. Key to this migration crisis is the reduction of migrants to symbols, cast alternately as victims, villains, threats, and burdens. Moving migrants to the centre of our analysis reveals a more complicated picture: people who face enormous barriers to entry and refuge in Europe find narrow margins in which to contest borders and negotiate their mobility. Their contestations and mobility constitute borders, state relations, and migration policies.

By analysing these dynamics throughout the twenty-first century, the book not only reveals the long history of constructed crises at the edge of Europe, but also how the purported 'solution'—increased border controls—fuels the crisis rather than deterring migration. Ruben Andersson (2014: 25) illustrates the absurdity of what he calls the migration industry 'as a perpetual mismatch between measures and targets that inflates the fears it seeks to address, raises the stakes, and spawns unforeseen conflicts while opening up an existential abyss for the travellers it targets'. Migrants continue to make long, dangerous journeys into Europe despite and because of the EU's border regime. With no opportunities to access legal channels, and with worsening global inequalities, environmental degradation, and conflict, people must traverse the Sahara and then the Mediterranean, relying on smugglers to facilitate their journeys.

The emphasis on controlling migration in the Mediterranean, along with the associated spectacles of enforcement and humanitarianism, are theoretically and empirically important in the creation of a unified, civilized 'Europe'. The crisis is neatly located at Europe's edge, emanating from the distanced shores of the Global South. The tensions and contradictions within the European Union are erased from the narrative, despite simultaneously being exacerbated by locating the crisis in the Mediterranean. Indeed, the projected chaos at Europe's edge works to construct 'Europe' as a coherent and singular actor. In order to complete this sleight of hand, the Mediterranean must be constructed as *mare nullius*, an empty space that neatly and absolutely separates Europe from Africa and Europeans from Africans, erasing the historical identity of the Sea as a space of connection and movement.

Janus-Faced Migration Controls: Humanitarian and Security Logics

To reach Europe, migrants display great ingenuity and tenacity, improvising in the face of enormous barriers and risks. Yet even when they are successful, their agency may be co-opted by the EU and its member states. For instance, member states like Malta point to arrivals as indicative of the 'migration crisis'. People who die at sea, as well as those who are rescued, are reduced to symbols in EU logics of humanitarianism and security.

In June 2015, the EU launched a naval operation, EUNavForMed, to 'better manage irregular migration and disrupt traffickers and smugglers' networks' off the Libyan coast (European Council 2017c).[1] The mission was renamed Sophia after a baby born on an EU frigate in August 2015 to Rahma Abukar Ali, a Somali woman rescued by the operation. Federica Mogherini, the EU's Foreign Minister, explained the decision:

> [I]nstead of calling it EUNAVFOR MED, I suggest we use the name: Sophia. To honour the lives of the people we are saving, the lives of people we want to protect, and to pass the message to the world that fighting the smugglers and the criminal networks is a way of protecting human life.   (EEAS 2017)

The EU has thus intertwined a humanitarian logic to its militarized migration governance in the Mediterranean (cf. Pallister-Wilkins 2015; 2017; Tazzioli 2016). The humanitarian discourse adopted by EU elites obscures the Union's role in the deaths of migrants at sea. Indeed, discussions and negotiations at the policy level analysed in Chapter 5 easily distract from the harrowing realities in the central Mediterranean today. Sophia was lucky to be rescued, to still be alive, to have been born on an EU frigate and not in a Libyan detention centre. Many suffer a different fate. In 2013, Yohanna, an Eritrean woman, gave birth as she drowned half a mile from Lampedusa. A hundred and fifty feet below the surface, divers found her and her new-born baby boy still

---

[1] The EU Naval Force's Mediterranean operation (EUNavForMed) is deployed in Libya's SAR area, but generally outside its territorial waters. It has a mandate to identify, capture, and destroy vessels used or suspected of being used by smugglers. It can also arrest people suspected of smuggling and transfer them to Italian authorities. In 2016, the EU extended its mandate to include the training of the Libyan coastguard and navy, and the implementation of the UN arms embargo on the high seas.

attached by the umbilical cord (The Local 2013). In July 2017, 181 people left Libya's western coast on a rubber dinghy. By the time Proactiva Open Arms, a Spanish NGO, rescued them thirteen were dead, including two pregnant women. Another woman among the dead left behind four children—the oldest five and the youngest just ten months—who shouted 'Mama! Mama!' through their tears as they were pulled onto the Spanish ship (Katz 2017). Over 3,000 people died in the Mediterranean in 2017.

The avoidable deaths of young children at the edges of Europe sometimes provoke considerable remorse. The picture of three-year-old Alan Kurdi's lifeless body washed up on a Turkish beach in 2015 was perhaps most emblematic of these fleeting moments when Europe has paused to take note of the horror unfolding at its edge. It prompted a surge in donations to NGOs working with refugees, including to the Migrant Offshore Aid Station conducting search and rescue operations in the central Mediterranean (Elgot 2015). Liisa Malkki reminds us that in the humanitarian imagination the figure of the child embodies basic human goodness. She is an 'exemplary human, and as politically harmless and neutral—the most neutral of neutrals' (Malkki 2015: 79). Very young children are therefore the perfect victims in the humanitarian narrative. Yet, these outpourings of regret have little bearing on the politics or practices surrounding migration in the Mediterranean. Security practices that make migrant journeys longer and more dangerous are still cloaked in the humanitarian language of 'saving lives'.

At sea, migrants continue to be cast largely as victims devoid of agency or aspirations, with a smaller number endowed with a dangerous level of agency, framed as villainous smugglers or traffickers. The depiction of migrants as victims allows governments to justify border controls as humanitarian measures to protect these travellers, despite their ineffectiveness at stopping migration flows or migrant deaths at sea.[2] Moreover, the depiction reduces migrants to biological, apolitical bodies that need to be saved. In this humanitarian context, it is only their corporeal survival that is a marker of success. The violence they may experience after rescue—from detention to socio-economic marginalization to deportation—becomes irrelevant. The humanitarian frame 'ultimately protects and encourages a limiting notion of humanity' (Ticktin 2006: 42; cf. Stierl 2018: 717).

At first glance, the humanitarian frame appears at odds with the security logic that encourages more migration controls, a narrowing of access to international protection, and increased deportations. In this narrative, migrants

---

[2] Similarly, in 2014, the Mexican and US governments both justified increased controls along the southern Mexican border under Plan Sur as an act of protection to deter migrants from 'putting themselves at risk' (Mainwaring and Brigden 2016: 413).

are more often characterized as having extreme forms of agency: immoral fraudsters and queue jumpers or dangerous criminals and potential terrorists. However, stripping migrants of agency at sea allows for this subsequent securitization. Reduced to symbols at sea, migrant lives are shipwrecked and easily transformed into a threat. Their subsequent marginalization within and deportation from the EU are justified in this context. Even as victims devoid of agency and aspirations, the imperative to return them to their 'homes' is likewise cast as a humanitarian act: this is after all where they 'belong' (Malkki 1992). The rhetoric of the nation as an exclusive home where citizens belong helps to sanction violent, security-driven measures such as deportation (Walters 2004).

Despite this bleak picture, important contestations take place every day on the edge of Europe. People continue to demonstrate that a border cannot be sealed, that Europe remains a sieve rather than a fortress, even as the human costs of squeezing through the gaps—the risk of death, the assurance of violence, rape, torture—reach new heights. Moreover, other non-state actors have moved into the Mediterranean space to rescue people in the face of state practices of non-assistance. A humanitarian fleet of NGOs has laid bare government inaction at the edge of Europe.

Contested Space: The Edge of Europe

The deadly politics of neglect and non-assistance that has characterized state action in the Mediterranean in the twenty-first century came to the fore when 400 people died in October 2013 within half a mile of the Italian island of Lampedusa. For years, migrants and NGOs condemned the Italian and Maltese governments for delaying the rescue of people in distress. Their accounts challenged state narratives and underscored the lack of accountability on the high seas (Interviews: 2006–15). In response, NGOs took to the seas to rescue people abandoned by states and to 'disrupt and challenge official framings and sovereign monopolisations of the sea as a delimited zone of never-ending emergency and tragedy' (Stierl 2018: 719).[3]

Based in Malta, the Migrant Offshore Aid Station (MOAS) launched the first non-state rescue vessel in the Mediterranean in 2014. MOAS is the brain-child of a wealthy US-Italian couple, the Catrambones, who came face to face with the migrant 'crisis' as they sailed on a private yacht near Lampedusa in

---

[3] The activities have a precedent in the *Cap Anamur*, a freighter chartered by a group of Germans in order to rescue people fleeing Vietnam in 1979. It rescued 10,375 'boat people' and provided medical treatment to a further 35,000 (Tremlett 2015).

2013. Regina Catrambone spotted a beige winter jacket 'floating on the water, like a ghost' and learned from the ship's captain that it probably belonged to a migrant, whose fate he feared was not to be rescued (Catrambone 2014). Describing the incident, Chris Catrambone remarked: 'Look at me out here cruising on my boat, at the same time people are out there dying....So our heaven is their hell, right? Our paradise is their hell.' Later that year, the deaths of so many near Lampedusa spurred the couple to buy a Canadian trawler, the *Phoenix*, outfit it for rescue, and establish MOAS. In August 2014, the *Phoenix* started its first sixty-day mission off the coast of Libya. In April 2017, it began its fifth mission and estimated that it had rescued 33,000 people (MOAS 2017; Tremlett 2015; Interview: Martin Xuereb, MOAS Director, 2014).

After 2015, the ranks of the humanitarian fleet swelled as more groups took to the sea to carry out search and rescue missions, from large, established organizations, like Médecins sans Frontières (MSF) and Save the Children, to smaller groups like Sea Watch, Proactiva Open Arms, and Jugend Rettet. The groups worked closely with the Rome Maritime Rescue Coordination Centre (MRCC), which often requested NGO assistance with rescue at sea. In 2016, NGOs carried out over 20 per cent of search and rescue operations in the central Mediterranean (European Commission 2017e: 4). In the first half of 2017, they were responsible for one-third of rescues (Henley and Giuffrida 2017).

Although all the groups were concerned with rescue at sea and the reduction of suffering and death at the edge of Europe, they constructed their humanitarian practices, the people they rescued, and Europe's role in the suffering they sought to alleviate in different ways (cf. Stierl 2018). MOAS, for instance, framed their operation as a pragmatic response to a 'problem': deaths at sea could be solved with more search and rescue operations. Migrants were seen solely as victims needing to be saved. On the other hand, groups like MSF and Sea Watch were explicit about the EU's responsibility for deaths at sea and published statements entitled 'Your Fences Kill. Provide Safe and Legal Passage' (MSF 2015; cf. Stierl 2018). Although the groups varied in their explicit criticism of the EU and member states, their presence exposed the vacuum left by governments unwilling to deploy the necessary resources to rescue people at sea or to create legal avenues for migrants.

These efforts at sea complement others that have sought to make state violence at the border visible, to provide counter-narratives to the limited one that casts migrants as victims or villains, and their journeys as unceasing and linear movements north. Migrants, artists, activists, and academics have engaged in counter-mapping efforts in order to challenge the politics of invasion and neglect surrounding migration. For example, Migreurop, a network of activists and researchers from Europe, Africa, and the Middle East, produces maps that document migrant deaths at the edge of and within Europe (see Figure 1.1). Memorials in Lampedusa and Evros remember people who have died at sea. Forensic Architecture used surveillance technology to reconstruct the fatal journey of migrants across the Mediterranean in 2011. Their video and written reports reveal how the many military vessels, aircrafts, and other actors in the central Mediterranean making up the NATO-led intervention in Libya all ignored the distress signals sent by people on board the 'Left-to-Die Boat'. State actors evaded their legal responsibilities to rescue at sea and contributed to the deaths of sixty-three people. Together, these maps, exhibitions, videos, and other technologies produce alternative representations of journeys, migration flows, borders, migration controls, resistance, and protest (Mainwaring and Brigden 2016: 248–50).

Although not physically present at sea, the WatchTheMed (2016) Alarm Phone has also filled the vacuum as a 'disobedient observer' in the Mediterranean. Launched in October 2014, the network is radically practical and political. It provides a twenty-four-hour hotline for travellers at sea to access information and advice. At travellers' request, it informs state rescue services of their whereabouts and monitors state responses to distress calls. In this capacity, it casts light on the politics of non-assistance at sea, a politics purposely obfuscated by state actors, and amplifies the voices and experiences of migrants so often dismissed as unreliable (Stierl 2016a). For example, in April 2017, WatchTheMed revealed how the Italian coastguard did not respond to a distress call from a boat carrying one hundred people for thirty hours. In that time, two cargo ships also approached the boat but did not rescue the migrants (Taylor 2017; WatchTheMed 2017).

In late 2016, the humanitarian organizations operating at sea came under direct attack as EU and member state officials criminalized and delegitimized their activities. In December, Frontex (2017b) characterized their efforts as a 'pull factor' that led to more people taking more dangerous journeys across the Mediterranean. A few months later, an Italian prosecutor accused the NGOs of 'colluding with smugglers' to destabilize the Italian economy, while the leader of Italy's far-right Lega called for NGO ships to be destroyed and their employees arrested. The populist, anti-establishment Five Star Movement labelled them a migrant 'taxi service' (Momigliano 2017a). The NGOs vehemently denied the accusations of collusion, while researchers pointed to a lack of evidence to substantiate the claims (Heller and Pezzani 2017). MSF's humanitarian advisor responded, 'What is the alternative but to let even more people die?' (Wintour 2017).

Yet, with a national election on the horizon in Italy, the mood turned decidedly against rescue at sea in 2017 and old divisions in Europe reappeared. The southern member state continued to argue that the number of migrant arrivals in Italy was unsustainable and that it was not getting enough support from the EU (European Commission 2017a). When support for EU relocation was not forthcoming, the Italian government threatened, in July 2017, to close its ports to people rescued by NGO boats (BBC 2017). It drafted a 'Code of Conduct' and insisted it be signed by all NGOs operating at sea. Though some, like MOAS and Save the Children, signed the Code, most groups, including MSF, refused. These groups criticized the Code for including principles that the NGOs already adhered to under international law. They also argued that two new provisions would undermine their operations. The first was the requirement of a police officer on board 'for information and evidence gathering with a view to conducting investigations related to migrant smuggling and/or trafficking in human beings' (Euronews 2017). MSF (2017b) and other groups argued that this would be a 'breach of fundamental humanitarian principles of independence, neutrality and impartiality'. The Code also prohibited the transfer of people from one boat to another, which effectively limited the ability of smaller groups to operate at sea as they regularly transferred migrants onto larger boats before continuing their search and rescue work. These smaller groups were also often more openly critical of the EU and its member states.

In the days following the defiant stance taken by many groups, Italian authorities seized *Iuventa*, a boat operated by Jugend Rettet, one of the NGOs refusing to sign the Code of Conduct. The Italians accused the German NGO of having contact with Libyan smugglers and using the boat 'to aid and abet illegal immigration'. Although the Italian state had relied upon and worked closely with these groups in its SAR activities for two years, the humanitarian face of state search and rescue at sea easily gave way to a securitized logic, criminalizing groups that save people's lives.

The criminalization of those who help migrants is not a new phenomenon. For example, in 2004, a ship operated by the relief group, Cap Anamur, rescued thirty-seven people stranded at sea in the Mediterranean. The boat was initially refused entry into Sicily. The Italian government only relented after a two-week stand-off which resulted in the physical and psychological deterioration of the migrants and crew members. Once in Italy, the ship's captain and first officer were arrested and charged with facilitating 'illegal immigration', along with the group's president. They were eventually acquitted in 2009 (BBC 2009; Cuttitta 2018). More recently, the Italian government launched an investigation into Father Mussie Zerai, an Eritrean priest nominated for the Nobel Peace Prize who lives in Italy and whose telephone number has been a lifeline for thousands of people crossing the Mediterranean over the past fifteen years (Iqbal 2017). A French farmer was also given a suspended jail term for helping migrants travel from Italy to France, before being exonerated by a higher court (Agerholm 2018). Although the criminalization of humanitarian work is not new, nor particular to the Mediterranean, it reveals the hypocrisy of state humanitarian rhetoric that cloaks securitized practices at sea.

Throughout the twenty-first century, EU member states in the central Mediterranean have tried to limit their responsibility for rescue and disembarkation at sea and to externalize this responsibility to states outside the EU, such as Libya, with little regard for the human consequences. For example, in early August 2017, the Proactiva ship, *Gulfo Azzurro*, rescued three Libyans under the direction of the Italian MRCC. However, when they tried to disembark them in Lampedusa, Italy refused the ship entry, citing a breach in the Code of Conduct. Malta, likewise, refused to allow them to disembark. In a return to the disputes over disembarkation seen between Italy and Malta before 2014, the boat remained at sea for seventy-two hours before Italy capitulated and let the boat dock (ANSAMed 2017). A few days later, the Libyan government in Tripoli, backed by Italy, formally established a search and rescue area and prohibited NGOs at sea from accessing the area, threatening to shoot at boats that ventured too near the coastline. The Italian MRCC then formally notified MSF about 'security risks', reminding them of the public threats made by the Libyan coastguard against humanitarian vessels in international waters. In these difficult circumstances, MSF, the largest NGO operating at sea, officially suspended their search and rescue activities in the Mediterranean. The group's Director of Operations stated,

> MSF refuses to be coopted into a system that aims at all cost to block people from seeking safety. We call on the EU and Italian authorities to stop implementing deadly containment strategies that trap people in a country at war with no regard for their protection and assistance needs. (MSF 2017c)

Sea-Eye and Save the Children also subsequently suspended their operations in the wake of the hostile stance taken by the Libyan coastguard (Henley and Giuffrida 2017).[4] A few weeks later, even MOAS suspended their operations

---

[4] Sea-Eye would resume its search and rescue work a month later but operate further from the Libyan coast (Spiegel 2017).

and reversed their long-standing narrative that expanding search and rescue was the solution to deaths at sea. In their statement, MOAS said that 'search and rescue is not the solution to the ongoing migration crisis' and that they did not want 'to become part of a mechanism where there is no guarantee of safe harbour or welcome for those being assisted and rescued at sea' (MaltaToday 2017).

The 2018 national election in Italy only increased state hostility towards NGO search and rescue missions at sea, as it brought the far-right Lega into power in coalition with the Five-Star Movement. In June 2018, the new government shut Italy's ports to NGO ships trying to disembark people they had rescued at sea. Malta followed suit, refusing to allow both the *Aquarius* and Proactiva's *Open Arms* permission to dock.[5] The Maltese government also charged the captain of the *Lifeline* with multiple offences and impounded his ship after he disregarded instructions and sailed the 230 people his crew had rescued at sea into Malta's Grand Harbour. Shortly afterwards, Malta grounded Sea Watch's spotter plane and detained the organization's ship for three months, denying it permission to leave port to carry out further search and rescue missions (Sea Watch 2018). As a result of the criminalization by EU governments, no NGO ships remained operational by July 2018.[6] More significantly, while these organizations were responsible for 40 per cent of people rescued in 2017 and up to May 2018, deaths rose sharply after they were forced to suspend their operations: 721 people drowned in the central Mediterranean in June and July 2018 (Amnesty International 2018: 5).

As research demonstrates, limiting search and rescue at sea does not deter people from journeying across the Mediterranean (e.g. Heller and Pezzani 2016a). Even before the civil war in Libya, migrants in Malta and Italy reported that they made the journey in order to escape difficult conditions in the country (Interviews: 2006–11). Since 2011, the situation in Libya has deteriorated and there are reports of the widespread torture and abuse of migrants (Amnesty International 2015b; Human Rights Watch 2017). In this context, people continue to report that the journey is driven primarily by the need to escape Libya (McMahon and Sigona 2016; UNHCR 2017a). In short, in the absence of legal channels into Europe or large-scale EU search and rescue operations at sea, more people will die if NGO boats are not allowed to operate. Moreover, their criminalization by the Italian state and the EU fans

---

[5] For more on the *Aquarius* and related limits of maritime, human rights, and EU law see Fink et al. 2018.

[6] Sea-Eye and Sea Watch would return to the sea in late 2018 in the face of continued state attempts to disrupt their search and rescue efforts.

the flames of far-right conspiracy theories and xenophobia. In 2017, for example, an anti-immigrant group, 'Defend Europe', an offshoot of the far-right Identitarian Movement, crowdfunded over £56,000 in order to charter a boat to stop migrants and 'criminal NGOs...that are nothing less than part of the international human trafficking ring' (Dearden 2017; Townsend 2017).[7]

Alongside efforts to criminalize and delegitimize search and rescue operations at sea, the EU and its member states are contributing to the 'discursive disappearance of the refugee' (Macklin 2005). In 2017, the EU repeatedly highlighted that the majority of people travelling across the Mediterranean were economic migrants and not refugees (e.g. European Commission 2017d). In June, Donald Tusk wrote a letter to all EU heads of state in order to lobby for monetary support to train and equip Libyan coastguards. In the letter, he emphasized that 'illegal arrivals' to Italy had increased by 26 per cent over the last year. When questioned about the language, he defended his decision: 'In most of the cases, and that is actually the case on the central Mediterranean route, we're talking clearly and manifestly about economic migrants. They get to Europe illegally, they do not have any documents which would allow them to enter the European soil' (Gutteridge 2017).

Such rhetoric erases the many thousands who will seek international protection in Europe. It obscures the fact that most refugees cannot access protection in Europe through legal channels and are forced to take long and dangerous journeys. It also does not account for the violence experienced in Libya by economic migrants and refugees alike, as well as the violence of poverty and other factors outside the Refugee Convention that might compel a person to move across borders. It fuels far right-wing movements and sensationalist headlines, such as 'EU admits hardly any migrants reaching Europe are refugees' (Gutteridge 2017; cf. Tomlinson 2017). Indeed, the focus on 'economic migrants' serves to justify EU efforts to externalize its borders to Libya by training Libyan borders guards, sending Italian naval ships into Libyan territorial waters to patrol the coastline, and funding Libyan detention centres (IOM 2017a; European Commission 2017f).

State rhetoric and practice thus erode the very idea that those who seek asylum may be refugees. This allows states to attach great importance to the principle of asylum in rhetoric, while simultaneously narrowing spaces of asylum by deploying enormous resources to prevent refugees and others from

[7] In a bizarre twist, Defend Europe's boat, the *C-Star*, was detained in Cyprus while en route to the central Mediterranean. Authorities there accused the crew of people smuggling, and five Asian crew members applied for asylum (Birnbaum 2017). Once in the central Mediterranean, the crew encountered technical difficulties. The Italian authorities instructed Sea-Eye, one of the ships whose activity the *C-Star* aimed to disrupt, to go to its aid (Dearden 2017).

ever arriving on their territory. States erect further obstacles for those who overcome barriers to entry. Acts of agency are vilified and used as grounds to reject asylum claims. Across the EU, 63 per cent of asylum claims were rejected between 2008 and 2017. States gave refugee status in less than 20 per cent of cases.[8] Matthew Gibney (2004: 229) labels this Western state response to refugees as 'organized hypocrisy'. The hypocrisy is only heightened by European involvement in and profit from the wars that produce refugees from Syria, Iraq, Afghanistan, Libya, and elsewhere.

Imagining Europe

Abdelmalek Sayad (1996: 10) argues that migration plays a 'mirror function' because it 'clarifies that which is latent...in the functioning of the social order, it unmasks that which is masked to reveal what many prefer to ignore and leave in a state of "innocence" or social ignorance' (translated and cited in Calavita 2005: 155). The edges of Europe reflect its very essence. Europe cannot be a space of refuge while it fortifies its borders with walls and patrols, closes safe corridors, and creates perilous paths that people must survive in order to reach European shores. Europe cannot be an 'area of protection' while thousands die along its borders every year and the Mediterranean remains the deadliest borderzone in the world.

The consequences of fortified borders must be critically examined. The proliferation of borders and border enforcement in the Mediterranean Sea and beyond do not stop migration flows. They make migrant journeys longer and more dangerous. Border controls confine people to war zones and poverty-stricken areas, where they suffer violence, torture, and rape.

EU policymakers have an opportunity to choose more progressive policies that do not exclude and kill. The first step in the creation of a European space that is a genuine area of protection is to shift the framework that constructs many migrants as the illegal other, reduced to symbols of social ills.[9] We must

---

[8] All of these figures are buoyed by the increase in refugees arriving in Europe after 2014. For instance, positive decisions were only given in 28 per cent of cases between 2008 and 2013. Figures are calculated based on Eurostat data on 'First instance decisions on applications'. See http://ec.europa.eu/eurostat

[9] Although the issue of 'illegal' migration can seem like a permanent feature of our global system, there have been other responses to boat migration in particular and migration more generally. It is only since the 1970s that the problematic figure of the 'illegal migrant' has been constructed in Europe and other countries in the Global North. At this time, the emergent doctrine of neoliberalism increasingly tied debt relief for nation states in the Global South to cuts in public expenditure and trade liberalization. Economic restructuring in South America, Asia, and Africa displaced many people from their traditional land and employment. Subsequent rural to urban migration in these areas easily funnelled into pathways towards affluent countries, where shrinking welfare states and high unemployment fuelled hostility towards particular migrants (McNevin 2009: 167).

recognize migrants as equals who contribute to our societies in many different ways. In part, this transformation rests on the portrayal of migrants as complex beings with agency, not just as victims or villains.

Through the recognition of a common humanity, an agency that connects us despite the different barriers we face and opportunities we have, we can elicit more empathy for people crossing the Mediterranean than we have seen within European politics and societies in the twenty-first century.[10] These expressions of agency, including crossing borders without authorization, should not disqualify people from international protection and other rights, especially in the absence of legal channels. To deny rights on the basis of people's agency makes mockery of Europe's commitment to human rights and the international refugee regime. The indifference with which policymakers sanction violent policies and exclusion belies a detached arrogance that is made possible through the othering and dehumanizing of migrants and the poor (cf. Gill 2016; Mountz 2010). For who could promote policies that cause deaths at sea if they believed that they could be one of the 'boat people', that it is but an accident of birth that they are born on the Mediterranean's northern rather than southern rim?

The imperative to represent migrants and refugees as more complex beings falls to many of us: the media, politicians, academics, and activists—who all potentially benefit from the construction of a migration crisis. We must all resist easy depictions that reinforce the migrant as the 'other'. Migrant experiences of borders and journeys should be valued as much as that of 'experts' in our respective fields.[11]

Beyond reframing, there are also immediate steps that politicians and policymakers must take. The lack of legal channels into Europe for most of the world's population creates the illegalized migration flows that member states rail against and fuels the vilified smuggling business. The decision to journey across the Mediterranean is fathomable if one considers the violence, poverty, and absence of opportunities in Libya and elsewhere, alongside the lack of other avenues into Europe. Omar, a thirty-year-old from the Gambia, reflected

---

[10] Vicki Squire (2017) has argued that using the language of structure and agency, even in critical terms, is politically problematic as it risks reproducing assumptions about the culpability or victimhood of a person. Although I am sympathetic to this concern, I maintain that constructing and seeing migrants as equally human is necessary in order to bring about more progressive migration policies and practices. If policymakers and publics in the Global North see themselves as actors with agency, understanding migrants in the same manner could generate more empathy.

[11] In recent years, the media has in many ways been at the forefront of attempts to convey migrant experiences of their journeys to the Global North. Using various audio-visual technologies, they have followed migrants en route (e.g. Hosseini et al. 2017; Mustafa Ali et al. 2017; Associated Press 2015; Kingsley 2015), as well as asking readers to imagine making the choices that people face during a journey through interactive pieces (e.g. BBC 2015b; Domokos et al. 2015).

on the dangers of crossing the sea and summed up the feelings of many migrants, 'It would have been better to die in the water on the way to Italy than to stay in Libya' (Mendel 2015). The creation of more legal channels for people, whether 'refugees' or 'economic migrants', is a moral and practical imperative in the face of deaths at sea, Europe's commitment to refugee protection, and its need for migrant labour.

In this endeavour, it is noteworthy that the borderless world simultaneously exalted in the discourse of globalization and denounced in the face of unauthorized migration flows already exists for the world's affluent classes. The wealthy businessman, the 'expat', the exchange student, and other elites move relatively seamlessly between countries. Open borders are not a utopian fantasy but a lived reality for the privileged in our global society. In contrast, the restrictions on the mobility of poorer classes, whether citizens or non-citizens, are a long-standing feature of our societies (cf. Anderson 2013: 12–28; Jones 2016: 70–88). In attempting to preserve this status quo and protect elite privilege, the EU's exclusive policies increase insecurities and inequality (cf. Long 2014).

We can also learn from historical moments in which the world responded differently to large-scale migration. During the Indochinese refugee crisis in the late 1970s, more than 3 million people fled Vietnam, Cambodia, and Laos. One million of them left on fishing boats. Inaction also characterized the global response for a number of years and thousands died at sea. However, in 1979, states undertook a genuine effort to resettle these 'boat people'. The United Nations High Commissioner for Refugees (UNHCR) granted them refugee status and Western states, led by the United States, established a programme that operated over the next decade to resettle hundreds of thousands of people. The programme's Rescue at Sea and Disembarkation Resettlement Schemes created an incentive for states and merchant ships to rescue and disembark refugees: in return, refugees were guaranteed resettlement to another country within ninety days.[12] The UNCHR also oversaw a reimbursement scheme for the costs incurred by ship owners who rescued people at sea (Pugh 2004: 51, 66; UNHCR 1985).

Although the programme was flawed, adopted for political reasons, and targeted a population largely accepted as 'refugees', it gives us an important

[12] The schemes collapsed when, in 1989, states introduced screening for every claimant, which effectively removed the guarantee of resettlement. In response, states once again refused to allow refugees to disembark on their territory.

template for alternative responses to the migration flows in the Mediterranean.[13] For example, the creation of an EU reimbursement scheme for ship owners engaged in rescue in the Mediterranean would transform the current climate in which fishermen and other mariners avoid rescue. Moreover, a permanent resettlement scheme within the EU would encourage peripheral member states to engage in more robust search and rescue operations and to allow disembarkation. This would then also limit the time and cost involved with rescue and disembarkation by merchant vessels. Ultimately, search and rescue operations will not stop people dying in the Mediterranean and more radical changes need to be made in order to provide safe passage for people. However, when people are in distress at sea, they should be rescued without delay, regardless of their class or skin colour.

The relationship between core and peripheral member states, characterized by mistrust and ill feeling especially with regard to migration, is at the heart of much EU inaction. The Dublin system exacerbates this tension by placing a disproportionate responsibility on peripheral member states. Although member states are currently negotiating another iteration of the Regulation, the proposal for Dublin IV put forward by the Commission in May 2016 falls short of the fundamental overhaul needed. Responsibility for asylum applications remains with the first country of arrival but is supplemented by a 'corrective allocation mechanism' when a member state experiences asylum claims over its allocated share as determined by member states' population and GDP (each given 50 per cent weight). If they receive more than 150 per cent of their assigned quota, the reallocation mechanism is automatically triggered. Member states that do not accept asylum seekers relocated under the mechanism would pay a 'solidarity contribution' of €250,000 per asylum seeker (Di Filippo 2016; European Commission 2016a; European Parliament 2017b).

Despite this 'corrective mechanism', greater responsibility is placed on the first country of arrival in other ways. They must, for instance, assess the inadmissibility of a claim if the asylum seeker constitutes a security risk, comes from a 'safe country of origin', or transits a 'safe third country'. The proposal also does away with clauses that release first member states from their responsibility after a certain period of time. Overall, the emphasis remains on containing people in regions of origin and returning them there if they manage to reach Europe. For instance, the first paragraph reads: 'Protection in the region

---

[13] There are also other contemporary examples of large-scale resettlement programmes. For example, over just three months in 1999, NATO airlifted more than 85,000 Kosovar Albanians to thirty different countries in Europe and North America (Gibney 1999; Hammerstad 2015).

and resettlement from there to the EU should become the model for the future, and best serves the interests and safety of refugees.' Asylum seekers are also, once again, reduced to objects in the proposal: they play no role in the 'corrective mechanism' through which they might be resettled in another member state, and the proposal does not indicate a mechanism by which this member state would be identified (European Commission 2016a; Di Filippo 2016; ECRE 2016).

The EU has an opportunity here to overhaul the entire system. It could, for example, create a centralized system to assess asylum applications. Relocation could be carried out on a proportionate basis to different member states, while also taking into account asylum seekers' wider family relationships, language skills, previous stays in member states, and other similar factors that are fundamental to successful integration (cf. Di Filippo 2016).

Member states on the periphery also have an opportunity to be progressive leaders in the field of migration. Having received many more boat people than other member states, they already have some leverage within the European Union. They would be on much firmer moral footing if they rescued people at sea without squabbling, if they had genuine integration plans, and if they did not externalize the problem to Libya, Turkey, and elsewhere. This would obviously benefit migrants, but it would also be beneficial for southern member state societies: employers would be less able to undermine national labour protections by hiring people without status; these societies would not include an underclass of marginalized non-citizens; and racism and xenophobia would decrease. Small states, like Malta, have a particularly good opportunity to increase their power by leading a genuine humanitarian effort with regard to migration in the Mediterranean. They have the capacity to rescue more people at sea and to integrate those who arrive on the island, rather than prioritizing deterrent measures that marginalize and criminalize.[14]

More broadly, the EU could limit activities that sustain the migration flows seen in the Mediterranean. EU politicians and policymakers pay lip service to tackling 'root causes' of migration, yet many member states are actively involved in wars and the arms trade, activities that produce refugee flows. For example, in the five years that followed the lifting of the Libyan arms embargo in 2005, the EU exported over €800 million in arms to Libya. Italy, France, the UK, and Germany were the biggest exporters (The Guardian 2011). Germany, the world's fourth largest arms exporter, sold Syria €13 million of weapons

---

[14] While Prime Minister Joseph Muscat has shut Maltese ports to NGO ships, he has simultaneously maintained that Malta needs 'foreign workers…to maintain current economic growth levels' (Cocks 2018).

between 2002 and 2013. In 2014, they also sold 8,000 assault rifles to Peshmerga fighters in the country (Knight 2015). Certainly, fewer people would travel across the Mediterranean if their homes and the countries they travel through were not ravaged by war and awash with arms.

Over forty years ago, at the 1975 Conference on Security and Co-operation in Europe in Helsinki, Malta argued relentlessly that peace and security in Europe without peace and security in the Mediterranean was 'nothing but an illusion'.[15] This observation is still relevant in the twenty-first century: peace and security in Europe depends on peace and security on all sides of the Mediterranean. Without it, people will continue to make the dangerous voyage across the sea. These people are not the migrant 'others' who, at best, deserve our compassion and charity. They are not simply victims or villains. Rather, they are equals and as human beings have a right to move. Acknowledging their agency and the complex realities they navigate is a first step towards a more progressive politics in the Mediterranean and in Europe. By acknowledging their agency, we acknowledge a common humanity and avow that they are not so different from us.

---

[15] In the negotiations, Prime Minister Dom Mintoff insisted that states on the southern edge of the Mediterranean, like Tunisia and Algeria, have a place at the table. He called for a commitment to peace in the Middle East and the withdrawal of Russian and American fleets from the Mediterranean. He also proposed a Euro–Arab union. These lobbying efforts led to the inclusion of a 'Mediterranean Chapter' in the Helsinki Final Act (Calleya and Wohlfeld 2016; OSCE 1975).

Reflections on Methods and Ethics

The ideas found in this book formed over many years, in part derived from formal data collection but also shaped by other exchanges and collaborations, impressions, chance encounters, and my own personal history in the Mediterranean. Much of ethnography is after all an improvisation, a bridge between art and science (Tilly 2006). In this appendix, I spend a little longer reflecting on how, in trying to understand the international through the local, I conducted fieldwork for the project, the questions and problems that arose, and the answers that remain elusive.

I started thinking about these issues and collecting data over a decade ago, initially in Malta for my MA research in 2006. I feel humbled in the face of this. There are lots of things that I could have done better, or in any case that I would now do differently. Following my MA, I began my DPhil which involved ethnographic research in Malta and Cyprus, mostly conducted between 2008 and 2010. Since then, I have continued to make regular field visits to Malta and to collect data, sometimes for other, related projects.[1]

Throughout these years, the main groups of people I interviewed in Malta were: migrants (sixty-six interviews); migrant rights' advocates usually working for international or local organizations (twenty-eight); politicians and policymakers (twenty-two); government officials working on the 'front line', including for instance border guards, detention officials, and open centre coordinators (thirteen); and fishermen (four).

I also conducted twenty-one interviews in Brussels with bureaucrats and politicians in the summer of 2010. The interviewees included officials within the European Commission, permanent representatives in the Council from various member states, and Maltese Members of the European Parliament. Within the Commission, the majority of interviews conducted were with officials in the Directorate General (DG) for Justice, Freedom and Security (JFS),[2] but also within the DG for External Relations. Here, the aim was to explore the evolution of EU migration and asylum policies. The interviewees also provided different views on Malta's power at the EU level. Within the Council, I interviewed representatives from Malta, but also from Cyprus, France, Germany, and Poland. I did not intend this exercise to be exhaustive but chose these countries for their particular interests in migration and asylum, and their comparative potential.

In total, the study draws on over 150 interviews. During this time, I conducted an additional fifty-six interviews in Cyprus with similar groups of people.[3] These are not drawn

---

[1] Some of these projects were done in collaboration with Derek Lutterbeck and Daniel Mainwaring in Malta (e.g. European Commission 2016c; 2015a; EU Agency for Fundamental Rights 2013). Both Lutterbeck and Mainwaring conducted some of the interviews for these projects, which were recorded and later transcribed. I have noted in the text where I have drawn on interviews which I analysed but did not conduct.

[2] While I was conducting interviews in June–July 2010, the DG JFS was split into the DG for Justice (made up of three units: Civil Justice, Criminal Justice, and Fundamental Rights and Citizenship) and the DG for Home Affairs (also made of up of three units: Internal Security, Immigration and Asylum, and Migration and Borders).

[3] These included migrants (thirty-one interviews); migrant rights' advocates usually working for international or local organizations (thirteen); politicians and policymakers (ten); and front-line government officials (two).

upon directly but inform the study. The majority of interviews were semi-structured with pre-existing questions that allowed for flexibility in responding to the interests of inter-viewees. Access to politicians, policymakers, front-line officials, and NGO representatives was fairly straightforward. I had established contact with many interviewees prior to field-work but employed snowball sampling once I was in the field.

In Malta, I also used a snowball sampling strategy to identify migrant participants. Initial contacts were often made through friends working in the field, NGOs, and open centre coordinators. I also met other participants more spontaneously at events and in public spaces. I consciously sought different entry points into the population to avoid bias. I also sought to schematically replicate overall demographic trends in contemporary migration flows to Malta in my sample. Thus, the majority of people interviewed were male (forty-nine out of sixty-six participants) and the nationalities represented included people from Somalia (twenty-three), Eritrea (fourteen), Ethiopia (five), Nigeria (five), Niger (four), Sudan (three), Côte D'Ivoire (three), Liberia (two), Sierra Leone (one), Gambia (one), Palestine (one), Libya (one), Togo (one), Ghana (one), and Iraq (one).[4]

I conducted interviews with migrants in English in an array of spaces: in open centres, in NGO centres, in people's homes, in parks, and on beaches. The vast majority were recorded with permission from interviewees and then subsequently transcribed. I then analysed transcripts and field notes thematically. I use pseudonyms throughout the manu-script to refer to interviewees.[5] Throughout the book, I have also omitted identifying information and been careful to limit or omit specific information that may be detrimental to the migrant and refugee population collectively.

I also conducted participant and non-participant observation. This primarily included spending time in migrant open centres, in NGO spaces, and in public spaces often frequented by migrants. It was here that I talked to people informally, befriended some of them, helped with events run by NGOs or open centres, sat in on English lessons, and generally gleaned more about people's lives than was possible in formal interviews. In Malta (and Cyprus), I gained access to detention centres, where I talked to people and conducted a small number of more formal interviews, the ethics of which I return to below. I wrote field notes after each visit. Access to detention in Malta is restricted by the government, ostensibly due to the fact that detention centres are located within operational military barracks. I only gained access by accompanying one of the small number of NGO representatives who were granted access to provide services inside detention centres.

As a young Masters student, with no experience of fieldwork, I jumped at the opportunity to visit detention centres in Malta. What I saw in these centres was shocking: people locked up for up to eighteen months only because they were asking for asylum and had sometimes inadvertently arrived in Malta; conditions that were terrible and abuse from guards that was a regular occurrence. These are, of course, not conditions unique to Malta but systemic within the global immigration detention system (cf. Mainwaring and Cook 2018). The visits were powerful moments for me that informed my research.

It was only afterwards that I began to reflect on the ethics of doing research in detention. In parallel to these visits, I talked to people about their detention experiences outside of detention. This was undoubtedly ethically less complicated: here I met on more equal footing with my interlocutors. I also avoided the risk that my presence in detention would

---

[4] A breakdown of nationalities of the people arriving by boat in Malta between 2002 and 2016 is provided in the last paragraph of the section 'Across the Mediterranean' in Chapter 3.
[5] There are two exceptions in Chapter 4: Ibrahim's experiences at sea were widely reported in the press (e.g. Yardley 2014), while Tefarra launched public legal proceedings against the Maltese government over his detention (Civil Court—Malta 2007). Both gave me explicit consent to use their real names.

be perceived as an endorsement of the system, given my ability to enter and exit relatively freely. Although it is important that the conditions of and people's experiences in detention are revealed and shared with the wider public, as researchers we have to think carefully about the ethics of doing research in immigration detention where consent is difficult to obtain, where more long-term relationships are hard to develop, and where we are very limited in our ability to give back in any meaningful way.

Gaining access to spaces that are not easily accessible or dangerous is often implicitly, if not explicitly, valued in academic circles. Like the investigative journalist who ventures further than others and takes more risks, she is admired. Sometimes these risks lead to new truths being uncovered, but often such decisions are self-motivated and lead to academic voyeurism (De Leon 2015: 11–16).

We must interrogate our choices. Will access to these spaces benefit our research career more than anything else? With regard to research on immigration detention, is it possible to interview people about their detention experiences outside of detention? What value is added by conducting research in detention, given the ethical compromises? Sometimes the answers are quite straightforward. This is perhaps especially true when there is a plethora of existing evidence of conditions in detention and people's experiences published by advocacy organizations and journalists. There are also good examples of research and advocacy like this: Alison Mountz's (2011a) critical and far-reaching study on immigration detention on islands did not involve interviews in detention, and largely interviewed staff and NGOs (cf. Hiemstra 2017). An Australian advocacy organization, Behind the Wire, gathered and published testimonies from people who were or had been in detention. *They Cannot Take the Sky* is a collection of narratives gathered over numerous meetings and interviews, edited only where strictly necessary and always in dialogue with the authors (Green et al. 2017).

My own identity undoubtedly shaped this research in terms of how I was seen and what I was able to see. I was born in Malta and spent the first ten years of my life there. Nevertheless, my physical appearance is dominated by genes inherited from my Welsh father and my accent marked by many years spent in North America. I am therefore often initially identified as a foreigner in Malta. And yet, my family history centres me on this small island in the middle of the Mediterranean. My grandfather, Dom Mintoff, was leader of the Labour Party and Prime Minister of Malta from 1971–84. He remains a controversial figure: saviour from imperialism and poverty to some, socialist devil to others. This family history coloured my interactions with policymakers in particular and probably facilitated access to a certain degree. More significant, I believe, was my ability to play both the insider and outsider. In interviews with policymakers in Malta, this allowed me to connect with my interlocutors culturally but also maintain some distance and thus an air of impartiality, helped by my position at a prestigious 'northern' university.

As a (then) young, middle class, white woman, I was unthreatening for the almost entirely male group of policymakers I interviewed. I was likewise unthreatening for my migrant interlocutors. Many adopted an informal manner in our interviews and other exchanges. Some likely performed a particular masculinity for me, perhaps exaggerating or at least emphasizing their agency. Even so, I was surprised at people's openness and generosity in sharing their journeys with me, including both moments of victory over borders and solidarity with others, as well as violent, traumatic experiences.

Migrants become adept at telling their stories, because their lives often depend on it. They depend on institutions and bureaucrats that distrust them and routinely question the credibility of their words, forcing them to reproduce the same narrative an untold number of times (Griffiths 2012). While taking these dynamics into account in my interactions and subsequent analysis, I also proceeded with the conviction that migrants were not just passive objects recounting their experiences, nor villains intent on lying. Neither did they view me as an objective, passive audience. After I introduced my research to Bisi, a young Nigerian man, he replied, 'I want to answer some questions. I will also ask you some questions. You want to know much about my condition and I want to know much about what you're doing, you know? You understand' (Interview: 2009). As Noelle Brigden (2018b: 3) eloquently observes, the interviews were 'performances through which two strangers craft a relationship'. As with all interactions, the 'truths' we told and identities we performed were partial and strategic, at the very least socially situated. Indeed, feminist scholars have long argued that 'there is no underlying truth to be discovered in interviews, only a series of narratives that people tell, performances offered at distinct moments for distinct reasons' (Mountz 2007: 46).[6]

People certainly had different motivations for engaging with me. For some, the interviews were a welcome disruption to the oppressive boredom of waiting (for status, for release from detention, etc.), an opportunity to tell their truths and, in that moment, reconstitute their identity and beliefs in a particular way. Others saw me as a potential ally for material gain or information and the space we created as a platform for political statements. Still others were at least partially motivated by a desire for friendship, camaraderie, or a sexual relationship. Although I approached these interactions with compassion and many were emotionally charged, there were times when it felt necessary to reinforce professional boundaries. I was often in very male spaces: detention centres and open centres for men, or public spaces dominated by men waiting for work, for instance. Here, my gender was hard to ignore and attracted attention.

I did not foresee many of the challenges that I faced while collecting data. Before embarking into the field, I duly submitted my research ethics form and in doing so read about your run-of-the-mill ethical issues: consent, access, confidentiality, handling sensitive information, and so on. And yet, as with so much in research, practice turned out to be much messier and more complex than theory. Below I discuss in more detail two of the thornier issues that I grappled with and indeed continue to negotiate: representations and reciprocity. I raise these issues not because I have found definitive answers to them, but rather because I believe an iterative and ongoing reflection on ethics is crucial to conducting sound research that seeks to avoid replicating hierarchies and injustices (Pratt 2000; Katz 1992). I demonstrate this by also including a brief discussion of how my own research practices changed over time.

Ethics in the Field: Representations and Reciprocity

Representation was an overarching issue I confronted both in the field and after I left. It is a complex and multifaceted issue (cf. Katz 1992). Here, I treat it briefly, examining both how I represented myself and my interviewees. While still in the field, I began interviews by informing my interlocutors about my research and my role as a researcher. Early on, I started to suspect that my role as a doctoral student and researcher was not entirely clear to my interviewees. Most often they seemed to associate me with one of the many NGOs also working in the field, thus raising their expectations of my ability to help them in practical ways and compromising informed consent. Over time, I got better at communicating my

---

[6] For compelling arguments that draw on Erving Goffman (1959) to depict fieldwork as performance, see work by Brigden (2018a: 2–4), Mountz (2007: 44), Katz (1992), and Pratt (2000).

role by avoiding the word 'student' and saying that I worked for the university, which became more straightforward when I was no longer a student.

Questions around representation only multiplied once I left the field. How was I to move from forming relationships, however short-lived, with people in the field, to using their words as a basis for research findings? I was concerned about the ethics of cutting, dissecting, and using participants' words, as well as just representing them as 'migrants' rather than the complex, insightful, spirited beings I knew them to be. Heath Cabot (2016) reminds us that images and voices of refugees give authority to academic and advocacy work yet can lead to exploitation and exclusion (cf. Coddington 2017). Although their voices form a currency in our work, refugees and migrants themselves rarely appear fully, sometimes because the people behind these voices are more complex than cherry-picked quotes or images. There are, however, good practices where people are challenging these hierarchies. In the UK, Freed Voices brings together men who are 'experts-by-experience'. Drawing on their own experiences in detention, they advocate for changes to and ultimately the abolition of immigration detention. Academics are co-authoring with migrants: not an easy, straightforward fix but an important challenge to whose knowledge is valued and how we write about research participants (e.g. Aparna et al. 2017; Castleden et al. 2010).

As well as reflecting on ethics and power dynamics at play in our research and our industry, we must also be humble: humble about what we know and don't know, humble in our research and in how we conduct it (cf. Cabot 2016). In this vein, I have included these pages in this book to share some of the challenges and missteps in my research. In my writing, I include extensive quotes from migrants when possible in order to avoid taking their words out of context. I also return to the original interview transcripts regularly to counter the distorting effects of time and of cutting and pasting interview quotes from one piece of work into another.

Ultimately, I agree with Aihwa Ong (1995: 354) that when working with marginalized groups, 'the most critical point is not that we reap material and social benefits from their stories [though we do] but that we help to disseminate their views and that we do so without betraying their political interests as narrators of their own lives.' There are nevertheless challenges to this endeavour. Although I have had the privilege of comparatively long stays in my field sites, my work is still marked by what could be called 'intrusive empiricism'[7]: relatively short research trips, where interviewees are generally only met with once, and where the realities of these vulnerable groups is thus only a short-term reality for the researcher. In one sobering exchange with Ibrahim, a young Palestinian man, he quietly noted, 'Everybody wants my story; nothing changes' (Interview: 2014).

Reciprocity was an ongoing and evolving consideration in my research. Here I distinguish two different yet interrelated components: the practical considerations one faces in the field, on the one hand, and the broader ethical implications of researching marginalized groups, on the other. During my fieldwork in Malta, I interviewed many people who were struggling to survive, given very limited financial support from the government and scarce opportunities to find secure forms of employment. During the course of these interviews, where people spent hours sharing their migration experiences, it became obvious that I— as a privileged, relatively wealthy migrant/researcher—had an obligation to give back in a more concrete manner than just providing advice. In some cases, this unequal exchange was obvious. Towards the end of a long interview, a young Nigerian man, who had been

---

[7] Les Back (2007: 16) uses this term especially in relation to journalistic exposés and reality TV ethnography and argues that it 'claims to know and judge the very soul of its subjects.... Intrusive empiricism is defined by revelation, occlusive detail, fast turnaround and an excess of "data"'.

unsuccessful in his first asylum claim, legitimately inquired, 'What kind of help do you have for us?'

Although my intuition was to pay these interviewees for the time they spent with me, just as I would be paid if I participated in research at my university, concerns about how a financial exchange would bias the research initially stopped me from doing so. Colleagues counselled that remuneration would bring about bias and reminded me that it was cathartic for those I interviewed to tell their stories and that my work would have positive consequences for future migrants. In the field, however, this was clearly not a universal truth: some of my interviewees seemed to gain very little from sharing their experiences with me, with the occasional, though not insignificant few appearing to be re-traumatized by the interview (cf. Rogers, Leydesdorff, and Dawson 1999). Moreover, given the slow-moving wheels of academia and academics, the research will not help those who I interviewed, even if it is my hope that it will improve the lot of future migrants. Yet, this is hardly an outcome I can guarantee and given academia's track record, not something on which I would care to bet.

In the face of this, I tried to compensate in other ways—I paid travel expenses, gave practical advice where I could, baked cakes, and offered meals, tea and coffee—which ultimately felt inadequate in exchange for the hours people spent sharing their experiences, experiences that would become the basis of my research and my career. So why was I counselled to not pay my interviewees for their time, as researchers would compensate me for my time? Was it merely a question of not wanting to bias the research? If so, the underlying assumption is that people give neutral or unbiased information when no financial or material assistance is required or exchanged—a gross simplification of the complex relationship between researcher and research subject, if not a complete falsehood. So why is it an academic taboo to pay (some) research subjects for their time? Is it more to do with the discomfort I felt as a privileged white woman confronted by the reality of global inequalities that I read about in books but with which I am so rarely faced? Is it due to a naive wish not to highlight the material power dynamics in the relationship, which are surely evident to both parties? And even if payment does bias research, when do ethical considerations, such as helping someone in need, override the role of a researcher?

The assumption that payment or other forms of giving bias respondents' answers and thus the research assumes a superficial, one-dimensional relationship between a wealthy, powerful researcher and a poor, vulnerable research subject. This characterization disregards the complexity of all relationships and the different power dynamics that evolve based on a multitude of factors beyond wealth and status (Lammers 2007). Moreover, it disregards the autonomy and power of the research subject to decide what information to divulge and how to divulge it, decisions shaped in part by the level of trust established. Indeed, a mutually agreed price or exchange might in fact allow for more trust and honesty. For all these reasons, I began to pay informants for participating in interviews after I had finished my doctoral research.

Beyond the individual level, there are also bigger questions that could be classed under the heading of 'reciprocity'. Given the current political climate around migration, what are our professional and ethical responsibilities as researchers engaging in this field? We live in an era of 'travel bans', the rise of far-right political movements, the fortification of borders, the de facto dismantling of the international refugee regime, mass detention of migrants, and a variety of other anti-immigrant, exclusionary policies. In this context, we face an increased responsibility to unearth and make known truths about migration. However, we must simultaneously grapple with the fact that documenting migration practice renders it legible to the state and therefore poses potential danger to populations who survive by being 'undocumented'. Moreover, in this politically charged milieu, is it enough to remain locked in our ivory towers, primarily focusing on writing that next academic article or book? How do we, individually and collectively, demonstrate solidarity with mobile populations and effect positive change in our societies?

There are a multitude of possible answers to these questions, shaped by our different capabilities and (other) responsibilities as mothers, children, friends, workers, and comrades. I have engaged with policymakers, taught students, tried to write a book that is accessible to people outside academia, written some blog pieces, and engaged in some activism.[8] Often, these activities continue to feel inadequate in the face of staggering injustice and inequality. Certainly, as academics, it is imperative that we continue to discuss and reflect on issues of ethics, power, and research.

---

[8] For an important discussion on the 'price of impact', see Andersson (2018).

Works Cited

Aalberts, Tanja E., and Thomas Gammeltoft-Hansen, 2014. 'Sovereignty at sea: the law and politics of saving lives in mare liberum'. *Journal of International Relations and Development* 17: 439–68.

Abulafia, David, ed., 2003. *The Mediterranean in History*, Los Angeles, CA: Getty Conservation Institute.

Acuto, Michele, 2014. 'Everyday International Relations: Garbage, Grand Designs, and Mundane Matters'. *International Political Sociology* 8(4): 345–62.

aditus foundation et al., 2012. 'NGO Statement on the Death of a Migrant in Detention', Malta: July 1. Available here: http://www.jrsmalta.org/content.aspx?id=328754#.V7QpG47QuRs

aditus foundation et al., 2013. 'Government must not return migrants back to Libya', Press Release. Available here: http://www.jrsmalta.org/content.aspx?id=358793#.WPSjvY61uRs

aditus foundation et al., 2016. 'Joint NGO input on Temporary Humanitarian Protection N', November. Available here: http://aditus.org.mt/Publications/THPNsubmissions_2016.pdf

Agamben, Giorgio. 1998. *Homo Sacer: Sovereign Power and Bare Life*, Stanford: Stanford University Press.

Agamben, Giorgio, 2005. *State of Exception*, Chicago: University of Chicago Press.

Agamben, Giorgio, 2013. 'The Endless Crisis as an Instrument of Power: In Conversation with Giorgio Agamben', Verso Blog, 4 June.

Agerholm, Harriet, 2018. 'Farmer who helped migrants enter country should not have been prosecuted because he showed "fraternity", French court rules'. *The Independent*, 6 July.

Agnew, John, 1994. 'The Territorial Trap: The Geographical Assumptions of International Relations Theory'. *Review of International Political Economy* 1(1): 53–80.

Agustín, Laura María, 2007. *Sex at the Margins: Migration, Labour Markets and the Rescue Industry*, London: Zed Books.

AIDA (Asylum Information Database), 2014. 'European Parliament LIBE Committee backs search and rescue rules for Frontex sea operations', European Council on Refugees and Exiles, 21 February. Available here: http://www.asylumineurope.org/news/25-05-2017/european-parliament-libe-committee-backs-search-and-rescue-rules-frontex-sea

AIDA (Asylum Information Database), 2017. 'Country Report: Malta'. European Council on Refugees and Exiles, 24 May. Available here: http://www.asylumineurope.org/reports/country/malta

Albahari, Maurizio, 2006. 'Death and the Moral State: Making Borders and Sovereignty at the Southern Edges of Europe', Working Paper No. 136, CCIS Working Paper Series, San Diego: Center for Comparative Immigration Studies, University of California, San Diego.

Albahari, Maurizio, 2016. *Crimes of Peace: Mediterranean Migrations at the World's Deadliest Border*, Philadelphia: University of Pennsylvania Press.

Ameen, Juan, 2009. 'Somalis protest at Safi'. *Times of Malta*, 11 January.

Amnesty International, 2004. 'Eritrea: "You have no right to ask"—Government resists scrutiny on human rights', AFR 64/003/2004, London: Amnesty International, 18 May.

Amnesty International, 2015a. 'Europe's Sinking Shame: The Failure to Save Refugees and Migrants at Sea', EUR 03/1434/2015, London: Amnesty International, 22 April.

Amnesty International, 2015b. '"Libya is full of cruelty": Stories of abduction, sexual violence and abuse from migrants and refugees', MDE 19/1578/2015, London: Amnesty International, 11 May.

Amnesty International, 2016. 'Hotspot Italy: How EU's Flagship Approach Leads to Violations of Refugee and Migrant Rights', EUR 30/5004/2016, London: Amnesty International.

Amnesty International, 2018. 'Between the devil and the deep blue sea. Europe fails refugees and migrants in the Central Mediterranean', EUR 30/8906/2018, London: Amnesty International.

Anderson, Bridget, 2008. '"Illegal Immigrant": Victim or Villain?'. Centre on Migration, Policy and Society Working Paper Series, 64, University of Oxford, UK.

Anderson, Bridget, 2010. 'Migration, Immigration Controls and the Fashioning of Precarious Workers'. Work, Employment & Society 24(2): 300–17.

Anderson, Bridget, 2012. 'Where's the Harm in That? Immigration Enforcement, Trafficking, and the Protection of Migrants' Rights'. American Behavioral Scientist 56(9): 1241–57.

Anderson, Bridget, 2013. Us and Them? The Dangerous Politics of Immigration Control. Oxford: Oxford University Press.

Anderson, Bridget, and Vanessa Hughes, eds., 2015. Citizenship and Its Others, Basingstoke: Palgrave Macmillan.

Anderson, Bridget, and Martin Ruhs, 2010. 'Researching illegality and labour migration'. Population, Space and Place 16(3): 175–9.

Andersson, Ruben, 2014. Illegality, Inc.: Clandestine Migration and the Business of Bordering Europe, Berkeley: University of California Press.

Andersson, Ruben, 2016. 'Europe's Failed "fight" against Irregular Migration: Ethnographic Notes on a Counterproductive Industry'. Journal of Ethnic and Migration Studies 42(7): 1055–75.

Andersson, Ruben, 2018. 'The Price of Impact: Reflections on Academic Outreach amid the "Refugee Crisis"'. Social Anthropology 26(2): 222–37.

Andreas, Michael, 2010. 'Copying Camouflage: In/visibility of Illegalized Immigration in Julio Cesar Morales' Series Undocumented Interventions'. In Images of Illegalized Immigration, edited by Christine Bischoff, Francesca Falk, and Sylvia Kafehsy, 57–70. New Brunswick: Transaction Publishers.

Andreas, Peter, 2003. 'Redrawing the Line: Borders and Security in the Twenty-first Century'. International Security 28(2): 78–111.

Andreas, Peter, and Timothy Snyder, 2000. The Wall around the West: State Borders and Immigration Controls in North America and Europe. Oxford: Rowman & Littlefield.

Andrijasevic, Rutvica. 2010. Migration, agency and citizenship in sex trafficking, New York: Palgrave Macmillan.

ANSA, 2017. 'Malta continues to prevent migrant ships from docking'. ANSA, 5 May.

ANSAmed, 2013. 'Immigration: EU Council divided over FRONTEX guidelines'. ANSA 15 October.

ANSAmed, 2017. 'Migrants: Proactiva ship still out of Italian waters'. ANSA, 9 August.

Anthias, Floya, and Gabriella Lazaridis, 1999. Into the Margins: Migration and Exclusion in Southern Europe, Aldershot: Ashgate.

Apap, Joanna, and Sergio Carrera, 2003. 'Maintaining Security Within Borders: Toward a Permanent State of Emergency in the EU?' CEPS Policy Briefs, Brussels: Centre for European Policy Studies.

Aparna, Kolar, Zeinab Mahamed, Ingmar Deenen, and Olivier Thomas Kramsch, 2017. 'Lost Europe(s)'. *Journal of Ethnography and Qualitative Research* 3: 435–52.

Aradau, Claudia, and Jef Huysmans, 2014. 'Critical methods in International Relations: The politics of techniques, devices and acts'. *European Journal of International Relations* 20(3): 596–619.

ARCI (Associazione Indipendente di Promozione Sociale e Civile), 2012. Aereoporto di Fiumicino, 27 April.

Ashutosh, Ishan, and Alison Mountz, 2011. 'Migration management for the benefit of whom? Interrogating the work of the International Organization for Migration'. *Citizenship Studies* 15(1): 21–38.

Associated Press, 2015. 'Fear, fatigue and separation: a journey with migrants willing to risk everything'. *The Guardian*, 6 April.

Aus, Jonathan P., 2006. 'Eurodac: A Solution Looking for a Problem?' *European Integration Online Papers (EIoP)* 10(6).

Baczynska, Gabriela, 2017. 'Malta suggests cash solution to end EU migration row'. *Reuters*, 24 April.

Baczynska, Gabriela, and Tom Körkemeir, 2016. 'EU agrees money-for-migration deal with Mali'. *Reuters*, 12 December.

Bakewell, Oliver, 2010. 'Some reflections on structure and agency in migration theory'. *Journal of Ethnic and Migration Studies* 36(10): 1689–708.

Baldwin-Edwards, Martin, 1997. 'The Emerging European Immigration Regime: Some Reflections on Implications for Southern Europe'. *Journal of Common Market Studies* 35(4): 497–519.

Balibar, Etienne, 1998. 'The Borders of Europe'. In *Cosmopolitics: Thinking and Feeling Beyond the Nation*, edited by Pheng Cheah and Bruce Robbins, 216–33. Minneapolis: University of Minnesota Press.

Balzan, Saviour, 2017. 'An act of humiliation and violence'. *MaltaToday*, 20 April.

Basaran, Tugba, 2015. 'The saved and the drowned: Governing indifference in the name of security'. *Security Dialogue* 46(3): 205–20.

Bauman, Zygmunt. 1998. *Globalization: The Human Consequences*, New York: Columbia University Press.

BBC, 2009. 'Italy acquits migrant rescue crew'. *BBC*, 7 October.

BBC, 2011a. 'France had right to halt migrant trains from Italy – EU'. *BBC*, 18 April.

BBC, 2011b. 'France blocks Italian trains carrying migrants'. *BBC*, 17 April.

BBC, 2014. 'Mediterranean migrants: EU rescue policy criticized'. *BBC*, 12 November.

BBC, 2015a. 'EU seeks UN support to tackle migrant smuggling'. *BBC*, 11 May.

BBC, 2015b. 'Syrian Journey: Choose your own escape route'. *BBC*, 1 April.

BBC, 2016. 'Migrant crisis: EU plans penalties for refusing asylum seekers'. *BBC*, 4 May.

BBC, 2017. 'Europe migrant crisis: Italy threatens to close ports as ministers meet'. *BBC*, 2 July.

Behdad, Ali, 2005. *A forgetful nation on immigration and cultural identity in the United States*, Durham: Duke University Press.

Beirens, Hanne, Sheila Maas, Salvatore Petronella, and Maurice van der Velden, 2016. 'Study on the Temporary Protection Directive: Executive Summary', European Commission, January.

Ben Jelloun, Tahar, 1997. *Le Pareti della Solitudine*, Turin: Giulio Einaudi Editore.

Betts, Alexander, ed., 2011. *Global Migration Governance*, Oxford: Oxford University Press.

Bilefsky, Dan, 2006a. 'Africans allowed ashore, but EU policy stays adrift'. *International Herald Tribune*, 21 July.

Bilefsky, Dan, 2006b. 'In Malta, migrant wave leads to backlash'. *International Herald Tribune*, 8 June.

Bilefsky, Dan, 2007a. 'EU official sees "failure" on migrants Members fall short in providing rescue equipment, he says'. *International Herald Tribune*, 7 June.

Bilefsky, Dan, 2007b. 'Malta angrily faults EU migration policies'. *International Herald Tribune*, 5 June.

Birnbaum, Michael, 2017. 'A far-right group chartered a boat to repel migrants on the Mediterranean. Then part of its crew filed for asylum'. *Washington Post*, 27 July.

Bleiker, Roland, David Campbell, Emma Hutchison, and Xzarina Nicholson, 2013. 'The Visual Dehumanisation of Refugees'. *Australian Journal of Political Science* 48(4): 398–416.

Boissevain, Jeremy, 1991. 'Ritual, Play and Identity: Changing Patterns of Celebration in Maltese Villages'. *Journal of Mediterranean Studies* 1(1): 87–100.

Bonnici, Julian, 2017. ' "Solidarity in the EU should go beyond migration" – Prime Minister Muscat'. *Malta Independent*, 24 March.

Borg, Carmel, and Peter Mayo, 2007. 'Toward an Antiracist Agenda in Education: The Case of Malta'. In *Race and Racialization: Essential Readings*, edited by Tania Das Gupta. Toronto: Canadian Scholars' Press.

Borges, Anelise, 2018. 'Italy's threat to Malta over immigrants'. *Euronews*, 20 August.

Bosswick, Wolfgang, 2000. 'Development of Asylum Policy in Germany'. *Journal of Refugee Studies* 13(1): 43–60.

Boswell, Christina, 2003. 'The "External Dimension" of EU Immigration and Asylum Policy'. *International Affairs* 79(3): 619–38.

Boswell, Christina, 2011. 'Migration Control and Narratives of Steering'. *The British Journal of Politics & International Relations* 13(1): 12–25.

Boubakri, Hassen, 2004. 'Transit Migration Between Tunisia, Libya and Sub-Saharan Africa: Study Based on Greater Tunis'. Conference paper presented at 'Migrants in Transit Countries: Sharing Responsibility for Management and Protection' in Istanbul, Turkey.

Boucher, Gerard, 2008. 'A Critique of Global Policy Discourses on Managing International Migration'. *Third World Quarterly* 29(7): 1461–71.

Braudel, Fernand, 1995a. *The Mediterranean and the Mediterranean World in the Age of Philip II: Vol 1*. Sian Reynolds, trans. Berkeley, CA: University of California Press.

Braudel, Fernand, 1995b. *The Mediterranean and the Mediterranean World in the Age of Philip II: Vol. II*. Sian Reynolds, trans. Berkeley, CA: University of California Press.

Braudel, Fernand, 2001. *Memory and the Mediterranean*, New York, NY: Vintage.

Brick, Kate, 2011. 'Regularizations in the European Union: The Contentious Policy Tool'. *Insight*, Migration Policy Institute, December.

Brigden, Noelle K., 2016. 'Improvised Transnationalism: Clandestine Migration at the Border of Anthropology and International Relations'. *International Studies Quarterly* 60(2): 343–54.

Brigden, Noelle K., 2018a. 'Gender Mobility: Survival Plays and Performing Central American Migration in Passage'. *Mobilities* 13(1): 111–25.

Brigden, Noelle K., 2018b. *The Migrant Passage: Clandestine Journeys from Central America*, Ithaca NY: Cornell University Press.

Broeders, Dennis, 2007. 'The New Digital Borders of Europe: EU Databases and the Surveillance of Irregular Migrants'. *International Sociology* 22(1): 71–92.

Brouwer, Evelien, 2008. *Digital Borders and Real Rights: Effective Remedies for Third-country Nationals in the Schengen Information System*, Leiden: Martinus Nijhoff.

Brown, Wendy, 2010. *Walled States, Waning Sovereignty*, New York: Zone Books.

Busuttil, Simon, 2002. 'Negotiations on property explained'. *Aġġornat*, Malta-EU Information Centre, Special Edition No. 7, February.

Butler, Judith, 2004. *Precarious Lives: The Power of Mourning and Violence*, London: Verso.

Butler, Judith, 2009. *Frames of War*, London: Verso.

Cabot, Heath, 2014. *On the Doorstep of Europe: Asylum and Citizenship in Greece*, Philadelphia: University of Pennsylvania Press.

Cabot, Heath, 2016. '"Refugee Voices": Tragedy, Ghosts, and the Anthropology of Not Knowing'. *Journal of Contemporary Ethnography* 45(6): 645–72.

Calavita, Kitty, 2005. *Immigrants at the Margins: Law, Race, and Exclusion in Southern Europe*, Cambridge: Cambridge University Press.

Calleja, Meinrad. 2000. *Aspects of Racism in Malta*, Bormla: Mid-Dlam Ghad-Dawl (Daritama).

Calleya, Stephen, and Monika Wohlfeld, 2016. 'Helsinki plus 40: The Mediterranean Chapter of the Helsinki Final Act and the Future of Mediterranean Co-operation'. Med Agenda—Special Issue, Mediterranean Academy of Diplomatic Studies, Malta, February.

Camilleri, Carla, 2018. *Compendium of Asylum Jurisprudence, Law and Poliy: A collection of Maltese asylum case law*, Hamrun, Malta: adius foundation.

Camilleri, Ivan, 2005. 'Malta wins key concession over funding'. *Times of Malta*, 9 June.

Camilleri, Ivan, 2010. 'Urgent talks in Malta on Frontex rules'. *Times of Malta*, 14 April.

Campbell, Zach, 2017. 'Abandoned at Sea'. *The Intercept*, 1 April.

Campesi, Giuseppe, 2011. 'The Arab Spring and the Crisis of the European Border Regime: Manufacturing Emergency in the Lampedusa Crisis'. EUI Working Paper. Italy: European Union Institute.

Carling, Jorgen, 2007. 'Migration Control and Migrant Fatalities at the Spanish-African Borders'. *International Migration Review* 41(2): 316–43.

Carrera, Sergio, 2007. 'The EU Border Management Strategy: FRONTEX and the Challenges of Irregular Immigration in the Canary Islands'. CEPS Working Document. Centre for European Policy Studies, Brussels.

Carrera, Sergio, Steven Blockmans, Jean-Pierre Cassarino, Daniel Gros, and Elspeth Guild, 2017. 'The European Border and Coast Guard: Addressing migration and asylum challenges in the Mediterranean?' CEPS Task Force Report, Centre for European Policy Studies, Brussels.

Carrera, Sergio, and Elspeth Guild, 2008. 'The French Presidency's European Pact on Immigration and Asylum: Intergovernmentalism Vs. Europeanisation? Security Vs. Rights?' CEPS Policy Brief, Centre for European Policy Studies, Brussels.

Caruana, Julian, 2016. 'Struggling to Survive: An Investigation into the Risk of Poverty among Asylum Seekers in Malta', Birkirkara, Malta: aditus foundation & Jesuit Refugee Services Malta.

Casas-Cortes, Maribel, Sebastian Cobarrubias, Nicholas De Genova, et al., 2015. 'New Keywords: Migration and Borders'. *Cultural Studies* 29(1): 55–87.

Cassarino, Jean-Pierre, ed., 2010. 'Unbalanced Reciprocities: Cooperation on Readmission in the Euro-Mediterranean Area'. *Viewpoints* Special Edition. Washington, DC: Middle East Institute.

Castleden, Heather, Vanessa Sloan Morgan, and Aelita Neimanis, 2010. 'Researchers' Perspectives on Collective/Community Co-Authorship in Community-Based Participatory Indigenous Research'. *Journal of Empirical Research on Human Research Ethics* 5(4): 23–32.

Castles, Stephen, 2005. 'Nation and Empire: Hierarchies of Citizenship in the New Global Order'. *International Politics* 42(2): 203–24.

Castles, Stephen, 2006. 'Guestworkers in Europe: A Resurrection?' *International Migration Review* 40(4): 741–66.

Castles, Stephen, 2010. 'Understanding Global Migration: A Social Transformation Perspective'. *Journal of Ethnic and Migration Studies* 36(10): 1565–86.

Castles, Stephen, Hein de Haas, and Mark J. Miller, 2014. *The Age of Migration: International Population Movements in the Modern World*. 5th edition. New York: Guilford Press.

Catrambone, Chris, 2014. '7 days, 371 lives', 24 October. Available here: http://www.christophercatrambone.com/7-days-371-lives/

Chalmers, Damian, Gareth Davies, and Giorgio Monti, 2010. *European Union Law: Cases and Materials*, Cambridge: Cambridge University Press.

Chen, Michelle, 2015. 'EU Officials Are Considering Bombing Libyan Smuggling Boats. That's the Last Thing Refugees Need'. *The Nation*, May 20.

Chimni, B.S., 1998. 'The Geopolitics of Refugee Studies: A View from the South'. *Journal of Refugee Studies* 11(4): 350–74.

Choi, Susanne, and Eleanor Holroyd, 2007. 'The Influence of Power, Poverty and Agency in the Negotiation of Condom Use for Female Sex Workers in Mainland China'. *Culture, Health & Sexuality* 9(5): 489–503.

Civil Court—Malta, 2007. 'Tefarra Besabe Berhe Vs Kummissarju Tal-Pulizija Noe Et', Civil First Hall, Malta, 8 May.

Civillini, Matteo, and Lorenzo Bagnoli, 2017. 'Skyrocketing costs for returning EU migrants'. *EU Observer*, 5 May.

Clandestino Project, 2009. 'Final Report'. Clandestino Undocumented Migration: Counting the Uncountable. Data and Trends across Europe. European Commission, November 23.

Cocks, Paul, 2018. 'Malta needs foreign workers, Joseph Muscat tells unions'. *MaltaToday*, 2 May.

Coddington, Kate, 2017. 'Voice Under Scrutiny: Feminist Methods, Anticolonial Responses, and New Methodological Tools'. *The Professional Geographer* 69(2): 314–20.

Coleman, Mathew, 2007. 'Immigration Geopolitics Beyond the Mexico–US Border'. *Antipode* 39(1): 54–76.

Collett, Elizabeth, 2008. 'The EU Immigration Pact—from Hague to Stockholm, via Paris', European Policy Centre, Policy Brief, October.

Collett, Elizabeth, 2016. 'The Paradox of the EU-Turkey Refugee Deal', Migration Policy Institute, March.

Collyer, Michael, 2010. 'Stranded Migrants and the Fragmented Journey'. *Journal of Refugee Studies* 23(3): 273–93.

Commonwealth of Australia, 2002. 'A Certain Maritime Incident', Senate Select Committee, 23 October.

Constitutional Court, 2014. *Essa Maneh et. v. Commissioner of Police*. Appeal Number 53/2008/1, Civil Court, First Hall, Malta, 29 April. Available here: http://www.refworld.org/cgi-bin/texis/vtx/rwmain/opendocpdf.pdf?reldoc=y&docid=51a86d424

Cooper, Harry, 2016. 'Malta slammed for cash-for-passports programme'. *Politico*, 17 August.

Cornelius, Wayne A., 2001. 'Death at the Border: Efficacy and Unintended Consequences of US Immigration Control Policy'. *Population and Development Review* 27(4): 661–85.

Cornelius, Wayne A., Philip L. Martin, and James F. Hollifield. 1994. *Controlling Immigration: A Global Perspective*, Stanford: Stanford University Press.

Corporate Watch, 2013. 'Collective Expulsion: The Case against Britain's Mass Deportation Charter Flights'. London: Corporate Watch Co-Operative.

Côté-Boucher, Karine, Federica Infantino, and Mark B. Salter, 2014. 'Border Security as Practice: An Agenda for Research'. *Security Dialogue* 45(3): 195–208.

Council of Europe, 2002. 'Towards a Migration Management Strategy', European Committee on Migration, Strasbourg, November.

Council of Europe, 2004. 'Report by Mr. Alvaro Gil-Robles, Commissioner for Human Rights, on His Visit to Malta, 20–21 October 2003', CommDH(2004)4, Strasbourg: Office of the Commissioner for Human Rights, Council of Europe, 12 February.

Council of Europe, 2005. 'Report to the Maltese Government on the Visit to Malta Carried Out by the European Committee for the Prevention of Torture and Inhuman or Degrading Treatment or Punishment from 18 to 22 January 2004', CPT/Inf (2005) 15, Strasbourg, 25 August.

Council of Europe, 2007. 'Report to the Maltese Government on the Visit to Malta Carried Out by the European Committee for the Prevention of Torture and Inhuman or Degrading Treatment or Punishment from 15 to 21 June 2005', CPT (2005) 76, Strasbourg, 10 September.

Council of Europe, 2010. 'Criminalisation of Migration in Europe: Human Rights Implications', Commissioner for Human Rights, Issue Paper 1, Strasbourg, 4 February.

Council of Europe, 2011. 'Report by Thomas Hammarberg, Commissioner for Human Rights of the Council of Europe, following his visit to Malta from 23–25 March 2011', CommDH (2011) 17, Strasbourg, 9 June.

Council of Europe, 2012. 'Lives lost in the Mediterranean Sea: who is responsible?', Parliamentary Assembly, Committee on Migration, Refugees and Displaced Persons, Doc 12895, 5 April.

Council of Europe, 2013. 'ECRI Report on Malta (fourth monitoring cycle)', European Commission Against Racism and Intolerance, CRI(2013)37, 15 October.

Coutin, Susan Bibler, 2005. 'Being En Route'. *American Anthropologist* 107(2): 195–206.

Crawley, Heaven, Franck Düvell, Katharine Jones, Simon McMahon, and Nando Sigona, 2017. *Unravelling Europe's 'Migration Crisis': Journeys over Land and Sea*, Bristol: Policy Press.

Crosbie, Judith, 2007. 'Malta tells EU member states to share immigration burden'. *European Voice*, 7 June.

Crouch, David, 2018. 'Swedish student who grounded deportation flight faces prosecution'. *The Guardian*, 19 October.

Cumbers, Andrew, Gesa Helms, and Kate Swanson, 2010. 'Class, Agency and Resistance in the Old Industrial City'. *Antipode* 42(1): 46–73.

Cuttitta, Paolo, 2006. 'The Changes in the Fight Against Illegal Immigration in the Euro-Mediterranean Area and in Euro-Mediterranean Relations'. Challenge Liberty & Security Working Paper.

Cuttitta, Paolo, 2018. 'Repoliticization Through Search and Rescue? Humanitarian NGOs and Migration Management in the Central Mediterranean'. *Geopolitics* 23 (3): 632–60.

Czaika, Mathias, and Hein De Haas, 2013. 'The Effectiveness of Immigration Policies'. *Population and Development Review* 39(3): 487–508.

Danewid, Ida, 2017. 'White Innocence in the Black Mediterranean: Hospitality and the Erasure of History'. *Third World Quarterly* 38(7): 1674–89.

Dauvergne, Catherine, and Sarah Marsden, 2014. 'Beyond Numbers Versus Rights: Shifting the Parameters of Debate on Temporary Labour Migration'. *Journal of International Migration and Integration* 15(3): 525–45.

Davies, Lizzy, 2013. 'Lampedusa boat tragedy is "slaughter of innocents" says Italian president'. *The Guardian*, 3 October.

Day, Kate, and Paul White, 2002. 'Choice or circumstance: The UK as the location of asylum applications by Bosnian and Somali refugees'. *GeoJournal* 56(1): 15–26

Day, Michael, 2014. 'The most lethal route in the world: 3,419 migrants died crossing Mediterranean from Africa to Europe this year'. *Malta Independent*, 10 December.

De Genova, Nicholas, 2002. 'Migrant "Illegality" and Deportability in Everyday Life'. *Annual Review of Anthropology* 31: 419–47.

De Genova, Nicholas, 2013. 'Spectacles of Migrant "Illegality": The Scene of Exclusion, the Obscene of Inclusion'. *Ethnic and Racial Studies* 36(7): 1180–98.

De Genova, Nicholas, 2016. 'The European Question: Migration, Race, and Postcoloniality in Europe'. *Social Text* 34(3): 75–102.

De Genova, Nicholas, ed., 2017. *The Borders of 'Europe': Autonomy of Migration, Tactics of Bordering*, Durham, NC: Duke University Press.

De Genova, Nicholas, and Nathalie Peutz, eds., 2010. *The Deportation Regime: Sovereignty, Space, and the Freedom of Movement*, Durham, NC: Duke University Press.

De Genova, Nicholas, and Martina Tazzioli, eds., 2016. 'Europe/Crisis: New Keywords of "the Crisis" in and of "Europe"'. *Near Futures Online* 1.

de Haas, Hein, 2007. 'The Myth of Invasion: Irregular migration from West Africa to the Maghreb and the European Union'. IMI Research Report. Oxford: International Migration Institute, University of Oxford.

de Haas, Hein, 2008. 'The Myth of Invasion: The Inconvenient Realities of African Migration to Europe'. *Third World Quarterly* 29(7): 1305–22.

De Leon, Jason. 2015. *The Land of Open Graves: Living and Dying on the Migrant Trail*, Oakland, CA: University of California Press.

Dearden, Lizzi, 2016b. 'Refugee crisis: Arrivals rocket in Italy amid warnings Turkey deal could force migrants on more dangerous routes'. *The Independent*, 30 March.

Dearden, Lizzie, 2016a. 'Refugee crisis: Concern over "unprecedented" arrivals in Greece and Italy after 2016 total passes 100,000'. *The Independent*, 23 February.

Dearden, Lizzie, 2017. 'Refugee rescue boat sent to help far-right anti-immigrant ship stranded in Mediterranean with mechanical failure'. *The Independent*, 11 August.

DeBono, Daniela, 2016. 'Returning and Deporting Irregular Migrants: Not a Solution to the "Refugee Crisis"'. *Human Geography* 9(2): 101–12.

Debono. James, 2013. 'MaltaToday survey | The Great Siege syndrome: one in five thinks Malta is being "invaded"'. *MaltaToday*, 12 August.

Delia, E. P., 1982. 'The Determinants of Modern Maltese Emigration'. *International Migration* 20(1–2): 11–25.

den Heijer, Maarten, 2016. 'Frontex and the Shifting Approaches to Boat Migration in the European Union'. In *Externalizing Migration Management: Europe, North America and the Spread of "Remote Control" Practices*, edited by Ruben Zaiotti, 53–71. Abingdon: Routledge.

DeRosa, Katie, 2012. 'Special Report: An investigation of Canada's refugee policy'. *Times Colonist*, 17 November.

Desjarlais, Robert R., 1997. *Shelter Blues: Sanity and Selfhood among the Homeless*, Philadelphia: University of Pennsylvania Press.

Di Filippo, Marcello, 2016. 'Dublin 'reloaded' or time for ambitious pragmatism?' EU Immigration and Asylum Law and Policy Blog, 12 October.

Diacono, Tim, 2015. 'Detention centre security proved no match for over 1,000 fleeing migrants'. *MaltaToday*, 15 January.

Diacono, Tim, 2017. 'Integration policy to be launched this year'. *MaltaToday*, 22 February.

Dines, Nick, Nicola Montagna, and Vincenzo Ruggiero, 2015. 'Thinking Lampedusa: Border Construction, the Spectacle of Bare Life and the Productivity of Migrants'. *Ethnic and Racial Studies* 38(3): 430–45.

Dinmore, Guy and Guilia Segreti, 2014. 'Italy's right calls for end to navy's rescue of African migrants'. *The Financial Times*, April 22.

Divers, ed., Leo R. Dobbs, 2014. 'UNHCR chief Guterres and Angelina Jolie warn of mounting crisis in the Mediterranean', UNHCR, 15 September.

Domokos, John, Harriet Grant, and Guardian Interactive Team, 2015. 'The refugee challenge: can you break into Fortress Europe?' *The Guardian*, 14 January.

Doty, Roxanne Lynn, 2011. 'Bare Life: Border-Crossing Deaths and Spaces of Moral Alibi'. *Environment and Planning D: Society and Space* 29(4): 599–612.

Doty, Roxanne Lynne, and Elizabeth Shannon Wheatley, 2013. 'Private Detention and the Immigration Industrial Complex'. *International Political Sociology* 7(4): 426–43.

Douglas, Mary, 1966. *Purity and Danger: An Analysis of Concepts of Pollution and Taboo*, London: Routledge.

Douzinas, Costas, 2007. 'The Many Faces of Humanitarianism'. *Parrhesia* 2: 1–28.

Düvell, Franck, 2011. 'Paths into Irregularity: The Legal and Political Construction of Irregular Migration'. *European Journal of Migration and Law* 13(3): 275–95.

Düvell, Franck, and Bastian Vollmer, 2009. 'Irregular Migration in and from the Neighbourhood of the EU. A Comparison of Morocco, Turkey and Ukraine'. Clandestino Undocumented Migration: Counting the Uncountable. Data and Trends across Europe. Brussels: European Commission.

EASO (European Asylum Support Office), 2012. 'EASO fact finding report on intra-EU relocation activities from Malta'. Available here: http://www.refworld.org/pdfid/52aef8094.pdf

ECRE (European Council on Refugees and Exiles), 2004. 'Broken Promises—Forgotten Principles: An ECRE Evaluation of the Development of EU Minimum Standards for Refugee Protection, Tampere 1999—Brussels 2004'. London: ECRE.

ECRE (European Council on Refugees and Exiles), 2006. 'Report on the Application of the Dublin II Regulation in Europe'. AD3/3/2006/EXT/MH, March.

ECRE (European Council on Refugees and Exiles), 2012. 'CJEU annuls Frontex Sea Borders Rule and says that EU Parliamentary approval is required'. Weekly Bulletin, 14 September.

ECRE (European Council on Refugees and Exiles), 2013. 'ECtHR blocks pushback of Somali migrants from Malta to Libya following outcry from civil society', ECRE News, 12 July.

ECRE (European Council on Refugees and Exiles), 2014a. 'Mare Nostrum to end – New Frontex operation will not ensure rescue of migrants in international waters', ECRE News, 10 October.

ECRE (European Council on Refugees and Exiles), 2014b. 'European Parliament LIBE Committee backs search and rescue rules for Frontex sea operations', ECRE News, 21 February.

ECRE (European Council on Refugees and Exiles), 2016. 'ECRE Comments on the Commission Proposal for a Dublin IV Regulation COM(2016) 270', October.

ECRE (European Council on Refugees and Exiles), 2017. 'Germany: suspension of Dublin procedures to Greece set to end on 15 March 2017', ECRE News, 13 January.

EDAL (European Database of Asylum Law), 2015. 'Germany: Transfer of Syrian family to Italy suspended', 29 May.

EDAL (European Database of Asylum Law), 2016. 'Belgium: Council for Aliens Law Litigation suspends Dublin transfer to Italy', 3 June.

Eder, Florian, 2016. 'New border force guards Europe's "broken fence"'. *Politico*, 6 October.

Edwards, Alice, 2011. 'Back to Basics: The Right to Liberty and Security of Person and "Alternatives to Detention" of Refugees, Asylum-Seekers, Stateless Persons and Other Migrants'. PPLA/2011/01.Rev.1. Geneva: UNHCR.

Elgot, Jessica, 2015. 'Charity behind migrant-rescue boats sees 15-fold rise in donations in 24 hours'. *The Guardian*, 3 September.

Ellermann, Antje, 2010. 'Undocumented Migrants and Resistance in the Liberal State'. *Politics & Society* 38(3): 408–29.

Emirbayer, Mustafa, and Ann Mische, 1998. 'What Is Agency?' *American Journal of Sociology* 103(4): 962–1023.

Erlanger, Steven, and Kimiko De Freytas-Tamura, 2015. 'Britain and France Point Fingers as Migrant Crisis Becomes a Political One'. *New York Times*, 31 July.

ESI (European Stability Initiative), 2017. 'The Refugee Crisis Through Statistics: A compilation for politicians, journalists, and other concerned citizens', 30 January.

Euractiv, 2016. 'EU, Mali sign deal to return refugees'. *Euractiv*, 12 December.

Euractiv, 2017. 'Germany proposes EU rules making migrant deportations easier'. *Euractiv*, 22 February.

Euro-Mediterranean Human Rights Network, 2014. 'Prioritising Border Control over Human Lives: Violations of the Rights of Migrants and Refugees at Sea', Policy Brief, June. Copenhagen, Denmark: Euro-Mediterranean Human Rights Network. Available at: http://www.statewatch.org/news/2014/jul/eu-migrants-at-sea.pdf

Euronews, 2017. 'Italy's code of conduct for NGOs involved in migrant rescue: text'. *Euronews*, 3 August.

European Commission, 2000. 'Communication from the Commission to the Council and the European Parliament on a Community immigration policy', COM(2000) 757, Brussels, 22 November.

European Commission, 2006. 'Reinforcing the management of the European Union's Southern Maritime Borders', COM(2006) 733 final, 30 November.

European Commission, 2007. 'Report from the Commission to the European Parliament and the Council on the evaluation of the Dublin system', SEC(2007) 742, COM(2007) 299, Brussels, 6 June.

European Commission, 2008. 'Strengthening the Global Approach to Migration: Increasing Coordination, Coherence and Synergies', COM(2008) 611 final, Brussels, 8 October.

European Commission, 2010. 'Study on the Feasibility of Establishing a Mechanism for the Relocation of Beneficiaries of International Protection', JLX/2009/ERFX/PR/1005, July.

European Commission, 2011a. 'The Global Approach to Migration and Mobility', COM(2011) 743, 17254/11, Brussels, 18 November.

European Commission, 2011b, 'Communication on Migration', COM (2011) 248 final, Brussels, 4 May.

European Commission, 2011c. 'Extraordinary Justice and Home Affairs Council and Commission Pledging Conference on Relocation and Resettlement', MEMO/11/285, Brussels, 12 May.

European Commission, 2011d. 'Statement by Commissioner Malmström on the compliance of Italian and French measures with the Schengen acquis', MEMO/11/538, Brussels, 25 July.

European Commission, 2011e. 'Statement by Cecilia Malmström, EU Commissioner in charge of Home Affairs, on the results of the Ministerial Pledging Conference 12 May', MEMO/11/295, Brussels, 13 May.

European Commission, 2013. 'Commission report calls for forward-looking policies on migration', Press Release, IP/13/552, Brussels, 17 June.

European Commission, 2014a. 'Frontex Joint Operation "Triton"—Concerted efforts to manage migration in the Central Mediterranean', Memo, Brussels, 7 October 2014.

European Commission, 2014b. 'Communication from the Commission to the Council and the European Parliament on EU Return Policy', COM(2014) 199, Brussels, 28 March.

European Commission, 2014c. 'The Use of Detention and Alternatives to Detention in the Context of Immigration Policies'. Synthesis Report for the EMN Focused Study.

European Commission, 2015a. 'A study on smuggling of migrants—Characteristics, responses and cooperation with third countries. Final report.' Brussels: European Commission, DG Migration & Home Affairs/European Migration Network.

European Commission, 2015b. 'European Commission Statement following the decision at the Extraordinary Justice and Home Affairs Council to relocate 120,000 refugees', Brussels, 22 September.

European Commission, 2015c. 'Refugee Crisis: European Commission Takes Decisive Action', Press Release, Strasbourg, 9 September.

European Commission, 2015d. 'EU Action Plan on Return', COM(2015) 453, Brussels, 9 September.

European Commission, 2015e. 'Proposal for a Regulation of the European Parliament and of the Council establishing a crisis relocation mechanism and amending Regulation (EU) No. 604/2013 of the European Parliament and of the Council of 26 June 2013 establishing the criteria and mechanisms for determining the Member State responsible for examining an application for international protection lodged in one of the Member States by a third country national or a stateless person', COM(2015) 450 final 2015/0208(COD), Brussels, 9 September.

European Commission, 2016a. 'Proposal for a Regulation of the European Parliament and of the Council establishing the criteria and mechanisms for determining the Member State responsible for examining an application for international protection lodged in one of the Member States by a third-country national or a stateless person (recast)', COM(2016) 270 final 2016/0133 (COD), Brussels, 4 May.

European Commission, 2016b. 'Evaluation of the Implementation of the Dublin III Regulation', DG Migration and Home Affairs, Brussels, 18 March.

European Commission, 2016c. 'A study on smuggling of migrants—Characteristics, responses and cooperation with third countries. Case Study 2: Ethiopia–Libya–Malta/Italy.' Brussels: European Commission, DG Migration & Home Affairs/European Migration Network.

European Commission, 2017a. 'European Agenda on Migration: Commission presents new measures for an efficient and credible EU return policy', Brussels, 2 March.

European Commission, 2017b. 'European Agenda on Migration: Good progress in managing migration flows needs to be sustained', Press Release, Brussels, 6 September.

European Commission, 2017c. 'Commission Recommendation of 7.3.2017 on making returns more effective when implementing the Directive 2008/115/EC of the European Parliament and of the Council', C(2017) 1600 final, Brussels, 7 March.

European Commission, 2017d. 'Central Mediterranean Route: Commission proposes Action Plan to support Italy, reduce pressure and increase solidarity', Press Release, Strasbourg, 4 July.

European Commission, 2017e. 'Irregular Migration via the Central Mediterranean: From Emergency Response to Systemic Solutions', European Political Strategy Centre Strategic Notes, Issue 22, 2 February.

European Commission, 2017f. 'EU Trust Fund for Africa adopts €90 million programme on protection of migrants and improved migration management in Libya', Press Release, 12 April.

European Commission, 2017g. 'Partnership Framework on Migration: Commission reports on results and lessons learnt one year on', Press release, Strasbourg, 13 June.

European Commission, 2017h. 'EU Trust Fund for Africa adopts €46 million programme to support integrated migration and border management in Libya', Press Release, Brussels, 28 July.

European Commission, 2018. 'State of the Union 2018: Stronger EU rules on return—Questions and Answers', Fact Sheet, Strasbourg, 12 September.

European Council, 1998. '2075th Council meeting, Justice and Home Affairs, Brussels, 19 March 1998', Press Release PRES/98/73, 26 March.

European Council, 2001. 'Council Directive 2001/55/EC of 20 July 2001 on minimum standards for giving temporary protection in the event of a mass influx of displaced persons and on measures promoting a balance of efforts between Member States in receiving such persons and bearing the consequences thereof'. *Official Journal of the European Union* L 212: 12–23, 7 August.

European Council, 2004. 'Council Regulation (EC) No. 2007/2004 of 26 October 2004 establishing a European Agency for the Management of Operational Cooperation at the External Borders of the Member States of the European Union'. *Official Journal of the European Union* L 349, 25 November.

European Council, 2006. '2768th Council Meeting, Justice and Home Affairs, Brussels, 4–5 December 2006', Press Release 15801/06, 4–5 December.

European Council, 2007. '2807th Council meeting, Justice and Home Affairs, Luxembourg, 12-13 June 2007', Press Release 10267/07, 13 June.

European Council, 2008. 'European Pact on Immigration and Asylum', 13440/08 ASIM 72, 24 September.

European Council, 2009a. 'Cyprus, Greece, Italy and Malta Paper: Combating illegal immigration in the Mediterranean', 5689/09, Brussels, 23 January.

European Council, 2009b. '2927th Council meeting, Justice and Home Affairs', Press Release 6877/09, Brussels, 26–27 February.

European Council, 2009c. 'Presidency Conclusions—Brussels, 18/19 June 2009', 11225/2/09 REV 2, 10 July.

European Council, 2010. 'Council Decision of 26 April 2010 supplementing the Schengen Borders Code as regards the surveillance of the sea external borders in the context of operational cooperation coordinated by the European Agency for the Management of Operational Cooperation at the External Borders of the Member States of the European Union'. *Official Journal of the European Union* L 111: 20–6, 4 May.

European Council, 2011. 'Council Directive 2011/51/EU amending Council Directive 2003/109/EC to extend its scope to beneficiaries of international protection'. *Official Journal of the European Union* L 132, 19 May.

European Council, 2012a. 'Council conclusions on a Common Framework for genuine and practical solidarity towards Member States facing particular pressures on their asylum systems, including through mixed migration flows', 3151st Justice and Home Affairs Council meeting, Brussels, 8 March.

European Council, 2012b. 'EU Action on Migratory Pressures—A Strategic Response', 8714/1/12, Brussels, 23 April.

European Council, 2015. 'Council Decision (EU) 2015/1601 of 22 September 2015 establishing provisional measures in the area of international protection for the benefit of Italy and Greece'. *Official Journal of the European Union* L 248: 80–94, 24 September.

European Council, 2016. 'Joint Commission-EEAS non-paper on enhancing cooperation on migration, mobility and readmission with Afghanistan' 6738/16, Brussels, 3 March.

European Council, 2017a. 'Commission Recommendation of 7.3.2017 on making returns more effective when implementing the Directive 2008/115/EC of the European Parliament and of the Council', 6949/17, Brussels, 8 March.

European Council, 2017b. 'Council Implementing Decision (EU) 2017/818 of 11 May 2017 setting out a Recommendation for prolonging temporary internal border control in exceptional circumstances putting the overall functioning of the Schengen area at risk'. *Official Journal of the European Union* L 122: 73–5, 13 May.

European Council, 2017c 'EUNAVFOR MED Operation Sophia: mandate extended until 31 December 2018', Press Release, 494/17, Security & Defence, 25 July.

European Council, 2018. 'Member States' notifications of the temporary reintroduction of border control at internal borders pursuant to Article 25 et seq. of the Schengen Borders Code'. Available here: https://ec.europa.eu/home-affairs/sites/homeaffairs/files/what-we-do/policies/borders-and-visas/schengen/reintroduction-border-control/docs/ms_notifications_-_reintroduction_of_border_control_en.pdf

European Court of Human Rights, 2010. *Louled Massoud V. Malta*, Application no. 24340/08, Strasbourg: 27 July.

European Court of Human Rights, 2011. *M.S.S. v. Greece and Belgium*, application no. 30696/09, 21 January.

European Court of Human Rights, 2012. *Hirsi Jamaa and Others v. Italy*, Application no. 27765/09, 23 February.

European Court of Human Rights, 2013a. *Aden Ahmed v. Malta*. Application no. 55352/12. Strasbourg, 23 July.

European Court of Human Rights, 2013b. *Suso Musa vs Malta*. Application no. 42337/12. Strasbourg, 23 July.

European Court of Human Rights, 2013c. 'Conditions in Maltese immigration detention centre constituted degrading treatment', Press Release, ECHR 231 (2013), 23 July.

European Migration Network, 2010. 'Annual Policy Report on Immigration and Asylum', Malta.

European Migration Network, 2013. 'Annual Policy Report 2012 on Migration and Asylum Policy in Malta'. European Commission.

European Parliament, 2009. 'Parliament considers the future of the European Common Asylum System', Press Release, 10 March.

European Parliament, 2010. 'What System of Burden-Sharing between Member States for the Reception of Asylum Seekers?', European Parliament Director General for Internal Policies: Policy Department C—Citizens' Rights and Constitutional Affairs, PE419-620, Brussels.

European Parliament, 2015a. 'Asylum in the EU: Facts and Figures', Briefing, March.

European Parliament, 2015b. 'Enhancing the Common European Asylum System and Alternatives to Dublin', Study for LIBE Committee, Directorate General for Internal Policies, Policy Department C: Citizens' Rights and Constitutional Affairs, Civil Liberties, Justice and Home Affairs, PE 519.234, July.

European Parliament, 2016. 'Migration and Asylum Infographic', European Parliamentary Research Service, 10 May. Available here: http://www.europarl.europa.eu/thinktank/infographics/migration/public/index.html?page=migration

European Parliament, 2017a. 'Resettlement of Refugees: EU framework', EU Legislation in Progress Briefing, April.

European Parliament, 2017b. 'Reform of the Dublin Regulation', EU Legislation in Progress Briefing, 10 March.

European Parliament and Council, 2007. 'Regulation (EC) No. 863/2007 of the European Parliament and of the Council of 11 July 2007 establishing a mechanism for the creation of Rapid Border Intervention Teams and amending Council Regulation (EC) No. 2007/2004 as regards that mechanism and regulating the tasks and powers of guest officers'. *Official Journal of the European Union* L 199, 31 July.

European Parliament and Council, 2008. 'Directive 2008/115/EC of the European Parliament and of the Council of 16 December 2008 on common standards and procedures in Member States for returning illegally staying third-country nationals'. *Official Journal of the European Union* L 348: 98–107, 24 December.

European Parliament and Council, 2010. 'Regulation (EU) No. 439/2010 of the European Parliament and of the Council of 19 May 2010 establishing a European Asylum Support Office'. *Official Journal of the European Union* L 132: 11–28, 29 May.

European Parliament and Council, 2011. 'Directive 2011/95/EU of the European Parliament and of the Council of 13 December 2011 on standards for the qualification of third-country nationals or stateless persons as beneficiaries of international protection, for a uniform status for refugees or for persons eligible for subsidiary protection, and for the content of the protection granted'. *Official Journal of the European Union* L 337: 9–26, 20 December.

European Parliament and Council, 2013a. 'Regulation (EU) No. 1051/2013 of the European Parliament and of the Council of 22 October 2013 amending Regulation (EC) No. 562/2006 in order to provide for common rules on the temporary reintroduction of border control at internal borders in exceptional circumstances'. *Official Journal of the European Union* L 295: 1–10, 6 November.

European Parliament and Council, 2013b. 'Regulation (EU) No. 604/2013 of the European Parliament and of the Council of 26 June 2013 establishing the criteria and mechanisms for determining the Member State responsible for examining an application for international protection lodged in one of the Member States by a third-country national or a stateless person (recast)'. *Official Journal of the European Union*, L 180: 31–59, 29 June.

European Parliament and Council, 2014. 'Regulation (EU) No. 656/2014 of the European Parliament and of the Council of 15 May 2014 establishing rules for the surveillance of the external sea borders in the context of operational cooperation coordinated by the European Agency for the Management of Operational Cooperation at the External Borders of the Member States of the European Union'. *Official Journal of the European Union* L 189: 93–107, 27 June.

European Parliament and Council, 2016. 'Regulation (EU) 2016/1624 of the European Parliament and of the Council of 14 September 2016 on the European Border and Coast Guard and amending Regulation (EU) 2016/399 of the European Parliament and of the Council and repealing Regulation (EC) No. 863/2007 of the European Parliament and of the Council, Council Regulation (EC) No. 2007/2004 and Council Decision 2005/267/EC'. *Official Journal of the European Union* L 251: 1–76, 16 September.

European Parliament LIBE Committee, 2010. 'What *system of burden-sharing* between Member States for the reception of asylum seekers?', Directorate General for Internal Policies, Policy Department C: Citizens' Rights and Constitutional Affairs, Civil Liberties, Justice and Home Affairs, PE 419.620, 22 January.

European People's Party, 2011. 'Migration: giving Europe the Frontex it needs. Simon Busuttil MEP'. *Euractiv*, 13 July.

European Union, 1997. 'Convention determining the State responsible for examining applications for asylum lodged in one of the Member States of the European Communities'. *Official Journal of the European Union* C 254, 19 August.

European Union, 2000. 'Convention Implementing the Schengen Agreement (CISA) of 14 June 1985'. *Official Journal of the European Union* L 239, 22 September.

European Union, 2007. 'Letter from Malta's Permanent Representative to the Chair of the EU's Committee on Civil Liberties', 2 July. Available here: http://www.europarl.europa.eu/meetdocs/2004_2009/documents/dv/letter_caruana_/Letter_Caruana_en.pdf

European Union, 2010. 'The Stockholm Programme—An Open and Secure Europe Serving and Protecting Citizens'. *Official Journal of the European Union* C 115: 1–38, 4 May.

European Union, 2011. 'Asylum policy: More trust through more solidarity between EU Member States', Press Release MEMO/11/861, 2 December.

European Union Agency for Fundamental Rights, 2010. 'European Union Minorities and Discrimination Survey (EU-MIDIS) Main Results Report'. Luxembourg: Publications Office of the European Union.

European Union Agency for Fundamental Rights, 2013. 'Fundamental Rights at Europe's Southern Sea Borders'. Luxembourg: Publications Office of the European Union.

European Union External Action Service (EEAS), 2017. 'Factsheet about EUNAVFOR MED mission—Operation SOPHIA', 161003_11, Brussels, September.

Eurostat, 2010. 'Asylum decisions in the EU27: EU Member States granted protection to 78 800 asylum seekers in 2009', Eurostat News Release 29/2010, 18 June.

Eurostat, 2016a. 'Asylum decisions in the EU: EU Member States granted protection to more than 330 000 asylum seekers in 2015', Press Release 75/2016, 20 April.

Eurostat, 2016b. 'Share of non-nationals in the resident population, 1 January 2016'. Available here: http://ec.europa.eu/eurostat/statistics-explained/index.php/File:Share_of_non-nationals_in_the_resident_population,_1_January_2016_(%25).png

Eurostat, 2017. 'Third country nationals returned following an order to leave—annual data (rounded)'. Available here: http://appsso.eurostat.ec.europa.eu/nui/show.do?dataset=migr_eirtn&lang=en

Faiola, Anthony, 2014. 'Amid flood of refugees to Europe, Italy opens a back door'. *The Washington Post*, 9 September.

Falzon, Mark-Anthony, and Mark Micallef, 2008. 'Sacred Island or World Empire? Locating Far-Right Movements in and Beyond Malta'. *Journal of Contemporary European Studies* 16(3): 393–406.

Fasani, Francesco, 2010. 'The quest for "La Dolce Vita"? Undocumented Migration in Italy'. In *Irregular Migration in Europe: Myths and Realities*, edited by Anna Triandafyllidou, 167–85. Aldershot: Ashgate.

Ferrer-Gallardo, Xavier, 2008. 'The Spanish–Moroccan Border Complex: Processes of Geopolitical, Functional and Symbolic Rebordering'. *Political Geography* 27(3): 301–21.

Fink, Melanie, Kristof Gombeer, and Jorrit Rijpma, 2018. 'In search of a safe harbour for the Aquarius: the troubled waters of international and EU law', EU Immigration and Asylum Law and Policy Blog, 9 July.

Flynn, Michael, 2014. 'There and Back Again: On the Diffusion of Immigration Detention'. *Journal on Migration and Human Security* 2(3): 165–97.

Fortress Europe, 2007. 'Escape from Tripoli: Report on the Conditions of Migrants in Transit in Libya', 25 October.

Frantze, Suzan, 2015. 'Not Adding Up: The Fading Promise of Europe's Dublin System', Migration Policy Institute, March.

Freeman, Colin, and Nick Squires, 2013. 'EU immigration: "Malta is the smallest state, and we are carrying a burden that is much bigger than any other country"'. *The Telegraph*, 21 July.

Frontex, 2007. 'Annual Accounts for 2006', Warsaw, Poland, May.

Frontex, 2008. 'Annual Report 2007', Warsaw, Poland, May.

Frontex, 2009. 'General Report 2008', Warsaw Poland, May.

Frontex, 2010a. 'General Report, 2009', Warsaw, Poland.

Frontex, 2010b. 'Final Accounts for 2009', Warsaw, Poland, June.

Frontex, 2014. 'Frontex launches call for participation of the EU Member States in Joint Operation Triton', 26 September.

Frontex, 2017a. 'Central Mediterranean Route'. Available at: https://frontex.europa.eu/along-eu-borders/migratory-routes/central-mediterranean-route/

Frontex, 2017b. 'Risk Analysis for 2017', Warsaw, Poland: Frontex.

Garcés-Mascareñas, Blanca, 2015. 'Why Dublin "Doesn't Work"'. Notes Internacionals, Barcelona Centre for International Affairs (CIDOB), 135, November.

Garside, Juliette, 2017. 'Malta's prime minister under pressure from MEPs over corruption claims'. The Guardian, 9 May.

Gatti, Fabrizio, 2017. 'Così l'Italia ha lasciato annegare 60 bambini: in esclusiva le telefonate del naufragio'. L'Espresso, 8 May.

Gayle, Damien, 2019. 'Stansted 15: no jail for activists convicted of terror-related offences'. The Guardian, 6 February.

GCIM (Global Commission on International Migration), 2005. 'Migration in an Interconnected World—New Directions for Action', Report of the Global Commission on International Migration', October.

Geddes, Andrew, 2003. The Politics of Migration and Immigration in Europe, London: Sage.

Geddes, Andrew, 2005. 'Europe's Border Relationships and International Migration Relations'. JCMS: Journal of Common Market Studies 43(4): 787–806.

Geddes, Andrew, and Peter Scholten, 2016. The Politics of Migration and Immigration in Europe, London: Sage.

Geiger, Martin, and Antoine Pécoud, eds., 2010. The Politics of International Migration Management, Basingstoke: Palgrave Macmillan.

Ghezelbash, Daniel, 2014. 'Forces of diffusion: what drives the transfer of immigration policy and law across jurisdictions?' International Journal of Migration and Border Studies 1(2): 139–53.

Ghosh, Bimal, ed., 2000. Managing Migration: Time for a New International Regime? Oxford: Oxford University Press.

Gibney, Matthew, 1999. 'Kosovo and beyond: popular and unpopular refugee'. Forced Migration Review 5: 28–30.

Gibney, Matthew, 2004. The ethics and politics of asylum: Liberal democracy and the response to refugees, Cambridge: Cambridge University Press

Giddens, Anthony, 1984. The Constitution of Society, Berkeley and Los Angeles: University of California Press.

Gill, Nick, 2016. Nothing Personal? Geographies of Governing and Activism in the British Asylum System, Chichester: John Wiley & Sons.

Gill, Rosalind C., 2007. 'Critical Respect: The Difficulties and Dilemmas of Agency and "Choice" for Feminism. A Reply to Duits and van Zoonen'. European Journal of Women's Studies 14(1): 69–80.

Global Detention Project, 2014a. 'Immigration Detention in New Zealand', Geneva: Global Detention Project, February.

Global Detention Project, 2014b. 'Immigration Detention in Malta', Geneva: Global Detention Project, January.

Global Detention Project, 2014c. 'Greece Immigration Detention Profile', Geneva: Global Detention Project, April.

Godenau, Dirk, 2014. 'Irregular Maritime Immigration in the Canary Islands: Externalization and Communautarisation in the Social Construction of Borders'. Journal of Immigrant & Refugee Studies 12(2): 123–42.

Goffman, Erving, 1959. The Presentation of Self in Everyday Life, Garden City, NY: Doubleday.

Gogou, Kondylia, 2017. 'The EU-Turkey deal: Europe's year of shame', Amnesty International, 20 March.

González-Enríquez, Carmen, and Anna Triandafyllidou, 2009. 'Comparing the New Hosts of Southern Europe'. *European Journal of Migration and Law* 11(2): 109–18.

Gonzi, Lawrence, 2007. 'Illegal Immigration: A Maltese View'. *European View* 5: 41–5.

Gonzi, Lawrence, 2011. 'Malta: PM Lawrence Gonzi on the impact of EU membership'. Global: The International Briefing, January.

Grabbe, Heather, 2000. 'The Sharp Edges of Europe: Extending Schengen Eastwards'. *International Affairs* 76(3): 519–36.

Graham, Nadian, 2017. '5 reasons why we stopped a UKgov deportation flight to Nigeria last night'. *openDemocracy UK*, 29 March.

Grant, Harriet, and John Domokos, 2011. 'Dublin regulation leaves asylum seekers with their fingers burnt'. *The Guardian*, 7 October.

Grant, Will, 2011. 'Berlusconi: "Human tsunami" arraigning in Lampedusa'. *BBC*, 10 April.

Grech, Helena, 2017. 'PM says point of migrant deal from informal summit is to send "strong signal", genuine refugees welcome'. *Malta Independent*, 8 February.

Grech, Herman, 2005. 'Are we Racist?' *Times of Malta*, 20 August.

Grech, Herman, 2007. 'Fisherman defies AFM orders to return migrants to Libya'. *Times of Malta*, 30 June.

Grech, Herman, 2010. 'Right back where they left'. Times of Malta, 25 July.

Grech, Herman, 2017. 'Man who took his own life had applied for assisted return, minister says'. *Times of Malta*, 21 February.

Grech, Herman, and Kurt Sansone, 2009. 'Shrinking Malta's search and rescue area is "not an option": Italy applying pressure directly and indirectly'. *Times of Malta*, 26 April.

Green, Michael, Andre Dao, Angelica Neville, Dana Affleck, and Sienna Merope, eds., 2017. *They Cannot Take the Sky*, Crowns Nest, Australia: Allen & Unwin.

Gregory, Derek. 2004. *The Colonial Present: Afghanistan, Palestine, and Iraq*, Oxford: Blackwell Publishing.

Griffiths, Melanie, 2012. '"Vile Liars and Truth Distorters": Truth, Trust and the Asylum System'. *Anthropology Today* 28(5): 8–12.

GUE/NGL, 2017. 'EU and Italian cooperation with Sudan on border control: what is at stake? Report GUE/NGL Delegation to Khartoum, Sudan 19–22 December 2016'. Available here: https://www.dielinke-europa.eu/kontext/controllers/document.php/628.8/5/22e.pdf

Gutteridge, Nick, 2017. 'EU admits hardly any migrants reaching Europe are refugees as it toughens deportation talk'. *Express*, 21 June.

Hadj-Abdou, Leila, 2014. 'Europe's "Rio Grande": (Im)mobility in the Mediterranean'. In *A New Paradigm: Perspectives on the Changing Mediterranean*, edited by Andy Mullins and Sasha Toperich. Center for Transatlantic Relations, Johns Hopkins University SAIS.

Hadjicostis, Menelaos, and Derek Gatopoulos, 2016. 'Top diplomats from European Union nations bordering the Mediterranean say unilateral actions by some countries to stem the huge influx of mi-grants won't solve the crisis'. *US News*, 26 February.

Hage, Ghassan, 2000. *White Nation: Fantasies of White Supremacy in a Multicultural Society*, New York, NY; Annandale, NSW: Routledge.

Hall, Stuart, Chas Critcher, Tony Jefferson, John Clarke, and Brian Roberts. 2013. *Policing the crisis: mugging, the state and law and order*, Basingstoke: Palgrave Macmillan.

Hammerstad, Anne, 2015. 'Lessons for dealing with today's migrant crisis from the last one'. *Reuters*, 10 September.

Hanafi, Sari, and Taylor Long, 2010. 'Governance, Governmentalities, and the State of Exception in the Palestinian Refugee Camps of Lebanon'. *Journal of Refugee Studies* 23(2): 134–59.

Hansen, Peo, and Stefan Jonsson, 2017. 'Eurafrica Incognita: The Colonial Origins of the European Union'. *History of the Present* 7(1): 1–32.

Hartling, Poul, 1979. 'Opening Statement by Mr. Poul Hartling, United Nations High Commissioner for Refugees, at the Meeting on Refugees and Displaced Persons in South-East Asia, 21 July 1979', United Nations, 21 July.

Havinga, Tetty, and Anita Böcker, 1999. 'Country of asylum by choice or by chance: Asylum-seekers in Belgium, the Netherlands and the UK'. *Journal of Ethnic and Migration Studies* 25(1): 43–61.

Hay, Colin, 2002. *Political Analysis: A Critical Introduction*, Abingdon: Palgrave Macmillan.

Haynes, Mike, 1999. 'Setting the Limits to Europe as an "Imagined Community"'. In *The European Union and Migrant Labour*, edited by Gareth Dale and Mike Cole, 17–42. Oxford: Berg.

Hayter, Theresa, 2000. *Open Borders: The Case Against Immigration Controls*, London: Pluto Press.

Heller, Charles, Nicholas De Genova, Maurice Stierl, Martina Tazzioli, and Huub van Baar, 2016. 'Crisis'. In 'Europe/Crisis: New Keywords of "the Crisis" in and of "Europe"', edited by Nicholas De Genova and Martina Tazzioli, 7–16. Zone Books: Near Futures Online.

Heller, Charles, and Lorenzo Pezzani, 2016a. 'Death by Rescue', Forensic Oceanography, Forensic Architecture Agency, Goldsmiths University. Available here: https://deathbyrescue.org/

Heller, Charles, and Lorenzo Pezzani, 2016b. 'Ebbing and Flowing: The EU's Shifting Practices of (Non-) Assistance and Bordering in a Time of Crisis', *Europe at a Crossroads*, Near Futures Online, Issue 1.

Heller, Charles and Lorenzo Pezzani, 2017. 'Blaming the Rescuers', Forensic Oceanography, Forensic Architecture Agency, Goldsmiths, University of London.

Heller, Charles, Lorenzo Pezzani, and Maurice Stierl, 2017. 'Disobedient Sensing and Border Struggles at the Maritime Frontier of EUrope'. *Spheres: Journal for Digital Cultures* 4.

Heller, Charles, Lorenzo Pezzani, and Situ Studio, 2012. 'Report on the "Left-To-Die Boat"', Forensic Architecture Agency, Goldsmiths University. Available here: http://www.forensic-architecture.org/wp-content/uploads/2014/05/FO-report.pdf

Henley, Jon and Angela Giuffrida, 2017. 'Three NGOs halt Mediterranean migrant rescues after Libyan hostility'. *The Guardian*, 14 August.

Herbert, Matthew, 2016. 'At the Edge: Trends and routes of North African clandestine migrants', Institute for Security Studies Paper 298, November.

Hiemstra, Nancy, 2012. 'Geopolitical Reverberations of US Migrant Detention and Deportation: The View from Ecuador'. *Geopolitics* 17(2): 293–311.

Hiemstra, Nancy, 2017. 'Periscoping as a Feminist Methodological Approach for Researching the Seemingly Hidden'. *The Professional Geographer* 69(2): 329–36.

Hier, Sean P., and Joshua L. Greenberg, 2002. 'Constructing a Discursive Crisis: Risk, Problematization and Illegal Chinese in Canada'. *Ethnic and Racial Studies* 25(3): 490–513.

Hodge, Paul, 2015. 'A Grievable Life? The Criminalisation and Securing of Asylum Seeker Bodies in the 'violent Frames' of Australia's Operation Sovereign Borders'. *Geoforum* 58: 122–31.

Hodges, Dan, 2014. 'Drown an Immigrant to Save an Immigrant: Why Is the Government Borrowing Policy from the BNP?' *Telegraph*, 28 October 28.

Hoffmann, Ulrike, 2013. 'The Influence of pro-Migrant Groups within the Shaping Process of the EU Asylum and Migration Policy', PhD Thesis, University of Salford.

Hollifield, James F, 1992. 'Migration and International Relations: Cooperation and Control in the European Community'. *International Migration Review* 26(2): 568–95.

Holzscheiter, Anna, 2005. 'Discourse as Capability: Non-State Actors' Capital in Global Governance'. *Millennium—Journal of International Studies* 33(3): 723–46.

Home Office, 2002. 'Secure Borders, Safe Haven: Integration with diversity in modern Britain'. London, UK: Author.

hooks, bell, 1990. 'Marginality as Site of Resistance'. In *Out There: Marginalization and Contemporary Cultures*, edited by Russell Ferguson, Martha Gever, Trinh T. Minh-ha, and Cornel West, 341–3. Cambridge, MA: MIT Press.

Hooper, John, 2007. 'UN rebuke as governments squabble over immigrants found clinging to tuna nets'. *The Guardian*, 29 May.

Horden, Peregrine, and Nicholas Purcell, 2000. *The Corrupting Sea: A Study of Mediterranean History*, Oxford, UK: Wiley-Blackwell.

Hosseini, Khalid, Adeel Akhtar, Liz Edwards, Francesca Panetta, Nicole Jackson, Shehani Fernando, Mona Mahmood, Anrick Bregman, Andrew Mason, Anetta Jones, Lisa Golden, Peregrine Andrews, So When, Kronos Quartet, and UNHCR, 2017. 'Sea Prayer: a 360 story inspired by refugee Alan Kurdi'. *The Guardian*, 1 September.

House of Commons, 2016. 'Libya: Examination of intervention and collapse and the UK's future policy options', HC 119, Third Report of Session 2016–17, Foreign Affairs Committee, UK, 14 September.

House of Lords, 2017. 'Operation Sophia: a failed mission', European Union Committee, HL Paper 5, 12 July.

Human Rights Watch, 2006. 'Stemming the Flow: Abuses Against Migrants, Asylum Seekers and Refugees'. Human Rights Watch.

Human Rights Watch, 2009. 'Pushed Back, Pushed Around: Italy's Forced Return of Boat Migrants and Asylum Seekers, Libya's Mistreatment of Migrants and Asylum Seekers'. Human Rights Watch, September.

Human Rights Watch, 2011. 'The EU's Dirty Hands: Frontex Involvement in Ill-Treatment of Migrant Detainees in Greece', 21 September.

Human Rights Watch, 2012. 'Boat Ride to Detention: Adult and Child Migrants in Malta', USA: Human Rights Watch, July.

Human Rights Watch, 2015. 'The Mediterranean Migration Crisis: Why People Flee, What the EU Should Do', 19 June.

Human Rights Watch, 2017. 'Libya: Armed Groups Detain, Torture, Kill', January.

Hyndman, Jennifer, and Alison Mountz, 2008. 'Another Brick in the Wall? Neo-Refoulement and the Externalization of Asylum by Australia and Europe'. *Government and Opposition* 43(2): 249–69.

IDC (International Detention Coalition), 2015. 'Does Detention Deter? Reframing immigration detention in response to irregular migration', No. 1, April.

ILO (International Labour Organization), 2004. 'Towards a Fair Deal for Migrant Workers in the Global Economy', International Labour Conference, 92nd Session, 2004.

Inder, Claire, 2010. 'International Refugee Law, "Hyper-Legalism" and Migration Management: The Pacific Solution'. In *The Politics of International Migration Management*, edited by Martin Geiger and Antoine Pécoud, 220–51. Basingstoke: Palgrave Macmillan.

Indymedia UK, 2011. 'Airplane Forced to Return to Paris to Stop Deportation'. *Indymedia UK*, 22 January.

Innes, Alexandria, 2015. Migration, Citizenship and the Challenge for Security: An Ethnographic Approach. Basingstoke, Hampshire: Palgrave Macmillan.

IOM (International Organization for Migration), 2005. 'International Agenda for Migration Management', Berne Initiative, Switzerland. Available here: http://publications.iom.int/system/files/pdf/iamm.pdf

IOM (International Organization for Migration), 2016. 'The Central Mediterranean route: Deadlier than ever', Global Migration Data Analysis Centre, Data Briefing Series. Issue No. 3, June.

IOM (International Organization for Migration), 2017a. 'UN Migration Agency (IOM) Improves Living Conditions for Detained Migrants in Libya', IOM News, 5 May.

IOM (International Organization for Migration), 2017b. 'Mediterranean Migrant Arrivals Top 363,348 in 2016; Deaths at Sea: 5,079', Press Release, 6 January.

IOM Malta, 2017. 'The United States Refugee Admissions Programme (USRAP)', Current Activities. Available here: https://malta.iom.int/the-united-states-refugee-admissions-programme-usrap

Iqbal, Nomia, 2017. 'Eritrean priest in Italy denies "people smuggling"'. BBC, 17 August.

Isin, Engin, 2008. 'Theorizing Acts of Citizenship'. In Acts of Citizenship edited by Engin Isin and Greg Nielsen, 15–43. New York: Zed Books.

Italian Refugee Council, 2007. 'CIR Report Regarding Recent Search and Rescue Operations in the Mediterranean'.

Johnson, Heather L., 2011. 'Click to Donate: Visual Images, Constructing Victims and Imagining the Female Refugee'. Third World Quarterly 32(6): 1015–37.

Johnson, Heather L., 2013. 'The Other Side of the Fence: Reconceptualizing the "Camp" and Migration Zones at the Borders of Spain'. International Political Sociology 7(1): 75–91.

Joly, Daniele, 1994. 'The Porous Dam: European Harmonization on Asylum in the Nineties'. International Journal of Refugee Law 6(2): 159–93.

Jones, Huw R., 1973. 'Modern Emigration from Malta'. Transactions of the Institute of British Geographers (60): 101–19.

Jones, Jonathan, 2015. 'The yacht and the dinghy in the Aegean: a perfect allegory for the migrant crisis'. The Guardian, 17 August.

Jones, Reece. 2012. 'Spaces of Refusal: Rethinking Sovereign Power and Resistance at the Border'. Annals of the Association of American Geographers 102(3): 685–99.

Jones, Reece, 2016. Violent Borders: Refugees and the Right to Move, London; New York: Verso.

Jones, Sam, Patrick Kingsley, and Mark Anderson, 2015. 'Escaping Eritrea: "If I Die at Sea, It's Not a Problem—at Least I Won't Be Tortured"'. The Guardian, 21 April.

Journalism++ SAS, Journalism++ Stockholm and Dataninja, Neue Zürcher Zeitung, El Confidencial, Sydsvenskan, Radiobubble, Alice Kohli, Jean-Marc Manach, and Jacopo Ottaviani, 2015. 'The Migrants' Files'. Available here: http://www.themigrantsfiles.com/

JRS (Jesuit Refugee Services), aditus foundation, Integra Foundation, and Malta Emigrants' Commission, 2016. ' "Journeys of Hope": We urge Malta to grant safe and legal access to refugees', Press Statement on World Refugee Day 2016, 1 July.

Juchno, Piotr, 2011. '75 thousand asylum seekers granted protection status in the EU in 2008', Statistics in Focus, Eurostat, Population and Social Conditions, 92/2009, 25 November.

Kambas, Michele, and Rene Maltezou, 2016. 'EU Med nations hold summit on growth, EU paymasters question motive'. Reuters, 9 September.

Karyotis, Georgios, 2007. 'European Migration Policy in the Aftermath of September 11'. Innovation: The European Journal of Social Sciences 20(1): 1–17.

Katrougalos, George, and Gabriella Lazaridis. 2003. Southern European Welfare States: Problems, Challenges and Prospects, Basingstoke: Palgrave Macmillan.

Katz, Andrew, 2017. ' "This is Hell on Earth": Eyewitness to a harrowing rescue on the Mediterranean'. Time, 26 July.

Katz, Cindi, 1992. 'All the world is staged'. Environment & Planning D: Society & Space 10: 495–510.

Kenyon, Paul, 2009. *I Am Justice: A Journey Out of Africa*, London: Preface Publishing.

Kessler, Oliver, and Xavier Guillaume, 2012. 'Everyday Practices of International Relations: People in Organizations'. *Journal of International Relations and Development* 15(1): 110–20.

King, Russell, 2009. 'Geography, Islands and Migration in an Era of Global Mobility'. *Island Studies Journal* 4(1): 53–84.

King, Russell, and Richard Black, 1997. *Southern Europe and the New Immigrations*. Brighton: Sussex Academic Press.

King, Russell, and Mark Thomson, 2008. 'The Southern European model of immigration: do the cases of Malta, Cyprus and Slovenia fit?' *Journal of Southern Europe and the Balkans* 10(3): 265–91.

Kingsley, Patrick, 2015. 'The Journey'. *The Guardian*, 9 June.

Kingsley, Patrick, and Ian Traynor, 2015. 'EU borders chief says saving migrants' lives "shouldn't be priority" for patrols'. *The Guardian*, 22 April.

Klein, Naomi, 2007. *The Shock Doctrine: The Rise of Disaster Capitalism*, London: Penguin.

Klepp, Silja, 2010. 'A Contested Asylum System: The European Union between Refugee Protection and Border Control in the Mediterranean Sea'. *European Journal of Migration and Law* 12(1): 1–21.

Klepp, Silja, 2011. 'A Double Bind: Malta and the Rescue of Unwanted Migrants at Sea, a Legal Anthropological Perspective on the Humanitarian Law of the Sea'. *International Journal of Refugee Law* 23(3): 538–57.

Knight, Ben, 2015. 'Weapons go to conflict zones, the money comes to Germany'. *DW*, 21 October.

Koser, Khalid, Martha Walsh, and Richard Black, 1998. 'Temporary Protection and the Assisted Return of Refugees from the European Union'. *International Journal of Refugee Law* 10(3): 444–61.

Koslowski, Rey, 1998. International Migration and European Security in the Context of EU Enlargement'. *Cambridge Review of International Affairs* 12(1): 30–48.

Koslowski, Rey, ed., 2011. *Global Mobility Regimes*, New York: Palgrave Macmillan.

Kovras, Iosif, and Simon Robins, 2016. 'Death as the Border: Managing Missing Migrants and Unidentified Bodies at the EU's Mediterranean Frontier'. *Political Geography* 55: 40–9.

Lammers, Ellen, 2007. 'Researching Refugees: Preoccupations with Power and Questions of Giving'. *Refugee Survey Quarterly* 26(3): 72–81.

Lavenex, Sandra, 2006. 'Shifting Up and Out: The Foreign Policy of European Immigration Control'. *West European Politics* 29(2): 329–50.

Legal Service of the Council, 1993. Advice 18 March 1993, 5546/93, JUR 25.

Leone-Ganado, Philip, 2017. 'Update 2—Malta demands safeguards as EU discusses migrants deal with Turkey'. *Times of Malta*, 17 March.

Long, Katy. 2014. *The Huddled Masses: Immigration and Inequality*, London: Thistle Publishing.

Loyd, Jenna M., and Alison Mountz, 2014. 'Managing Migration: Scaling Sovereignty on Islands'. *Island Studies Journal* 9(1): 23–42.

Luhmann, Niklas, Malika Bouhénia, and Fabrice Giraux, 2007. '"Everybody just tries to get rid of us." Access to health care and human rights of asylum seekers in Malta. Experiences, results and recommendations', Médecins du Monde, France, November

Lutterbeck, Derek, 2006. 'Policing Migration in the Mediterranean'. *Mediterranean Politics* 11(1): 59–82.

Lutterbeck, Derek, 2009. 'Small Frontier Island: Malta and the Challenge of Irregular Immigration'. *Mediterranean Quarterly* 20(1): 119–44.

Lutterbeck, Derek, 2013. 'Across the Desert, Across the Sea: Migrant Smuggling into and from Libya'. In *Migration, Security and Citizenship in the Middle East*, edited by Peter Seeberg and Zaid Eyadet, 137–66. New York: Palgrave Macmillan.

Maas, Willem, 2010. 'Unauthorized Migration and the Politics of Regularization, Legalization, and Amnesty'. In *Labour Migration in Europe*, edited by Georg Menz and Alexander Cavides, 232–50. Basingstoke: Palgrave.

Macklin, Audrey, 2005. 'Disappearing Refugees: Reflections on the Canada-U.S. Safe Third Country Agreement'. *Columbia Human Rights Law Review* 36(2): 101–61.

Maher, Kristen Hill, 2002. 'Who Has a Right to Rights? Citizenship's Exclusions in an Age of Migration'. In *Globalization and Human Rights*, edited by Alison Brysk, 19–43. Berkeley. CA: University of California Press.

Mahler, Sarah J., 1998. 'Theoretical and Empirical Contributions: Toward a Research Agenda on Transnationalism'. In *Transnationalism from Below*, edited by Michael Peter Smith and Luis Eduardo Guarnizo, 64–100. New Brunswick: Transaction Publishers.

Mahler, Sarah J., 2000. 'Constructing International Relations: The Role of Transnational Migrants and Other Non-State Actors', *Identities* 7(2): 197–232.

Mainwaring, Ćetta, 2012a. 'Resisting Distalization? Malta and Cyprus' Influence on EU Migration and Asylum Policies'. *Refugee Studies Quarterly* 31(4): 38–66.

Mainwaring, Ćetta, 2012b. 'Constructing a Crisis: The Role of Immigration Detention in Malta'. *Population, Space and Place* 18(6): 687–700.

Mainwaring, Ćetta, 2014. 'Small States and Nonmaterial Power: Creating Crises and Shaping Migration Policies in Malta, Cyprus, and the European Union'. *Journal of Immigrant and Refugee Studies* 12(2): 103–22.

Mainwaring, Ćetta, 2015. 'War is Peace and other forms of doublethink: EU proposes military operation to stop refugees', Glasgow Refugee Asylum and Migration Network (GRAMNet) Blog, 20 May.

Mainwaring, Ćetta, 2016a. 'Migrant Agency: Negotiating Borders and Migration Controls'. *Migration Studies* 4(3): 289–308.

Mainwaring, Ćetta, 2016b. 'Transnational migration and control: immigration detention on the edge of Europe'. In *Detaining the Immigrant Other: Global and Transnational Issues*, edited by Rich Furman, Douglas Epps, and Greg Lamphear, 117–28. Oxford: Oxford University Press.

Mainwaring, Ćetta, and Noelle Brigden, 2016. 'Beyond the Border: Clandestine Migration Journeys'. *Geopolitics* 21(2): 243–62.

Mainwaring, Ćetta, and Maria Lorena Cook, 2018. 'Immigration Detention: An Anglo Model', *Migration Studies*, early online print.

Mainwaring, Ćetta, and Stephanie J. Silverman, 2017. 'Detention-as-Spectacle'. *International Political Sociology* 11(1): 21–38.

Malkki, Liisa, 1992. 'National Geographic: The Rooting of Peoples and the Territorialization of National Identity among Scholars and Refugees'. *Cultural Anthropology* 7(1): 24–44.

Malkki, Liisa. 2015. *The Need to Help: The Domestic Arts of International Humanitarianism*, Durham: Duke University Press.

Malta, 1970. 'Immigration Act', Chapter 217. 21 September.

Malta, 2001. 'Refugees Act', Chapter 420, 1 October.

Malta, 2009. 'Building Bridges on Asylum: Malta's Bid for the European Asylum Support Office'. Malta: Government of Malta.

Malta Independent, 2017. 'US halts refugee resettlement programme with Malta'. *Malta Independent*, 2 February.

MaltaToday, 2009a. 'Immigration is "national crisis", 84% say'. *MaltaToday*, 5 April.

Malta Today, 2009b. 'Libya's bridge to Europe'. *Malta Today*, 29 April.

Malta Today, 2017. 'MOAS quits the Med: 'Search and rescue is not the solution to the ongoing migration crisis'. *Malta Today*, 4 September.

Maltese Council Presidency, 2017. 'Malta Summit—External aspects of migration', Informal meeting of EU heads of state, EU summit, Valletta, Malta, 3 February. Available here: http://www.statewatch.org/news/2017/jan/External-aspects-migration-final%20 copy-Malta.pdf

Mann, Itamar. 2016. *Humanity at Sea: Maritime Migration and the Foundations of International Law*, New York: Cambridge University Press.

Mares, Peter. 2002. *Borderline: Australia's Response to Refugees and Asylum Seekers in the Wake of the Tampa*, Sydney: UNSW Press.

Maritime Safety Committee, 2004. 'Resolution MSC.153(78)', 20 May. Available here: www.imo.org/blast/blastDataHelper.asp?data_id=15526&filename=153(78).pdf

Marr, David, and Marian Wilkinson. 2001. 'Going Overboard', *The Sydney Morning Herald*, 10 November.

Martin, Aryn, and Michael Lynch, 2009. 'Counting Things and People: The Practices and Politics of Counting'. *Social Problems* 56(2): 243–66.

Martin, Ivan, 2017. 'We do our bit to help Italy with migration, says OPM', *Times of Malta*. 2 July.

Martin, Philip, and Jonas Widgren, 2002. 'International Migration: Facing the Challenge'. *Population Bulletin* 57(1): March.

Martin, Susan F., ed., 2014. *Humanitarian Crises and Migration: Causes, Consequences and Responses*, Abingdon: Routledge.

Mattern, Janice Bially, 2005. 'Why "Soft Power" Isn't So Soft: Representational Force and the Sociolinguistic Construction of Attraction in World Politics'. *Millennium—Journal of International Studies* 33(3): 583–612.

McAdam, Jane, 2014. 'The concept of crisis migration'. *Forced Migration Review* 45: 10–11.

McMahon, Simon, 2017. 'Is Spain really facing a new migration crisis?', *The Conversation*, 25 August.

McMahon, Simon, and Nando Sigona, 2016. 'Boat migration across the Central Mediterranean: drivers, experiences and responses', Unravelling the Mediterranean Migration Crisis (MEDMIG), Research Brief No. 3, September.

McNevin, Anne, 2009. 'Contesting Citizenship: Irregular Migrants and Strategic Possibilities for Political Belonging'. *New Political Science* 31(2): 163–81.

McNevin, Anne, 2013. 'Ambivalence and Citizenship: Theorising the Political Claims of Irregular Migrants'. *Millennium—Journal of International Studies* 41(2): 182–200.

Mendel, Gideon, 2015. '"I'd rather die at sea than stay there": migrants on crossing the Med'. *The Guardian*, 16 May.

Merom, Gil, 1999. 'Israel's National Security and the Myth of Exceptionalism'. *Political Science Quarterly* 114(3): 409–34.

Metz, Helen Chapin, 2004. *Libya*, Whitefish, MT: Kessinger Publishing.

Mezzadra, Sandro, 2011. 'The gaze of autonomy: capitalism, migration and social struggles'. In *The Contested Politics of Migration*, edited by Vicki Squire, 121–42. New York: Routledge.

Michael, Maggie, 2017. 'Backed by Italy, Libya enlists militias to stop migrants', *Associated Press*. 29 August.

Miller, Mark J., and Demetrios G. Papademetriou, 1983. 'Immigration and U.S. Foreign Policy'. In *The Unavoidable Issue: US Immigration Policy in the 1980s*, edited by Demetrios G. Papademetriou and Mark J. Miller. Philadelphia: Institute for the Study of Human Issues.

Ministry for Foreign Affairs, 2009. 'Ministerial Statement regarding the immigrants who were rescued by the M/V Pinar-E off Lampedusa', Press Release, Malta, 21 April.

Ministry for Home Affairs and National Security, 2015. 'Strategy for the Reception of Asylum Seekers and Irregular Migrants', Malta, December.

Ministry for Home Affairs and National Security, 2016. 'Review of Temporary Humanitarian Protection—N(ew) for failed asylum seekers', Press Release 162593, Malta, 19 November.

Ministry for Justice and Home Affairs, 2005. 'Irregular Immigrants, Refugees and Integration: Policy Document', Malta.

Mitchell, Christopher, 1989. 'International Migration, International Relations and Foreign Policy', *International Migration Review* 23(3): 681–708.

Mitchell, Jon P., 2002. *Ambivalent Europeans: Ritual, Memory and the Public Sphere in Malta*, Abingdon, Oxon: Routledge.

MOAS (Migrant Offshore Aid Station), 2017. 'Moas Launches 2017 Maritime Search and Rescue Mission with Phoenix and Maritime Patrol Aircraft', Press Release, 3 April.

Momigliano, Anna, 2017a. 'In Italy, conspiracy theories about collusion between smugglers and charities rescuing migrants are spreading'. *The Washington Post*, 2 May.

Momigliano, Anna, 2017b. 'Italian forces ignored a sinking ship full of Syrian refugees and let more than 250 drown, says leaked audio'. *The Washington Post*, 9 May.

Montanari, Armando, and Antonia Cortese, 1993. 'South to North Migration in a Mediterranean Perspective'. In *Mass Migrations in Europe: The Legacy and the Future*, edited by Russell King, 212–33. London: Belhaven Press.

Morawska, Ewa, 2004. 'Gappy Immigration Control, Resourceful Migrants and Pendel Communities'. In *Controlling a New Migration World*, edited by Virginie Guiraudon and Christian Joppke, 173–99. London: Routledge.

Mountz, Alison, 2007. 'Smoke and Mirrors: An Ethnography of the State'. In *Politics and Practice in Economic Geography*, edited by Adam Tickell, Eric Sheppard, Jamie Peck, and Trevor Barnes, 38–48. London: Sage.

Mountz, Alison, 2010. *Seeking Asylum: Human Smuggling and Bureaucracy at the Border*, Minneapolis, MN: University of Minnesota Press.

Mountz, Alison, 2011a. 'The Enforcement Archipelago: Detention, Haunting, and Asylum on Islands'. *Political Geography* 30(3): 118–28.

Mountz, Alison, 2011b. 'Where Asylum-Seekers Wait: Feminist Counter-Topographies of Sites between States'. *Gender, Place & Culture* 18(3): 381–99.

Mountz, Alison, 2015. 'In/visibility and the securitization of migration shaping publics through border enforcement on islands'. *Cultural Politics*, 11(2): 184–200.

Mountz, Alison, and Nancy Hiemstra, 2014. 'Chaos and Crisis: Dissecting the Spatiotemporal Logics of Contemporary Migrations and State Practices'. *Annals of the Association of American Geographers* 104(2): 382–90.

MSF (Médecins Sans Frontières), 2009. ' "Not Criminals": Médecins Sans Frontières exposes conditions for undocumented migrants and asylum seekers in Maltese detention centres', April.

MSF (Médecins Sans Frontières), 2015. 'EU: your fences kill. Provide safe and legal passage', Open Letter, 11 September.

MSF (Médecins Sans Frontières), 2017a. 'MSF Response to European Council's "Malta Declaration" on Migration', 4 February.

MSF (Médecins Sans Frontières), 2017b. 'MSF committed to saving lives on Mediterranean but will not sign the Italian "Code of Conduct" ', 31 July.

MSF (Médecins Sans Frontières), 2017c. 'Hindrance of humanitarian assistance will create a deadly gap in the Mediterranean Sea', 12 August.

Mufti, Aamir, 2014. 'Stathis Gourgouris Interviews Aamir Mufti'. *Greek Left Review*, 14 July.

Murphy, Connor. 2017. 'Italy unfazed by Libyan strongman's threats to bomb navy', *Politico*, 3 August.

Mustafa Ali, Rania, Ayman Al Husseen, Anders Hammer, Erik Thorvald Aster, Michael Tait, and Mat Heywood,2017. 'Escape from Syria: Rania's odyssey—video'. *The Guardian*, 2 August.

Neslen, Arthur, 2017. 'Poland Faces €100,000-a-Day Fines over Illegal Logging in Białowieża Forest'. *The Guardian*, 21 November.

Nielsen, Nikolaj, 2017. 'Mixed review for EU asylum spots in Greece and Italy'. *EU Observer*, 25 April.

Noll, Gregor, 2003. 'Visions of the Exceptional: Legal and Theoretical Issues Raised by Transit Processing Centres and Protection Zones'. *European Journal of Migration and Law* 5: 303–41.

NSO (National Statistic Office), 2015. 'World Refugee Day News Release 2015', New Release, Malta, 20 June.

NSO (National Statistic Office), 2018. 'Inbound Tourism: December 2017', News Release 016/2018, Malta, 1 February.

NSO (National Statistics Office), 2009. 'Departing Tourists: December 2008', Information Society and Tourism Unit, 27 January.

NSO (National Statistics Office), 2011. 'World Refugee Day: 2011', News Release, Malta, 17 June.

Nye, Joseph, 1990. 'Soft Power'. *Foreign Policy* 80: 153–71.

Nye, Joseph. 2004. *Soft Power: The Means to Success in World Politics*, Cambridge, MA: Public Affairs.

Nyers, Peter, 2003. 'Abject Cosmopolitanism: the politics of protection in the anti-deportation movement'. *Third World Quarterly* 24(6): 1069–93.

Nyers, Peter, 2010. 'No One Is Illegal Between City and Nation'. *Studies in Social Justice* 4(2): 127–43.

O'Dowd, John, 2011. 'Mutual Recognition in European Immigration Policy: Harmonised Protection or Co-ordinated Exclusion?' In *The Future of Asylum in the European Union: Problems, Proposals and Human Rights*, edited by Flora A. N. J. Goudappel and Helena S. Raulus, 73–110. The Hague: Springer.

OECD (Organization for Economic Cooperation and Development), 2014. 'Is Migration Good for the Economy?' Migration Policy Debates, May.

Ohmae, Kenichi, 1994. *The Borderless World: Power and Strategy in the Global Marketplace*, London: HarperCollins.

Ong, Aihwa, 1995. 'Women Out of China: Traveling Tales and Traveling Theories in Postcolonial Feminism'. In *Women Writing Culture*, edited by Ruth Behar and Deborah A. Gordon, 351–72. Berkeley: University of California Press.

OSCE (Organization for Security and Co-operation in Europe), 1975. 'Conference on Security and Co-operation in Europe: Final Act', Helsinki. Available here: http://www.osce.org/helsinki-final-act?download=true

Oxfam, 2005. *Foreign Territory: The Internationalisation of EU Asylum Policy*, Oxford: Oxfam GB.

Oxford, Connie G., 2005. 'Protectors and Victims in the Gender Regime of Asylum'. *NWSA Journal* 17(3): 18–38.

PA, 2011. 'Italy strikes deal to limit mass migration'. *Times of Malta*, 6 April.

Pace, Roderick, 2002. 'A Small State and the European Union: Malta's EU Accession Experience'. *South European Society and Politics* 7(1): 24–42.

Pace, Roderick, 2006. 'Malta and EU Membership: Overcoming "Vulnerabilities", Strengthening "Resilience"'. *Journal of European Integration* 28(1): 33–49.

Pallister-Wilkins, Polly, 2015. 'The Humanitarian Politics of European Border Policing: Frontex and Border Police in Evros'. *International Political Sociology* 9(1): 53–69.

Pallister-Wilkins, Polly, 2017. 'Humanitarian Rescue/Sovereign Capture and the Policing of Possible Responses to Violent Borders'. *Global Policy* 8(S1): 19–24.

Panke, Diana, 2010. *Small States in the European Union: Coping with Structural Disadvantages*, Farnham: Ashgate.

Paoletti, Emanuela, 2008. 'A Critical Analysis of Migration Policies in the Mediterranean: The Case of Italy, Libya and the EU'. *Agora Without Frontiers* 13(4): 292–322.

Papadopoulos, Dimitris, Niamh Stephenson, and Vassilis Tsianos, 2008. *Escape Routes: Control and Subversion in the Twenty-First Century*, London: Pluto Press.

Papadopoulos, Dimitris, and Vassilis Tsianos, 2013. 'After citizenship: autonomy of migration, organisational ontology and mobile commons'. *Citizenship Studies* 17(2): 178–96.

Papastavridis, Efthymios, 2011. 'Rescuing "Boat People" in the Mediterranean Sea: The Responsibility of States under the Law of the Sea'. *EJIL: Talk!* 31 May.

Parliamentary Question, 2009. 'Detention Centres—spiża totali', no. 6959, House of Representatives, Malta, Legislature XI, 11 March.

Parliamentary Question, 2014. 'Ċentri ta' Detenzjoni—ħarbiet irreġistrati', No. 13155, House of Representatives, Malta, XII Legislature, 22 December.

Parliamentary Question, 2017. 'Third Country Nationals li jaħdmu f'Malta', No. 32196, House of Representatives, Malta, XII Legislature, 21 March.

Peel, Michael, and Mehreen Khan, 2018. 'EU states warned over billions banked through "golden visa" schemes'. *Financial Times*, 10 October.

Peers, Steve, 2010. 'Extending EU long-term resident status to refugees and persons with subsidiary protection status'. *Statewatch Analyses* 12(32/10), December.

Peregin, Christian, 2011. 'Migrants riot as police and army fight back'. *Times of Malta*, 17 August.

Perkowski, Nina, 2016. 'Deaths, Interventions, Humanitarianism and Human Rights in the Mediterranean "Migration Crisis"'. *Mediterranean Politics* 21(2): 331–5.

Perraudin, Frances, 2015. ' "Marauding" migrants threaten standard of living, says foreign secretary'. *The Guardian*, 10 August.

Phillips, Janet, 2014. 'Boat arrivals in Australia: a quick guide to the statistics', Parliament of Australia: Social Policy Section, Department of Parliamentary Services.

Phillips, Leigh, 2009. 'Malta to host EU asylum agency'. *EU Observer*, 2 December.

Pianigiani, Gaia, and Declan Walsh, 2017. 'Can E.U. Shift Migrant Crisis to the Source? In Libya, the Odds Are Long'. *The New York Times*, 17 February.

Pisani, Maria, 2011. 'There's an Elephant in the Room and She's "Rejected: and Black": Observations on rejected female asylum seekers from sub-Saharan Africa in Malta'. *It's Academic* 2: 24–51.

Politi, James, 2015. 'A question of identity for EU's migrants'. *Financial Times*, 15 June.

Politi, James, and Davide Ghiglione, 2016. 'Amnesty accuses Italy of abusing asylum seekers in "hotspots"'. *Financial Times*, 3 November.

Pop, Valentina, 2011. 'EU ignores Malta on special status for refugees'. *EU Observer*, 31 March.

Popham, Peter, 2007a. 'Europe's Shame'. *The Independent*, 28 May.

Popham, Peter, 2007b. 'Even in death, migrants were let down by Europe'. *The Independent*, 4 June.

Poutignat, Phillipe, and Jocelyne Streiff-Fénart, 2010. 'Migration Policy Development in Mauritania: Process, Issues, and Actors'. In *The Politics of International Migration Management*, edited by Martin Geiger and Antoine Pécoud, 202–19. Basingstoke: Palgrave Macmillan.

Pratt, Geraldine, 2000. 'Research performances'. *Environment & Planning D: Society & Space* 18: 639–51.

Preibisch, Kerry, 2010. 'Pick-Your-Own Labor: Migrant Workers and Flexibility in Canadian Agriculture'. *International Migration Review* 44(2): 404–41.

Puggioni, Raffaela, 2005. 'Refugees, Institutional Invisibility, and Self-help Strategies: Evaluating Kurdish Experience in Rome'. *Journal of Refugee Studies* 18(3): 319–39.

Pugh, Michael, 2004. 'Drowning not Waving: Boat People and Humanitarianism at Sea'. *Journal of Refugee Studies* 17(1): 50–69.

Rajaram, Prem Kumar, and Carl Grundy-Warr, 2004. 'The Irregular Migrant as Homo Sacer: Migration and Detention in Australia, Malaysia and Thailand'. *International Migration* 42(1): 33–63.

Rankin, Jennifer, 2017. 'Migration: EU Rejects Proposals for Turkey-Style Deal for Libya'. *The Guardian*, 25 January 25.

Rasmussen, Sune Engel, 2016. 'EU's secret ultimatum to Afghanistan: accept 80,000 deportees or lose aid'. *The Guardian*, 28 September.

Rekacewic, Philippe, 2013. 'Mapping Europe's war on immigration'. *Le Monde Diplomatique*, 16 October.

Republic of Cyprus, 2014. 'The Minister of Foreign Affairs participated in the Informal Ministerial Meeting of the Mediterranean Group "Med Group"', Ministry of Foreign Affairs, Press Release, 17 April.

Roitman, Janet, 2013. *Anti-Crisis*, Durham: Duke University Press.

Rother, Stefan, 2013. 'Global Migration Governance without Migrants? The Nation-State Bias in the Emerging Policies and Literature on Global Migration Governance'. *Migration Studies* 1(3): 363–71.

Ruhs, Martin, and Philip Martin, 2008. 'Numbers vs. Rights: Trade-Offs and Guest Worker Programs'. *International Migration Review* 42(1): 249–65.

Salt, John, 2002. 'Current Trends in international Migration in Europe', CDMG (2002) 26, Council of Europe, December.

Salter, Mark B, 2004. 'Passports, Mobility, and Security: How Smart Can the Border Be?' *International Studies Perspectives* 5(1): 71–91.

Salter, Mark B, 2006. 'The Global Visa Regime and the Political Technologies of the International Self: Borders, Bodies, Biopolitics'. *Alternatives: Global, Local, Political* 31(2): 167–89.

Salter, Mark B, 2008. 'When the Exception Becomes the Rule: Borders, Sovereignty, and Citizenship'. *Citizenship Studies* 12(4): 365–80.

Sambrook, Clare, 2013. 'Jimmy Mubenga and the Shame of British Airways'. *openDemocracy*, 12 October.

Sammut, Carmen, 2007. 'The Ambiguous Borderline Between Human Rights and National Security: The Journalist's Dilemma in the Reporting of Irregular Immigrants in Malta'. *Global Media Journal: Mediterranean Edition* 2(1): 1–9.

Sansone, Kurt, 2017a. 'Government climbs down from criticised migrants' policy: THPn holders to continue enjoying existing benefits'. *Times of Malta*, 22 February.

Sansone, Kurt, 2017b. 'Malians released after controversial three-month detention. Government still plans to deport the nine men'. *Times of Malta*, 14 February.

Sayad, Abdelmalek, 1996. 'La Doppia Pena del Migrante: Riflessioni sul "Pensiero di Stato"'. *Aut Aut* 275.

Schembri, Gabriel, 2017. 'Former soldier recalls colleague kicking Malian escaped migrant who died in 2012'. *Malta Independent*, 14 March.

Schengen Executive Committee, 2000. 'Decision of the Executive Committee of 21 April 1998 on the activities of the Task Force (SCH/Com-ex [98] 1 rev. 2)'. *Official Journal of the European Union* L 239: 191–2, 22 September.

Schuster, Liza, 2003a. 'Common Sense or Racism? The Treatment of Asylum-Seekers in Europe'. *Patterns of Prejudice* 37(3): 233–56.

Schuster, Liza, 2003b. *The Use and Abuse of Political Asylum in Britain and Germany*, London: Routledge.

Schuster, Liza, 2005. 'A Sledgehammer to Crack a Nut: Deportation, Detention and Dispersal in Europe'. *Social Policy & Administration* 39(6): 606–21.

Schuster, Liza, 2011. 'Turning refugees into "illegal migrants": Afghan asylum seekers in Europe'. *Ethnic and Racial Studies* 34(8): 1392–407.

Schuster, Liza, and Nassim Majidi, 2013. 'What Happens Post-Deportation? The Experience of Deported Afghans'. *Migration Studies* 1(2): 221–40.

Scicluna, Chris, 2017. 'Maltese PM Muscat wins second term in snap election'. *Reuters*, 4 June.

Scott, James C., 1985. *Weapons of the Weak: Everyday Forms of Peasant Resistance*, New Haven: Yale University Press.

Sea Watch, 2018. 'Sea-Watch 3 leaves Malta', News, 20 October.

Sewell, William H., 1992. 'A Theory of Structure: Duality, Agency, and Transformation'. *American Journal of Sociology* 98(1): 1–29.

Sharma, Nandita, 2005. 'Anti-Trafficking Rhetoric and the Making of a Global Apartheid'. *NWSA Journal* 17(3): 88–111.

Shaw, Wendy S., R.D.K. Herman, and G. Rebecca Dobbs. 2006. 'Encountering Indigeneity: Re-Imagining and Decolonizing Geography'. *Geografiska Annaler: Series B, Human Geography* 88(3): 267–76.

Sigona, Nando, 2015. 'Seeing Double? How the EU miscounts migrants arriving at its borders'. *The Conversation*, 16 October.

Simon, Julien, 2006. 'Irregular Transit Migration in the Mediterranean: Facts, Figures and Insights'. In *Mediterranean Transit Migration*, edited by Nina Sørensen, 25–65. Copenhagen: Danish Institute for International Studies.

Soares, Isa, and Oliver Joy, 2014. 'Malta foreign minister: Country "cannot offer" migrants opportunities'. *CNN*, 9 January.

Solé, Carlota, 2004. 'Immigration Policies in Southern Europe'. *Journal of Ethnic and Migration Studies* 30(6): 1209–21.

Spiegel, 2017. 'Sea-Eye nimmt Rettungsmission wieder auf'. *Spiegel*, 9 September.

Spindler, William, and Leo Dobbs, 2007. 'UNHCR calls for action to save 53 boat people off Malta', UNHCR, 23 May.

Squire, Vicki, ed., 2011. *The Contested Politics of Mobility: Borderzones and Irregularity*, London; New York: Routledge.

Squire, Vicki, 2014. 'Desert "trash": Posthumanism, border struggles, and humanitarian politics'. *Political Geography* 39(5): 11–21.

Squire, Vicki, 2017. 'Unauthorised migration beyond structure/agency? Acts, interventions, effects'. *Politics* 37(3): 254–72.

Stahnke, Julia, Paul Bickle, Philip Faigle, Karsten Polke-Majewski, and Sascha Venohr, 2015. 'Europe Deporting'. *Zeit Online*, 7 August.

Statewatch, 2007. 'Italy/Tunisia: Fishermen on trial for rescuing migrants'. *Statewatch News*, 7 September.

Steel, Zachary, Derrick Silove, Robert Brooks, Shakeh Momartin, Bushra Alzuhairi, and Ina Susljik, 2006. 'Impact of Immigration Detention and Temporary Protection on the Mental Health of Refugees'. *The British Journal of Psychiatry* 188(1): 58–64.

Steinberg, Philip E. 2001. *The Social Construction of the Ocean*, Cambridge: Cambridge University Press.

Stierl, Maurice, 2016a. 'A Sea of Struggle—Activist Border Interventions in the Mediterranean Sea'. *Citizenship Studies* 20(5): 561–78.

Stierl, Maurice, 2016b. 'Contestations in death—the role of grief in migration struggles'. *Citizenship Studies* 20(2): 173–91

Stierl, Maurice, 2017. 'Excessive Migration, Excessive Governance: Border Entanglements in Greek EU-rope'. In *The Borders of "Europe": Autonomy of Migration, Tactics of Bordering*, edited by Nicholas De Genova, 210–32. Durham, NC: Duke University Press.

Stierl, Maurice, 2018. 'A Fleet of Mediterranean Border Humanitarians'. *Antipode* 50(3): 704–24.

Tagliabue, John, 1998. 'More Kurds Reach Italy; Northern Europe Upset'. *New York Times*, 2 January.

Taylor, Diane, 2017. 'Refugees stranded for 30 hours before rescue in Mediterranean'. *The Guardian*, 21 April.

Taylor, Savitri, 2005. 'From Border Control to Migration Management: The Case for a Paradigm Change in the Western Response to Transborder Population Movement'. *Social Policy and Administration: An International Journal of Policy and Research* 39(6): 563–86.

Tazzioli, Martina, 2015. 'The Politics of Counting and the Scene of Rescue'. *Radical Philosophy* 192: 1–6.

Tazzioli, Martina, 2016. 'Border Displacements. Challenging the Politics of Rescue between Mare Nostrum and Triton'. *Migration Studies* 4(1): 1–19.

Teitelbaum, Michael S., 1984. 'Immigration, Refugees, and Foreign Policy'. *International Organization* 38(3): 429–50.

The Guardian, 2011. 'EU arms exports to Libya: who armed Gaddafi?' *The Guardian*, 2 March.

The Local, 2013. 'Migrant mother gave birth as she drowned'. *The Local*, 10 October.

Thielemann, Eiko R., 2003. 'Between Interests and Norms: Explaining Burden-Sharing in the European Union Special Issue: European Burden-Sharing and Forced Migration'. *Journal of Refugee Studies* 16(3): 253–73.

Thiollet, Helene, 2011. 'Migration as Diplomacy: Labor Migrants, Refugees, and Arab Regional Politics in the Oil-Rich Countries'. *International Labor and Working-Class History* 79: 1–22.

Thompson, Stuart A., and Anjali Singhvi, 2017. 'Efforts to Rescue Migrants Caused Deadly, Unexpected Consequences'. *New York Times*, 14 June.

Thomson, Mark, 2006. 'Migrants on the Edge of Europe: Perspectives from Malta, Cyprus and Slovenia', Sussex Migration Working Paper, No. 35. University of Sussex, Brighton.

Ticktin, Miriam, 2006. 'Where ethics and politics meet: The violence of humanitarianism in France'. *American Ethnologist* 33(1): 33–49.

Times of Malta, 2009. 'Updated: Malta wins bid to host EU Asylum Office'. *Times of Malta*, 30 November.

Times of Malta, 2011. 'Update 5: Migrants' rescue: Malta awaits Nato's explanation'. *Times of Malta*, 14 July.

Times of Malta, 2012. 'Hal Far "tent village" being dismantled'. *Times of Malta*, 19 April.

Times of Malta, 2013. 'Policy of migrant detention defended'. *Times of Malta*, 24 October.

Times of Malta, 2017. 'All migrants checked by police found to carry correct documentation'. *Times of Malta*, 12 April.

Times of Malta, Malta Independent, and MaltaToday, 2017. 'Editorial: Disintegrating the integrated'. *Times of Malta*, 1 February.

Tomlinson, Chris, 2017. 'European Union Admits Massive Rise of Illegal Migrants, But Not Refugees'. *Breitbart*, 23 June.

Torres, Diego, 2017. 'Southern Europe demands the North pay part of migration bill'. *Politico*, 4 October.

Tory-Murphy, Leanne, 2018. 'Migrants Malta Does Not Want Are Powering Its Economy'. *NewsDeeply*, 6 August.

Townsend, Mark, 2008. 'Libya Key Transit for UK-Bound Migrants'. *The Observer*, 13 January.

Townsend, Mark, 2017. 'Far right raises £50,000 to target boats on refugee rescue missions in Med'. *The Guardian*, 4 June.

Trauner, Florian, and Imke Kruse, 2008. 'EC Visa Facilitation and Readmission Agreements: A New Standard EU Foreign Policy Tool?' *European Journal of Migration and Law* 10(4): 411–38.

Travis, Alan, 2014. 'UK Axes Support for Mediterranean Migrant Rescue Operation'. *The Guardian*, October 27.

Tremlett, Giles, 2015. 'The millionaire who rescues migrants at sea'. *The Guardian*, 8 July.

Trevisanut, Seline, 2010. 'Search and Rescue Operations in the Mediterranean: Factor of Cooperation or Conflict'. *International Journal of Marine and Coastal Law* 25: 523–42.

Triandafyllidou, Anna, 2001. *Immigrants and National Identity in Europe*, London: Routledge.

Triandafyllidou, Anna, ed., 2010. *Irregular Migration in Europe: Myths and Realities*, London: Routledge.

UNHCR (United National High Commissioner for Refugees), 1985. 'Problems Related to the Rescue of Asylum-Seekers at Sea', EC/SCP/42, 8 July.

UNHCR (United National High Commissioner for Refugees), 2005. 'UNHCR says Maltese troops seemed to use excessive force to quell peaceful demo by detained asylum seekers', 19 January.

UNHCR (United National High Commissioner for Refugees), 2006. 'UNHCR welcomes positive outcome for 51 boat people off Malta', 21 July.

UNHCR (United National High Commissioner for Refugees), 2009a. 'UNHCR interviews migrants pushed back to Libya', Briefing Note, 14 July.

UNHCR (United National High Commissioner for Refugees), 2009b. 'Asylum Levels and Trends in Industrialized Countries, 2008', 24 March.

UNHCR (United National High Commissioner for Refugees), 2010a. 'UNHCR Information Note on National Practice in the Application of Article 3(2) of the Dublin II Regulation in particular in the context of intended transfers to Greece', Brussels, 16 June.

UNHCR (United National High Commissioner for Refugees), 2010b. 'Asylum Levels and Trends in Industrialized Countries, 2009', 23 March.

UNHCR (United National High Commissioner for Refugees), 2011a. 'Malta Fact Sheet 2002–2010', Malta: UNHCR.

UNHCR (United National High Commissioner for Refugees), 2011b. 'The 1951 Convention Relating to the Status of Refugees and its 1967 Protocol', Geneva, Switzerland.

UNHCR (United National High Commissioner for Refugees), 2012a. '2011 Malta Fact Sheet', Malta: UNHCR.

UNHCR (United National High Commissioner for Refugees), 2012b. 'Detention Guidelines: guidelines on the applicable criteria and standards relating to the detention of asylum-seekers and alternatives to detention', Division of International Protection, United Nations, Geneva, Switzerland.

UNHCR (United National High Commissioner for Refugees), 2015. 'Malta Asylum Trends 2014', Malta: UNHCR.

UNHCR (United National High Commissioner for Refugees), 2017a. 'Mixed Migration Trends in Libya: Changing Dynamics and Protection Challenges', UNHCR.

UNHCR (United National High Commissioner for Refugees), 2017b. 'Desperate Journeys', Bureau for Europe, UNHCR, February.

UNHCR (United National High Commissioner for Refugees), 2017c. 'Italy: UNHCR Update #10', UNHCR, 16 March.

UNHCR (United National High Commissioner for Refugees), 2017d. 'Global Trends: Forced Displacement in 2016'. Geneva, Switzerland: UNHCR.

UNHCR-Malta, 2018. 'Malta Asylum Trends: Real Time', UNHCR, Malta. Available here: http://www.unhcr.org.mt/charts/

UNICEF (United Nations International Children's Emergency Fund), 2017. 'A Deadly Journey for Children: The Central Mediterranean Migration Route', February.

United Nations, 2010. 'Report of the Working Group on Arbitrary Detention—Addendum: Mission to Malta (19 to 23 January 2009)', Human Rights Council, 13th Session, A/HRC/13/30/Add.2, 18 January.

United Nations, 2013. 'Report of the Special Rapporteur on the Human Rights of Migrants, François Crépeau', Human Rights Council, 23rd Session, A/HRC/23/46, 24 April.

United Nations, 2015. 'Report by the Special Rapporteur on the human rights of migrants, François Crépeau Mission to Malta (6–10 December 2014)', Human Rights Council, 29th Session, A/HRC/29/36/Add.3, 12 May.

United Nations, 2016. 'World Statistics Pocketbook, 2016 edition', Series V, No. 40, Department of Economic and Social Affairs Statistics Division. New York: United Nations. Available here: https://unstats.un.org/unsd/publications/pocketbook/files/world-stats-pocketbook-2016.pdf

UNODC (United Nations Office on Drugs and Crime), 2011. 'Smuggling of Migrants by Sea', Issue Paper, Anti-Human Trafficking and Migrant Smuggling Unit, United Nations.

Valenzia, Geoffrey, 2014. 'Inkjesta bis-shha tal-artikolu 4 tal-Att Dwar l'Inkjesti rigwardanti l'harba tal- immigrant Abdalla Mohammed (maghruf ukoll bhala Mamadou Kamara) ta'32 sena mill-Mali li gie certifkat mejjet wara li ttiehed ic-Centru tas-Sahha ta'Rahal Gdid minn ufficjali assenjati mas- Servizz ta'Detenzjoni'. Malta.

Van Hear, Nick, 2012. 'Forcing the Issue: Migration Crises and the Uneasy Dialogue between Refugee Research and Policy'. *Journal of Refugee Studies* 25(1): 2–24.

Van Liempt, Ilse, and Jereon Doomernik, 2006. 'Migrant's Agency in the Smuggling Process: The Perspectives of Smuggled Migrants in the Netherlands'. *International Migration* 44(4): 165–90.

Vance, Andrea, 2010. 'Key says no to refugee detention centre'. *Stuff*, 29 October.

Vaughan-Williams, Nick, 2008. 'The generalized biopolitical border? Re-conceptualising the limits of sovereign power'. *Review of International Studies* 35(4): 729–49.

Vaughan-Williams, Nick. 2009. *Border Politics: The Limits of Sovereign Power*, Edinburgh: Edinburgh University Press.

Vaughan-Williams, Nick. 2015. *Europe's Border Crisis: Biopolitical Security and Beyond*, Oxford: Oxford University Press.

Vella, Matthew, 2007. 'Dropping the shibboleths on migration'. *MaltaToday*, 13 June.

Vella, Matthew, 2017. 'Controversial Malta plan mooted 'legal way' of pushing back migrants'. *MaltaToday*, 27 January.

Venturini, Alessandra, 2004. *Postwar Migration in Southern Europe, 1950–2000: An Economic Analysis*, Cambridge: Cambridge University Press.

Vincenti, Daniela, 2018. 'IOM chief: There is no migration crisis but a political emergency'. *Euractiv*, 12 February.

Wall Street Journal, 2014. 'Italy Puts Plaque Underwater for Lampedusa Victims'. *Wall Street Journal*, 10 July.

Walters, William, 2004. 'Secure Borders, Safe Haven, Domopolitics'. *Citizenship Studies* 8(3): 237–60.

Walters, William, 2008. 'Bordering the Sea: Shipping Industries and the Policing of Stowaways'. *Borderlands* 7(3): 1–25.

Walters, William, 2009. 'Europe's Borders'. In *Sage Handbook of European Studies*, edited by Chris Rumford, 485–505. London: Sage.

Walters, William, 2011. 'Foucault and Frontiers: Notes on the Birth of the Humanitarian Border'. In *Governmentality: Current Issues and Future Challenges*, edited by Ulrich Bröckling, Susanne Krasmann, and Thomas Lemke, 138–64. London: Routledge.

Walters, William, 2016. 'The Flight of the Deported: Aircraft, Deportation, and Politics'. *Geopolitics* 21(2): 435–48.

WatchTheMed, 2016. 'Moving On: One Year Alarmphone', http://www.statewatch.org/news/2016/jan/eu-med-crisis-alarmphone-one-year-report-red.pdf

WatchtheMed, 2017. '15/04: A deadly void in the Central Med: Rescue of 100 travellers delayed 24 hours', Watch the Med Alarm Phone Investigations, 17 April.

Weiner, Myron, 1985. 'On International Migration and International Relations'. *Population and Development Review* 11(3): 441–55.

Wikileaks, 2016. 'EUNAVFOR MED Op SOPHIA—Six Monthly Report', 17 February.

Willen, Sarah S., 2007. 'Toward a Critical Phenomenology of "Illegality": State Power, Criminalization, and Abjectivity among Undocumented Migrant Workers in Tel Aviv, Israel'. *International Migration* 45(3): 8–38.

Wintour, Patrick, 2017. 'NGO rescues off Libya encourage traffickers, says EU borders chief'. *The Guardian*, 27 February.

Wintour, Patrick, Lorenzo Tondo, and Stephanie Kirchgaessner, 2018. 'Southern mayors defy Italian coalition to offer safe port to migrants'. *The Guardian*, 10 June.

Xuereb, Matthew, 2010. 'EU 'Understands Malta' Over Pull-out from Frontex'. *Times of Malta*, 1 May.

Yardley, Jim, 2014. 'Shipwreck was Simple Murder, Migrants Recall'. *The New York Times*, 20 October.

Yardley, Jim, and Gaia Pianigiani, 2013. 'Out of Syria, Into a European Maze'. *The New York Times*, 29 November.

Yardley, Jim, and Elisabetta Povoledo, 2013. 'Migrants Die as Burning Boat Capsizes Off Italy'. *The New York Times*, 3 October.

Zammit, David, 2016. 'Vernacularising Asylum Law in Malta'. In *Europeanization through Private Law Instruments*, edited by Rainer Arnold and Valentina Colcelli, 73–110. Regensburg: Universitatsverlag Regensburg GmbH.

Zolberg, Aristide R., 1981. 'International Migrations in Political Perspective'. In *Global Trends in Migration: Theory and Research on International Population Movements*, edited by Mary M. Kritz, Charles B. Keely, and Silvano M. Tomasi. New York: Center for Migration Studies of New York.

Zolberg, Aristide R.,1984. 'International Migration and Foreign Policy: When Does a Marginal Issue Become Substantive?' In *In Defense of the Alien*, edited by Lydio F. Tomasi. Vol. 6, Part 3: International Migration and Foreign Policy. New York: Center for Migration Studies.

Zolberg, Aristide R., Astri Suhrke, and Sergio Aguayo, 1986. 'International Factors in the Formation of Refugee Movements'. *International Migration Review* 20(2): 151–69.

Index